M000072957

Black Churches and Local Politics

Clergy Influence, Organizational Partnerships, and Civic Empowerment

Edited by
R. Drew Smith and
Fredrick C. Harris

ROWMAN & LITTLEFIELD PUBLISHERS, INC.
Lanham • Boulder • New York • Toronto • Oxford

ROWMAN & LITTLEFIELD PUBLISHERS, INC.

Published in the United States of America
by Rowman & Littlefield Publishers, Inc.
A wholly owned subsidiary of The Rowman & Littlefield Publishing Group, Inc.
4501 Forbes Boulevard, Suite 200, Lanham, Maryland 20706
www.rowmanlittlefield.com

PO Box 317
Oxford
OX2 9RU, UK

British Library Cataloguing in Publication Information Available

Library of Congress Cataloging-in-Publication Data

Black churches and local politics : clergy influence, organizational
partnerships, and civic empowerment / edited by R. Drew Smith and
Fredrick C. Harris.
   p. cm.
   Includes bibliographical references and index.
   ISBN 0-7425-4521-0 (cloth : alk. paper)—ISBN 0-7425-4522-9 (pbk. :
alk. paper)
   1. African American churches—Political activity. 2. African American
clergy—Political activity. 3. African Americans—Politics and
government. 4. Christianity and politics—United States. 5. Municipal
government—United States. I. Smith, R. Drew, 1956- II. Harris,
Fredrick C. BR563.N4B569 2005
   322'.1'08996073—dc22

                                       2005001206

Printed in the United States of America

∞™ The paper used in this publication meets the minimum requirements of
American National Standard for Information Sciences—Permanence of Paper
for Printed Library Materials, ANSI/NISO Z39.48-1992.

Black Churches
and Local Politics

Contents

Part II: Black Churches and Electoral Politics

Part III: Epilogue

Preface

This volume is third in a series of volumes on black churches and public life developed as part of the Public Influences of African-American Churches Project (PIAAC). The aim of the PIAAC Project, which is based at the Leadership Center at Morehouse College, is to examine the relationship between African American churches and American political life since the civil rights movement. A primary objective of the project has been to increase scholarly research in this subject area—working with approximately thirty scholars over the past few years in a multidisciplinary examination of black church activism with respect to electoral, public policy, and other civic involvements.

Convening this team of scholars has been a rich and rewarding experience that has produced important opportunities for scholarly interaction, including the collaboration between Fredrick C. Harris and myself in the editing of the current volume. He brought a record of pioneering scholarship on black religion and politics to the multiple roles he fulfilled within the PIAAC Project as consultant to the project during its formative stages, as a project scholar, and then as coeditor of this volume. The PIAAC Project is indebted to him and to each of the project scholars for all that they contributed to this effort. Our hope is that the multidisciplinary collaborations initiated within this project will generate additional research and dialogue on black religion and public life, both on the part of this team of scholars and by a wider range of scholars concerned with the intersections between American religion and public life.

Special thanks should be offered as well to the numerous church leaders across the country that provided information and access for our scholars and our project, to the Pew Charitable Trusts for its generous funding of this initial cycle of work (especially to Luis Lugo for his commitment to research on religion and American public life), to Walter Fluker and colleagues at the Leadership Center at Morehouse College, to Christopher Anzalone at Rowman & Littlefield Publishers, and to the *Western Journal of Black Studies* for permission to reprint here a revised version of an article by Michael Leo Owens published previously in volume 21 (1997) of that journal.

Introduction: Black Churches, Activist Traditions, and Urban Political Contexts

Fredrick C. Harris

Political engagement among activist black clergy and congregations is part and parcel of the nation's urban political landscape. Though most black churches in urban America are not directly active in the politics of their communities, an activist cadre of clergy and congregations mobilizing urban black communities for social change has been constant from the antebellum period to Reconstruction and then on to the modern civil rights movement.[1] These activist clergy and congregations have operated as valuable political assets for both black communities and urban political elites who rely strongly on the resources of activist clergy and churches in their pursuit of electoral goals and policy initiatives that affect black communities.

It is not inconsistent then that in the aftermath of the Second World War, the emerging modern civil rights movement in the South, as well as black activism outside the region, had at its disposal a militant vanguard of clergy and congregations advocating for social change. This vanguard included Charles Hill of the Hartford Avenue Baptist Church in Detroit,[2] William Holmes Borders of the Wheat Street Baptist Church in Atlanta, Gardner Taylor of the Concord Baptist Church in Brooklyn, New York, J. Raymond Henderson of the Second Baptist Church of Los Angeles, and Smallwood Williams of the Bible Way Pentecostal Church in the nation's capital, to name but a few. Black religious leaders and congregations in cities hosted protest rallies, challenged civic leadership on racial segregation, and encouraged black voter participation prior to the more widely known and church-based Montgomery Bus Boycott.

However, their activism was not confined to civil rights activism, nor was it confined to the public pronouncements of the male-dominated clergy sector. Urban black congregations with a commitment to social uplift also provided important social services to black communities with little or no support from the state or philanthropic agencies. Organized by activist women in congregations and the church-affiliated black women's clubs, urban black churches provided kindergartens, recreation centers, health awareness, and religious and formal education for adults and youth. Church-based social reformers such as Nannie Burroughs of the National Baptist Convention and Arenia Mallory of the Church of God in Christ used networks in their respective denominations to organize women on the local level and coordinate social activism in black communities across the nation.[3] Given this legacy of political and social activism, it is also not surprising that the protest campaigns that emerged in the mid-1950s in Baton Rouge, Louisiana, Montgomery, Alabama, and Tallahassee, Florida, were organized by black clergy and congregations. After all, black churches embodied critical organizational resources for collective action, specifically a ready-made leadership structure, networks for communicating information about political activities, a membership with transferable organizing skills, a physical space to assemble and discuss issues of the day, and a self-generated financial capacity that could generate funds for protest.[4]

There has been much debate about whether black churches have remained engaged in the social and political activism of black communities. By the early 1970s religion scholar C. Eric Lincoln was heralding an expansion of black church activism, noting that the opiate-driven Negro church that sociologist E. Franklin Frazier wrote about a decade earlier had "died an agonized death in the harsh turmoil" of the 1960s.[5] What resurrected from the ashes of the old paradigm of gradualism and a strict adherence to spirituality was a reconstructed normative commitment to the obligations of black churches to political and social activism. With the passage of the Voting Rights Act of 1965 and the ascendancy of black elected officials that followed, this obligation included participation in electoral politics. But despite ideas of black liberation influential within many segments of black civil society, a wholesale commitment to political and social activism by black religious institutions did not take a strong hold. As C. Eric Lincoln and Lawrence Mamiya explain in their analysis of urban black churches in the post–civil rights era: "The present picture of black urban churches is a complicated, mixed picture of some effects of privatization among unchurched sectors of the black population, and the withdrawal of some black churches into the sphere of personal piety and religiosity; but there are a number of signs of a continuing tradition of activism and involvement in the political, economic, educational, and cultural aspects of black life among the majority of black clergy and churches."[6]

At the same time that the normative commitments of black churches were being transformed by the civil rights and black power movements, the position of African Americans in urban politics was also changing. With the decline of white ethnic-based political machines and the exodus of whites from the city to the suburbs, African Americans were becoming incorporated into urban political systems as elected officials, municipal employees, and city managers.[7] Nonetheless, as blacks were elected to positions of power in city government—including the position of mayor in many major cities—black ascent into political power was deemed a "hollow prize." The prize of black empowerment and incorporation dwindled in the 1970s, 1980s, and into the 1990s as urban America began a downward economic spiral. Plagued by declining industry, higher concentrations of poverty and racial segregation, diminishing tax bases, and white flight to suburban communities, cities had to contend with fewer resources to address the social needs of mostly black and Latino inner-city communities.

Within the context of increasing political empowerment and declining economic fortunes of inner-city communities, activist black clergy and congregations have developed strategies that address social and economic dislocation in poor communities and take advantage of black political empowerment in urban America. Armed with a legacy of social and political activism, activist black clergy and congregations have continued their participation in the post–civil rights era, embracing strategies and tactics that take into account new urban realities. Some activist ministers and congregations center their activism on social and economic development, choosing to use their political influence and connections to politicians to lobby for community development. Others emphasize political empowerment, in which activist clergy and congregations employ tactics that challenge local and state governments on minority employment, police-community relations, affordable housing, public schools, and social services.[8] Both strategies ultimately have the same goal in mind—the economic, social, and political empowerment of African Americans—but they employ different strategies for improving the conditions of black America.

Whether the strategy is centered on community development or political empowerment, activist clergy and congregations have political resources at their disposal to mobilize African Americans into action. As John Mark Hanson and Steven Rosenstone point out in their research on political mobilization, individuals and groups are mobilized into action two ways— either directly or indirectly. With direct mobilization, organizations and institutions draw people into politics by targeting individuals for action while indirect mobilization occurs when individuals are stimulated to participate as a consequence of their exposure to political ideas and information.[9]

As mobilizing agents in black communities, activist clergy and congregations directly mobilize individuals through such activities as providing transportation for voters on election day, recruiting volunteers for community service, or hosting meetings that address political or community concerns. Activist ministers and congregations also indirectly stimulate activism by hosting candidate visits, informing congregants about community and political events, and exposing inactive individuals to church members who are already active in politics and community affairs. These direct and indirect appeals from activist congregations are a powerful facilitator of black political participation. As previous research has shown, the frequency of discussions about politics from the pulpit, visits to churches by political candidates, and direct appeals to become politically active occur more often in black churches than in Anglo and Latino churches. And both direct and indirect effects on participation from ministers and churches are considerably more likely to increase the political participation of blacks than the participation of Anglos and Latinos.[10]

This volume on black churches and urban politics uses case studies from various cities to examine the strategies and tactics of activist black clergy and congregations. These case studies illustrate how black activist clergy and congregations negotiate the political terrains of their respective cities. The cases show that the political culture of a city—whether that culture is shaped by machine politics, a legacy of political protest, racial and ethnic factionalism, or power residing in the mayor's office rather in the city council chamber—can influence the tactics of activist clergy and congregations. The cases also show how strategies and tactics vary across congregations as well as within and across cities. Not only do activist churches emphasize political empowerment or economic development, their tactics to pursue their goals may take different forms. They can form coalitions with other churches and/or political organizations, lobby public officials, use personal appeals to persuade politicians, or mobilize voters for candidates who support the congregation's agenda. By taking stock of the strategies that activist black clergy and congregations adopt and the tactics they use to reach their goals, the cases in this volume highlight nuances in black clergy and church activism that are captured beyond a single case or a focus on national politics.

PERSONAL INFLUENCE, COALITIONS, AND PRESSURE GROUPS

The first section of this volume examines three ways that black activist clergy and congregations voice their concerns in urban politics. The tactics explored are the use of personal influence by activist ministers, the formation of coalitions with churches and community organizations, and the deployment of pressure groups that lobby government institutions and leaders on behalf of minority communities. These various tactics of civic engagement often overlap, as activist clergy may use their personal influence to affect the decision making of political elites and simultaneously participate in coalitions or pressure groups.

Personal persuasion by black ministers is a political tactic that stretches back to black politics during Reconstruction and continues on as blacks were introduced to the politics of Northern cities during the Great Migration. Some Southern ministers during the era of Jim Crow also used their personal influence to extract what political favors they could from white economic and political elites. These ministers—whether they were using personal persuasion to extract personal or community benefits from political machines in the North or preventing physical or economic harm to blacks in the segregationist South—acted as "brokers" for black communities.[11] As brokers they built individual relationships with political and economic elites. As some analysts have noted, brokerage politics by black ministers often undermines the collective interests of black communities as brokers' advocacy on behalf of group interest may give way to individual interest. Since their power resides in religious institutions, black communities have found it difficult to hold some ministerial brokers accountable in representing the communities' economic and political interests.[12]

Another tactic black activist clergy and congregations use in pursuing political activism is involvement in coalitions. Coalitions are formed either with other black churches, with churches of other racial makeups, or with community or political organizations. As religion scholar Nancy Ammerman notes, religious institutions are ideal for the formation of coalitions since congregations are themselves "connected communities" with various resources that can link them to surrounding communities. Congregations generate the loyalties and networks that facilitate cooperation within congregations and across congregations. As Ammerman explains, "Whether it is the local ministerial alliance that administers emergency relief or the downtown churches who jointly sponsor concerts and other civic events, local congregations often recognize that the problems and possibilities of their neighborhoods and cities are bigger than they can tackle alone."[13] Tackling social and economic problems in black communities by forming congregational alliances or links with community groups is just another way that black clergy and congregations participate in urban politics.

Whether these activists are a part of ministerial alliances or stakeholders in coalitions, activist ministers and congregations operate as pressure groups advocating on behalf of minority and poor communities. While they do not possess the same level of financial resources that unions or corporations have in leveraging local political power, black activist clergy and congregations have human resources at their disposal. For instance, activist ministers can direct members of their congregation to put pressure on their elected representatives, or they can deploy protest tactics to demand policy change. As part of a ministerial delegation, activist clergy can meet with public officials, using their moral authority to pressure politicians in city hall, the county legislature, or the state capitol "to do the right thing."

Alton Pollard's chapter explores the contemporary activism of Atlanta's black clergy and congregations. Against the backdrop of black church advocacy for social change in Atlanta during the civil rights movement, Pollard documents the civic engagement of Atlanta-area clergy and churches in addressing urban poverty and opposition to the city's highly touted business set-aside programs for minorities and women. Known as the "City Too Busy to Hate" in the 1960s, host to the headquarters of the Southern Christian Leadership Conference (SCLC), and viewed today as the "Mecca" of black political empowerment, Atlanta's reputation as a progressive city seems to hamper the efforts of activist black congregations in addressing the economic realities facing Atlanta's inner-city communities. While using protest tactics to challenge the legal assault to business set-asides, activist clergy and congregations turn to uplift strategies when dealing with the poor. Pollard concludes that these leaders and congregations have not recognized the "shift in the political terrain" since the movement, where contemporary struggles for black advancement in the city have "moved from the steps of the courthouse and city hall to the inner chambers of power."

Demonstrating the use of personal persuasion as a political tactic, the chapter by Yvette Alex-Assensoh shows how individual ministers have "made a way out of no way" for blacks in Columbus, Ohio. In this examination of local activism by five ministers, Alex-Assensoh suggests that the clout of activist clergy, who use their "personal characteristics as technical skills," can yield benefits to black communities. Indeed, the governing structure of politics in Columbus facilitates the development of personal alliances between activist ministers and mayoral regimes since the city operates on a strong mayoral system where power resides in the mayor's office rather than with the elected representatives of the council. Sherri Wallace presents in chapter 3 with analysis of late Reverend Bennett W. Smith of Buffalo, New York, who pastored the St. John Baptist Church and served as president of the politically conscious Progressive Baptist Convention. Using the technique of persuasion, Reverend Smith pressed for political empowerment, social services, and economic development for blacks in Buffalo. As the analysis in the chapter reveals, it was much easier for Reverend Smith to promote economic development than to influence political change in the city. Mayoral regimes in the city preferred dealing with the city's black community through social services and development projects rather than as a force for political change.

James Jennings's chapter examines cooperation and conflict between faith-based coalitions in Boston's minority communities. Responding to the rise of youth violence in Boston's inner-city communities, the Ten Point Coalition for a National Church Mobilization to Combat Black on Black Violence was formed mostly by inner-city congregations in Boston as a way to develop strategies to combat youth violence. The coalition worked in cooperation with an array of organizations, including public health agencies, the police department, probation officers, and community development organizations. In what has come to be referred to as the "Boston Miracle," the Ten Point Coalition has been credited with helping to reduce murders in Boston's inner-city communities during the 1990s.

In contrast to the strategy of the Ten Point Coalition is the Black Ministerial Alliance of Greater Boston—the oldest black ministerial group in the city. More politically active than the Ten Point Coalition, the Black Ministerial Alliance has publicly criticized the city's mayor, opposed the restoration of the death penalty in Massachusetts, cosponsored voter registration drives, and lobbied the city's housing authority regarding racially motivated crimes at housing developments. While these two coalitions represent different spheres of civic engagement among activist clergy and congregations, political differences have stifled cooperation between the two coalitions. Differences within the coalition have been over political issues and over support for various black public figures.

Clarence Taylor's chapter on Miami also chronicles the coalitional tactics of activist clergy and congregations operating within associations focused, respectively, on social services and on political empowerment. The African-American Council of Christian Clergy (AACCC) was founded for the purpose of advocating for social services in Miami's black communities. The organization has been subsidized by public funding from local and state governments. Founded in the 1980s, People United to Lead the Struggle for Equality (PULSE) is a coalition of activist black churches, black labor organizations, tenant associations, social fraternities, and senior citizen groups. The coalition emerged as an advocacy group in the aftermath of rioting that erupted in the wake of police brutality incidents in Miami's black communities. Taylor points out ideological differences in the approaches of activist black churches operating within these two coalitions, concluding that PULSE "recognizes and challenges structural inequality" while AACCC "contends that the major problem facing blacks is that they are not prepared to function in a competitive society."

BLACK CHURCHES, POLITICAL PARTIES, AND ELECTORAL POLITICS

As some of the case studies in this volume indicate, direct involvement in electoral politics can be a two-edged sword for activist black clergy and churches. On the one hand, being induced into the political process enhances opportunities for engaging activist congregations. On the other hand, inducements by political actors may place unforeseeable constraints on activist black churches that receive financial assistance and symbolic rewards from political parties and urban regimes. These churches may be hampered in mobilization efforts that challenge the regime's policies and practices that are antithetical to moral principles of activist black clergy and congregations. Therefore, the inducements into the political process by urban regimes may open opportunities to activist churches in some contexts, constrain activism in others, and combine opportunities and constraints in many situations.[14]

In chapter 6, Ronald Walters and Tamelyn Tucker-Worgs delineate the limitations of black political power in the nation's capital, noting that the civil rights legacy of activist black clergy and churches in the District has been sustained mainly as a result of their association and involvement with national protest activities that are drawn to the city. However, given the changing needs of blacks in the District, church-based activism has extended to electoral politics, issue advocacy, and community development. In particular, the governing regime of multiterm mayor and former civil rights activist Marion Barry cultivated the electoral support of traditionally active congregations and induced into electoral politics other congregations that had not been previously active.

The vitality of political parties in urban politics is a factor that places constraints or presents opportunities for church-based electoral mobilization. In general, the mobilizing capacity of political parties has diminished over the past decades as television and media-centered politics have replaced face-to-face campaigning and political organizing. In chapter 7, Fredrick Harris explores how machine-style politics in Chicago have hampered reform-oriented, independent politics in Chicago's black communities. Through the political manipulation of social service funding from local, state, and federal-sponsored programs, the machine rewarded friendly congregations and punished activist clergy and churches that opposed the machine. As Harris explains, while social service funding "encouraged the civic engagement of ministers and churches, [it], paradoxically, strengthened the power of patronage-style politics in black communities and eventually undermined efforts by blacks to elect reform-oriented candidates or to engage in activism that would challenge the machine."

In reviewing the role of church-based political activism in Cleveland's historic 1967 election of Carl Stokes, the nation's first black big-city mayor, Mittie Chandler's chapter foregrounds that election to examine the continuation of clergy activism. Chandler fast-forwards to the unsuccessful congressional campaign of Reverend Marvin McMickle, an activist black pastor vying for the seat of retired congressman Louis Stokes (who was elected to Congress shortly after the election of his brother Carl Stokes). While noted for the activist tradition of previous ministers who led the same congregation, Reverend McMickle's poor showing in the race was credited to his weak ties to the Democratic Party establishment.

In chapter 9, Ronald Brown and Carolyn Hartfield's analysis of black activist clergy in Detroit, the authors examine a rarely used tool for church-based political activism—political action committees (PACs). Though Detroit is a predominately black and Democratic city that has had a black mayor for more than forty years, two separate church-based PACs operate in the city: the Black Slate Action Committee and the Fannie Lou Hamer Political Action Committee. In contrast to other church-based forms of electoral activism, these activist clergy use a formalized political organization to endorse political candidates, provide voter guides, and support voter turnout. Steeped in black nationalist ideology, these two church-based political action committees have a commitment to articulating the concerns of the poor and powerless in Detroit. While they operate on the premise of maintaining an independent politics, their independence seems to be compromised by Democrats who contribute to the PACs in exchange for political endorsements. As the authors note, these church-based PACs have to avoid "being used by a more powerful ally, the Democratic Party" in their efforts to effect social change.

In chapter 10, Michael Leo Owens's case study of Queens, New York, shows how weak party organization provided an opening for the insurgent congressional campaign of activist pastor Floyd Flake. Owens examines an alternative black political organization, the Southeast Queens Clergy for Community Empowerment (SQCCE), which evolved out of the 1984 presidential candidacy of Jesse Jackson. Challenging the candidacy of the local Democratic Party, the SQCCE-backed candidacy of Reverend Floyd Flake outmobilized the party regulars. As Owens points out, with black clergy "increasingly involving themselves and their churches in urban electoral politics, the type of alternative black political organization that will tend to predominate will be church-based, black nonparty organizations." Therefore, Owens concludes, activist black churches have an advantage in challenging local party structures that have lost their capacity to effectively mobilize voters.

As a conclusion to this volume, R. Drew Smith's epilogue discusses Republican efforts during George W. Bush's administration to promote government funding of faith-based initiatives and what that policy may mean for black churches engaged in church-based community and political action. As he argues, the policy has contributed to tensions between traditional activist clergy and clergy who have emerged in politics more recently out of an interest in funding opportunities for addressing the needs of the poor and underserved black communities.

The case studies in this volume provide an in-depth look into an often discussed but rarely studied subject—the involvement of activist black clergy and congregations in local politics. As these case studies indicate, that activism varies. It ranges from individual activism by ministers using personal persuasion in influencing policy, to the formation of coalitions between churches and civic organizations that collectively pool their resources to challenge inequalities and improve their communities. Activism also involves the most continuous and controversial aspect of church-based civic engagement—electoral politics. Not only does church-based electoral activism come close to violating the Constitution's mandate for the separation of church and state, but the engagement—whether through alignments with political machines or political action committees—may threaten to make some activist black clergy and congregations appendages of political organizations. The collective resources of activist churches can weaken local party organizations or can be used to leverage resources to develop depressed communities economically. Whatever the strategy or tactic of black activist clergy and congregations, the cases included here illustrate the vibrancy and complexity of black churches in urban politics.

NOTES

1. See Eric Foner, *Reconstruction: America's Unfinished Revolution, 1863–1877* (New York: Harper and Row, 1988); and C. Eric Lincoln and Lawrence H. Mamiya, *The Black Church in the African American Experience* (Durham: Duke University Press, 1990).

2. The late Reverend Charles Hill was the predecessor to the Reverend Charles Adams. During Hill's pastorate, the name of the church was Hartford Avenue Baptist Church rather than the church's current name, the Hartford Memorial Baptist Church.

3. See Lincoln and Mamiya, *Black Church*; and Evelyn Brooks Higginbotham, *Righteous Discontent: The Women's Movement in the Black Baptist Church, 1880–1920* (Cambridge: Harvard University Press, 1993); and Cheryl Townsend Gilkes, *If It Wasn't for the Women . . .: Black Women's Experience and Womanist Culture in Church and Community* (Maryknoll, N.Y.: Orbis Books, 2001).

4. See Aldon D. Morris, *The Origins of the Civil Rights Movement: Black Communities Organizing for Change* (New York: Free Press, 1984).

5. E. Franklin Frazier and C. Eric Lincoln, *The Negro Church in America/The Black Church Since Frazier* (New York: Schocken Books, 1974).

6. Lincoln and Mamiya, *Black Church*, 163.

7. Rufus P. Browning, Dale Rogers Marshall, and David H. Tabb, *Protest Is Not Enough: The Struggle for Blacks and Hispanics for Equality in Urban Politics* (Berkeley: University of California Press, 1984).

8. See Katie Day's analysis of black ministers' political strategies in Philadelphia, "The Construction of Political Strategies among African-American Clergy," in *Christian Clergy in American Politics*, edited by Sue E. S. Crawford and Laura Olson (Baltimore: Johns Hopkins University Press, 2001).

9. Steven Rosenstone and John Mark Hansen, *Mobilization, Participation, and Democracy in America* (New York: MacMillan, 1993).

10. See for example, Crawford and Olson, *Christian Clergy*, regarding the role of religious leaders in electoral and community-based politics; and Fredrick C. Harris,

Something Within: Religion in African-American Political Activism (New York: Oxford University Press, 1999) regarding the effects of church-based political activism on blacks, Anglo-whites, and Latinos.

11. See Foner, *Reconstruction*, and Harold Gosnell, *Negro Politicians: The Rise of Negro Politics in Chicago* (Chicago: University of Chicago, 1967).

12. See Adolph Reed, *The Jesse Jackson Phenomenon: The Crisis of Purpose in Afro-American Politics* (New Haven: Yale University Press, 1986).

13. Nancy Tatom Ammerman, *Congregation and Community* (New Brunswick: Rutgers University Press, 1997), 60. Also see Ammerman and see Fredrick C. Harris, *Something Within*, for discussions about religiously based resources and political and community activism.

14. See Harris, *Something Within*.

I

PERSONAL INFLUENCE, COALITIONS, AND PRESSURE GROUPS

1

Black Churches, Black Empowerment, and Atlanta's Civil Rights Legacy

Alton B. Pollard III

Atlanta is frequently portrayed in the popular media as the Mecca of African America, an urban enclave of unparalleled power, prosperity, and opportunity for America's denizens of African descent. While other leading urban centers like Chicago, New York, Los Angeles, and Oakland are no longer led by black mayors, Atlanta's majority black electorate has routinely returned African Americans to the mayoral seat the last thirty years. At the same time, the city has begun to experience a steady upturn and not so subtle demographic shift in its overall population during the last decade, fueled by favorable publicity, Sun Belt location, reportedly progressive politics, racial-ethnic diversification, and, most importantly, exuberant economic growth.[1]

Atlanta, the city once hailed as "too busy to hate," has understandably become a national showcase of black political power.[2] But all appearances notwithstanding, substantive race-related problems stemming from a long history of white racial hegemony and black civic exclusion and disfranchisement continue to negatively impact a substantial segment of the city's black population. Public policy decisions of the past, rooted in the perverse demagoguery of Southern white supremacy, bear a not-so-subtle responsibility for many of the economic injustices plaguing present-day Atlanta. Today, in the post–civil rights era, the central challenge facing the African American community in the city of Atlanta, as elsewhere, is how best to translate the hard-fought gains of black political power into a resurgent movement for black economic power.

This chapter focuses specifically on the role of Atlanta's African American churches in the public sphere by examining their strategic involvement in the current political struggle.[3] At the center of this investigation is a single question: do the city's black religious institutions function as viable agents of political change and economic incorporation since the civil rights movement? Answering this question requires careful explication of the contours of black church involvement in issues of social advocacy and public policy. In the end, many of the strategies that Atlanta's black churches use to influence the social sphere fall short of the level of direct political involvement; upon closer scrutiny, some churches have even been unwitting accomplices in reinforcing the status quo. Still, in the aggregate, the social witness of the churches explored in these pages points to the kind of ecclesiastical vision and infrastructure needed for more effective and systematic public engagement.

MOBILIZING FOR AFFIRMATIVE ACTION

One sweltering August night in 1999 on Auburn Avenue, at the historic Ebenezer Baptist Church, where the revered Martin Luther King Jr. once preached, approximately 150 people gathered to pray, testify, deliver speeches, and sing hymns in support of Mayor Bill Campbell's city-wide affirmative action program. They closed the evening with the signature song of the civil rights struggle, "We Shall Overcome." Meanwhile, about forty minutes north of inner-city Atlanta, in suburban Gwinnett County, an equally sizeable gathering of people met in a banquet hall, feasted on hors d'oeuvres, listened to the sounds of a Dixie jazz band, and wrote out checks to the conservative Southeastern Legal Foundation—a group strongly denounced by Mayor Campbell as a logical successor to the citizens' councils of old—in support of a lawsuit against the city of Atlanta's affirmative action program.[4] These parallel events offer an instructive perspective on the contested nature of Atlanta politics, economics, and culture, where most members of the black community are as determined to see the aims of affirmative action realized as some whites are to end them.

The affirmative action struggle in Atlanta is a constructive starting point, therefore, for us to consider the effect of black churches on the local political and economic environment. Cynthia Hewitt, in a study of the correlation between ethnic hegemony and economic empowerment in Atlanta, indicates that after nearly thirty years of affirmative action the city's black community has successfully challenged white market dominance in a number of government-linked industries—construction, real estate and finance, transportation and utilities, education and social services, and municipal employment.[5] On the other hand, the preponderance of Atlanta's industries remain largely outside the sphere of local government and its ability to influence market-structuring decisions and outcomes. These are businesses with which the city does not heavily interface and cannot therefore regulate, yet which continue to erect subtle but substantial barriers to black economic inclusion and empowerment. At present, spreading from the government sector to churches and other indigenous organizations, African Americans are actively seeking to advance their economic interests on at least three major fronts: (1) the forcing open of white-dominated labor markets, (2) the expansion of black business opportunities, and (3) equal housing and community opportunities. In the final analysis, however, the ability of black Atlantans to challenge the white monopolization of capital can only rely in part on the African American community's resolve to maintain a degree of social regulation of the economy through affirmative action. The majority black electorate will also have to decide at some point to pursue an alternative civic discourse where a more progressive redistribution of resources for the many can be advanced.

Nevertheless, Atlanta's current campaign to save affirmative action, what one leading black elected official describes as "the defining issue of our time," calls to our attention in significant ways the importance of the black church, real and potential, in public policy matters.[6] City government is of course a public secular institution whose mayor, currently Shirley Franklin, is the leading public official. As a microcomponent of the larger system of local, state, and federal governance, city hall is expected to be discreet in matters of church-state separation. Yet the earlier illustrated appearance of the black church in Atlanta city politics, specifically sought by political leadership to combat the current crisis, is indicative of how much the two spheres do intersect. Black activist culture, political, economic, or otherwise, often intersects with and corresponds closely to black religious culture. In Atlanta as in other African American communities, especially across the South, religion and politics are only partially differentiated at best; institutional boundaries are permeable; notions of separation of church and state are unintelligible and even reprehensible, in the face of continuing social injustices. In the unremitting struggle of African Americans to secure social and political gains made over the years, the popular belief in affirmative action as a form of moral agency as well as a political commitment should not be underestimated. As one local historian insightfully observed, "Black Atlantans' support for the city's affirmative action program is just as strong as the Jewish community's support for the state of Israel."[7]

In short, political activity in present-day Atlanta is enacted through a specific cultural landscape, which is heavily influenced—but by no means dominated—by the African American church. This does not mean, however, that the public significance of Atlanta's black churches is confined to their cultural role as the repository and reservoir of African American strength and commonality. Their more concrete and acknowledged importance lies instead in their historic ability to garner and mobilize support for social and political causes. Despite the fact that the actual number of black churches in the city of Atlanta remains an evasive quantity, their influence in the public sphere is somewhat easier to disclose and interpret.[8]

Generally speaking, the public influence of the city's black churches may be described as broadly apparent but clearly inconsistent, largely because of a lack of any systematic strategy or collective purpose. Public activities range from the wielding of political influence (electoral and protest) to neighborhood organizing and advocacy and economic development. Andrew Billingsley, in a recent survey of 150 Atlanta black churches, found that 131 congregations, or a full 87 percent, were actively engaged in some form of social or political engagement.[9] Building on his findings, I have found a commensurate commitment to the larger community among congregations of every size and description, from storefronts with memberships of fewer than one hundred to megachurches with memberships reported upwards of five thousand (the median membership of Atlanta's black congregations is between two hundred and one thousand). Still, when it comes to engaging the public square on such key policy matters as affirmative action, the tendency among faith-based institutions is for a few prominent churches and church-based organizations to be in the vanguard.[10] To the point, Atlanta's black faith community has a storied tradition of involvement in social activism, but the glaring absence of collaborative, sustained, and systemic engagement with the present social order belies the city's historic reputation as the "cradle of the civil rights movement."

THE ROLE OF TRADITIONAL ACTIVIST CHURCHES

The churches in the Auburn Avenue community became famous for their efforts to empower Atlanta blacks prior to and during the civil rights years. Auburn Avenue, or "Sweet Auburn" as it is more affectionately known, lies a mere one half mile east of downtown Atlanta. A part of the former Fourth Ward, it is equal parts thoroughfare and neighborhood, encompassed by Edgewood Avenue and Butler Street, Hilliard, Jackson and Houston (John Wesley Dobbs to the north and south) and the south end of Piedmont and Boulevard.[11] In 1957, *Fortune Magazine* named Sweet Auburn "the richest Negro Street in the world." Indeed, during the era of segregation Auburn Avenue was the epicenter of black Atlanta cultural and commercial life, boasting an impressive array of black-owned hotels, businesses, shops, restaurants, and social organizations. By the 1970s the neighborhood that former Mayor Jackson could once proudly point to as "a living lab for Martin Luther King, Jr.'s dreams" had become a casualty of integration, a deserted street of dreams for African Americans, many of whom now harbored mainstream and sometimes even suburban aspirations.[12] In the 1980s, construction of the Martin Luther King Jr. National Historic Site and the Martin Luther King Jr. Center for Nonviolent Social Change brought in tourists but did nothing to revive local fortunes. After years of decline and neglect, Sweet Auburn is once again showing modest but hopeful signs of economic recovery. The entrepreneurial wealth of Auburn Avenue mainstay Atlanta Life Insurance Co. is a source of local pride, and the venerable Butler Street YMCA has opened a new $1.6 million facility. However, poverty in the area is still deeply entrenched, especially among the elderly. In no uncertain terms, the willingness of Auburn Avenue's historic black churches—Ebenezer Baptist, Wheat Street Baptist, and Big Bethel African Methodist Episcopal—to commit themselves and their resources to the revitalization of Auburn Avenue will have a significant bearing on the community's return to stability.

Ebenezer Baptist Church

Serving as a house of worship and freedom shrine, Ebenezer is revered by visitors as ground zero for the civil rights movement. The church stands as a living monument to the progress of a people and a nation. Some have questioned, however, if the Ebenezer of today has any social currency other than its celebrated past.[13] Much of Ebenezer's reputation for activism predates the modern civil rights movement, to a time when black leadership typically came from the ranks of the elite—educators, entrepreneurs, and more often than not, the clergy. The Reverend Alfred Daniel (A. D.) Williams and his son-in-law Reverend Martin Luther King Sr. were in the forefront of the African American struggle for equality at a time when black politics were quite understandably defensive, whites were the only candidates, and black voters (who, despite segregation, still numbered several thousand in Atlanta) relied heavily on the pulpit to learn which candidate was considered the least detrimental to blacks. Called to the pulpit of Ebenezer in 1894, Williams served as the first president of the Atlanta branch of the NAACP, organizing the voter registration drive among blacks that helped defeat a bond referendum providing for the construction of white schools only. Two years later, a second bond issue was passed, but amended this time to include five new schools (and the first black high school) for the African American community. Williams preached a petit bourgeois message of black achievement, pushing where possible for the economic and political opportunities that were to give rise to Atlanta's early black middle class.

In 1935, Ebenezer's third pastor, Martin Luther King Sr., led a march on city hall to demand greater voting rights for blacks. In the 1940s, with the financial backing of Ebenezer and the active assistance of King, Atlanta's black teachers waged a protracted but successful legal battle to receive equal pay with their white counterparts. Auburn Avenue's power brokers, the black churches and businesses, in tandem with the city's black colleges, worked closely together in the fight against political disfranchisement, providing each other with fiscal support and counsel. Still, the pace of social change was slow, and excruciatingly so for the black poor. By 1960, Ebenezer and

"Daddy King," as King Sr. was widely known, had come to symbolize the old guard, an outmoded politics of gradualism, and a generation of leaders who, despite their firm commitment to social change, seldom negotiated from a position of strength. That same year, Martin Luther King Jr. resigned after five years as pastor of the Dexter Avenue Baptist Church in Montgomery, Alabama, to join his father as copastor at Ebenezer. Largely as a result of the far-flung social witness of Martin Luther King Jr. and his espousal of nonviolent resistance, Ebenezer took on a new ecumenical and worldwide fame.

The extraordinary history of Ebenezer Baptist Church makes it altogether impossible to ignore, therefore, as an institution of continuing social and political relevance. Cloaked in the aura of the civil rights era, the church has become a progressive beacon of hope for human rights causes everywhere. From protests against the war in the Persian Gulf in the early 1990s to current support for the city of Atlanta's affirmative action program, Ebenezer's sponsorship of political forums and rallies influences the court of public opinion. In the last few years alone, former Presidents Bill Clinton and Jimmy Carter, former Vice President Al Gore, Archbishop Desmond Tutu, and former Atlanta Mayors Maynard Jackson and Andrew Young have addressed various public policy matters from Ebenezer's pulpit. As earlier indicated, the church took an active part in former Mayor Bill Campbell's efforts to defend affirmative action. It has also supported the eleven former and current employees of suburban Atlanta defense contractor Lockheed Martin Corporation, now plaintiffs in a lawsuit charging the company with racial discrimination against black employees in promotions, performance evaluations, and compensation. Despite these and similar activities, the daunting perception in the local community remains, that Ebenezer does little to promote substantive change.

The most dramatic proof of Ebenezer's lack of concern would appear to lie within a five-block radius of the church, where several aging high-rise and low-rise complexes are located. These cater mostly to the elderly black poor, as does a nursing home across Auburn Avenue from the King Center. According to the Fulton County Services Office of Aging Division, approximately ten thousand seniors live in and around the Auburn Avenue community. This is by far the greatest concentration of seniors in the county, some 32 percent of whom fall below the poverty line.[14] Predictably, the attendant dilemmas of gentrification have begun to set in as old houses undergo renovation and new ones are built just east of the original King homestead two blocks from the church. With some of the new houses now priced in the hundreds of thousands, Ebenezer's detractors question the church's commitment to the elderly and to organizing low-income working families for social and economic empowerment.

For Ebenezer, the decision to build its new facility directly across the street from the original sanctuary is the most salient expression of their commitment to the people of Auburn Avenue and to the larger Atlanta community. Dr. Joseph L. Roberts Jr., Ebenezer's senior pastor for more than a quarter century, stresses that the church had a sacred obligation to remain on Auburn Avenue. When white-owned banks reneged on funding the new $8 million church several years ago, five black-owned banks collaborated to fund it.[15] According to the local print media, Ebenezer would have been more bankable had it elected to move to the more affluent suburbs.[16] Instead, the continuing physical presence of the church in the heart of the city, with the backing of the black banking community, allows it to remain a significant factor in the revitalization of the King Historic District and Sweet Auburn community.

Despite the fact that the majority of Ebenezer's members are middle or upper class and no longer reside in the neighborhood, Dr. Roberts vigorously maintains the actions of the church prove "it is not where you live, but where you spend your time and resources that is very important." Ebenezer has an institutional commitment to systemic and structural change that begins and ends with public advocacy for "the least of these" (Matthew 25:45): "We're continuing [King's] legacy by saying that you can transform the city by expending funds in it so that the people who live here will have the parable of hope."[17]

A little-known case in point is Ebenezer's letter-writing campaigns for the poor, in which members of the church have appealed to the federal government to make hunger legislation more helpful to those in need. Members have also been participants in a campaign advocating worldwide debt cancellation, especially as it relates to the near-indentured status of poor nations relative to wealthier nations. At the community level the Intergenerational Resource Center, Inc. started as an adult day care for Ebenezer families and now operates as an independent nonprofit organization serving the larger community. The center's offerings, including care and rehabilitation services for the elderly and disabled young adults and a respite program for caregivers, has made it the second largest adult day-care provider in Fulton County.

Still, even Dr. Roberts acknowledges that Ebenezer's ministries of social transformation are far outpaced by its more therapeutic ministries for social outreach. In addition to the above-named advocacy projects, the congregation has plans to build a $6 million community resource center adjacent the church, delivering an array of legal, medical, psychological, and special services. As well, the church has partnered with the Public Assistance Coalition, lobbying to increase aid to dependent children to the level of the cost-of-living index. Nevertheless, it is in terms of social outreach that Ebenezer's presence is most pronounced. Prominent among these ministries are a crisis food closet, eviction prevention, transportation assistance, homeless care, employment counseling and referral, HIV/AIDS ministry, job training programs, and support services for teenage mothers. Every Saturday morning the elderly of Auburn Avenue and other residents benefit from the Kingdom Food Cooperative, a marketplace sponsored by the church, providing fresh produce at cost to a community not served by a major grocery store. On every first Sunday the church conducts voter registration drives. To quote Dr. Roberts, "Even while challenging systems, the needs of persons must be ameliorated." This focus on human development is consistent with Ebenezer's therapeutic mission, not to duplicate available social services but to provide services where none previously existed.[18]

Wheat Street Baptist Church

One and a half blocks to the west of Ebenezer, on the corner of Auburn Avenue and William Holmes Borders Drive, is the Wheat Street Baptist Church. Founded during Reconstruction, seven persons began holding Sunday services under a brush arbor at what is now Howell Street, near Auburn Avenue. The small congregation relocated several times before finally moving to Wheat Street, which would be renamed Auburn Avenue a few short years later. The Reverend William Holmes Borders, a new professor of religion and philosophy at Morehouse College, became pastor in 1937 and immediately raised the bar for community involvement by black churches in the city. Like fellow civil rights pioneer Martin Luther King Sr., Borders took seriously the power of the ballot, leading black voter registration drives in the late 1930s. Borders was also instrumental in the creation of the Atlanta Negro Voters League (ANVL), an organization consisting of black Democrats and Republicans who were dedicated to establishing a black united front in local elections. Meeting at Wheat Street, the Butler Street YMCA (which began at Wheat Street a half century earlier), and other locations, such community stalwarts as Borders, John Wesley Dobbs, Grace Towns Hamilton, Warren Cochrane, A. T. Walden, and others interviewed candidates and endorsed the one whom they believed best supported black interests or, at the very least, they considered less harmful to black people. On the eve of every election, the league then issued its own "ticket" from the pulpit of Wheat Street. Come election day, the vast majority of the black electorate reportedly chose to follow ANVL recommendations.

The astute leadership of people like Borders was critical in an era when blacks had little to hope for and even less to bargain with. In the 1940s, he raised $11,000 to bury blacks lynched in Monroe, Georgia. In 1947, Borders and other black ministers persuaded then Mayor William Hartsfield to hire Atlanta's first black police officers. Ten years later, he spearheaded the first successful campaign to desegregate the city's transit lines, hotels, and restaurants. In the early 1960s, Wheat Street was the scene of major political rallies. In both the 1960 mayoral campaign and the 1962 congressional race, Atlanta's disciplined black electorate supported the candidate who went on to win. Nevertheless, as has already been seen, discontent within Atlanta's black community was quickly rising over the slow pace of social and political change.

It was Border's far-sighted leadership in 1956 that reintroduced Atlanta's black churches to a cardinal principle in the historic struggle for social equality—namely, organizing for economic enfranchisement and change. After complaints by church members and residents of the community about harassment by dishonest lenders, Borders organized the Wheat Street Federal Credit Union, the South's first church-sponsored and the first black church-sponsored credit union in the country. Today the credit union, which began with nine church members contributing $5 each, has more than one thousand members, holds assets approaching $1.5 million, and has approved more than fifty thousand loan applications totaling approximately $10 million. In 1964, the church obtained a federal loan and opened Wheat Street Gardens, a community that includes 280 two-bedroom apartments for low-income families. Wheat Street Gardens, the nation's first black church-operated rental complex, was quickly followed by Wheat Street Gardens II and III and, in the 1970s, by Wheat Street Towers, a retirement high-rise. However, when Wheat Street Gardens II and III, plagued by a series of financial mishaps and structural difficulties, fell into disrepair in the early 1980s, the federal government foreclosed.

Today, Wheat Street is led by Dr. Michael N. Harris, the sixth pastor in the church's history. Wheat Street owns more than $33 million in real estate in the Auburn Avenue neighborhood. In a continuation of the work of Borders, the Wheat Street Charitable Foundation, the economic development arm of the church, has purchased several single-family dwellings, an office building, and two mini-shopping centers in addition to the housing complexes the church already owns. Plans are now underway to renovate the two shopping centers along Auburn Avenue. The church is also a principal sponsor of the William Holmes Borders Comprehensive After Care Treatment Center, a drug rehabilitation program begun by Borders in 1983 at Wheat Street that now operates as an independent facility. The church has an impressive track record where affordable housing, commercial development, and ministries of social outreach are concerned. Far less clear, however, is whether Wheat Street is also committed to fighting for affirmative action, or any other form of broad-based economic empowerment, at the public policy level.

Big Bethel African Methodist Episcopal Church

At the other end of Auburn Avenue is Big Bethel A.M.E. Church, the oldest African American congregation in Atlanta. Formed as a Methodist church prior to the incorporation of Atlanta in 1847, the congregation associated

with the African Methodist Episcopal Church after the Civil War. The first
public school for blacks in Atlanta was started in the basement of Big Bethel
in 1879. Two years later, Morris Brown College, the only college in Georgia
founded solely by blacks, held its first classes in Big Bethel before moving to
its own campus. The church was also instrumental in the founding of Turner
Theological Center, one of the constituent schools of the Interdenominational Theological Center. Long affixed to the front of the church was one of
the city's landmark signs, just recently replaced: a large neon cross bearing
the message "Jesus Saves."

The church has had a long tradition of effective leadership in its history.
During segregation, Big Bethel was the church of many of Georgia's first
black elected officials, educators, and entrepreneurs. Like its sister churches
along the Auburn Avenue corridor, Ebenezer and Wheat Street, Big Bethel
was a focal point for political rallies and voter registration drives and the center of community cohesion. In the words of local Atlanta historian and minister Herman "Skip" Mason, "there was no such thing as the separation of
church and state at Big Bethel."[19] Today, a litany of problems has plagued the
area within sight of the church, including daylight drug sales, panhandling,
dilapidated and boarded-up buildings owned by absentee landlords, and a
paucity of local merchants. Under the leadership of Big Bethel's current pastor, Dr. James L. Davis, the church is once again raising its profile in the community.

The church, located in the heart of the Auburn Avenue business district,
never considered participating in the mainstream trend of relocating to the
suburbs. Davis interprets his congregation's commitment in this way: "If
we're going to stay on Auburn Avenue, we find it necessary to save the community if we're going to save the church."[20] The expressed mission of Big
Bethel—neighborhood revitalization and community development—began
in earnest in 1993 with the church's first real-estate acquisitions in forty years.
Since that time the church has purchased thirteen neighborhood properties
for about $1 million. In the first two years, a vacant lot that had been the fo-
cal point of illicit activities was transformed into a recreational site for church
and community youth. Directly across the street from the church, a gas station, plagued with environmental challenges, became a parking lot employ-
ing two full-time attendants and housing an auto detailing business. In 1996,
the former Vibrations nightclub on Auburn Avenue was resurrected as the
new Job Training Center. The nearby E.D.M.I. Corporation was established
to offer young adults vocational preparation. Current church plans call for
the recently purchased Casino nightclub and adjacent pool hall to be renovated and leased to a dance company. Not only is it anticipated that the Bal-
lethnic Dance Company will enrich the community's cultural reputation, but
it is also expected to attract over one hundred people daily to Sweet Auburn.
The church's most immediate priority, however, involves a property on Bell

Street between Auburn and Edgewood Avenues, which is slated to house the One Stop Social Service and Family Life Center, providing the Auburn Avenue community with a multipurpose outreach facility. Envisioned as a facility for persons in transition, site proposals call for a day-care center, mailboxes, showers, GED classes, and other practical necessities. The church has a number of other advocacy projects under consideration, including building a day-care center for children with AIDS on land the church recently purchased.

Big Bethel's commitment has not yet translated into mass economic opportunity for the surrounding community, yet the church seems well aware that its ministry of expansion must empower poor and working-class African Americans. Members are encouraged to give $30 monthly specifically for the Nehemiah Ministry and to seize ownership of a prophetic entrepreneurial vision to restore the people and proud heritage of Auburn Avenue. Recently, as part of its revitalization efforts, Big Bethel also completed a $1.8 million renovation of the church edifice. Finally, the church has established a series of social outreach ministries ranging from employment networking and homeless intervention to tutorial programs.

EXTENDING ECONOMIC OPPORTUNITY

In this analysis of the historic black churches along Auburn Avenue, economic empowerment emerged as the chief means and pragmatic form that their comprehension of the affirmative action struggle has taken. With the possible exception of Ebenezer, each of these congregations has further determined that intermediate, entrepreneurial solutions to achieving economic capacity—job training programs, small business incubators, investment projects, public-private collaborations, and credit unions—are the best means to effect change and intervene in an uncertain political environment. It is instructive to contrast the religious commitment that the churches of Auburn have made to extend economic empowerment into the surrounding community with some of the more popular church-backed programs of today. The most prominent of these teachings is the prosperity gospel, a message that is typically (but certainly not exclusively) associated with evangelical and charismatic churches and emphasizes personal health and wealth. Frequently presented as a perk of church membership, prosperity has yet to give any indication that its message also possesses broad restorative potential for the black community.

The one caveat to consider in relation to the aforementioned churches and economic empowerment is the case of Ebenezer, whose ecclesiastical currency ramifies beyond Auburn Avenue, extending outward to influence city policymaking and to support affirmative action policy in particular. Clearly, not every church is willing or prepared to fight at the level of securing affirmative action as a matter of public policy. In the cases of Wheat Street and Big Bethel, it is quite plausible that while Atlanta's affirmative action policies have proven to be of immeasurable benefit to the African American community as a whole, their impact on the Old Fourth Ward has never been substantial enough to give impetus to a like-minded marshalling of resources. Instead, these two congregations have elected to try to raise the quality of life for the people of Sweet Auburn on their own terms. While it remains to be seen what kind of impact their investments will finally have on community revitalization, it is hoped that their commitment to the demands of economic justice has only just begun.

Considering Atlanta's charged political environment in which affirmative action and other programs designed to promote the economic well-being of women and people of color are under attack, such church-sponsored initiatives as those found on Auburn Avenue are of critical importance to black progress and serve as a source of reference for similar faith-based initiatives. Nevertheless, if the revival of Auburn Avenue as envisioned by Ebenezer, Wheat Street, and Big Bethel is to rightfully succeed, then it is imperative that a greater partnership develop than currently exists—between the congregations and in collaboration with other local institutions—to address the root problems of the entire community. It is enough to note, for instance, that each of the churches has only infrequently established alliances with leading neighborhood development organizations like the Sweet Auburn Business and Improvement Association or the Historic District Development Corporation (a nonprofit agency) to attack the overarching systematic needs of the community. In the end, as Wayne Santoro so adroitly notes, it is not organizations per se "but rather better organized black communities" which make political entities more accountable for the passage, implementation, and retention of economic policies advantageous to their black constituents.[21] How well the black churches of Auburn Avenue are prepared to organize and continuously pressure for community policies—beyond the competing demands of church polity—ultimately matters.

The lack of viable cooperation between the churches of Auburn Avenue and between these churches and extant political agencies also has broad implications at the public policy level. Although the respective churches and their members have made important, and even signal, contributions to the local black community, it is hardly axiomatic that their efforts will lead to a significant structural witness. In order to operate as a radical transformative presence these congregations (no less churches everywhere) will have to commit themselves to more extensive forms of political engagement, to forms that critically attend to the underlying structural and systemic forces at work against community building. For the black marginalized and excluded, particularly along Auburn Avenue, the maldistribution of social goods and services is one such factor that has been weakly contested for too long. Similarly, a critique of the structural and leadership issues that encourage churches to focus on the entrepreneurial, often to the neglect of the political, may be another. To take Santoro one step further, then, the problems facing Auburn Avenue and many other black communities not only require that churches and other social institutions be better organized but that they be authentic change agents mobilizing against state and corporate efforts at black privation. Only time will tell whether these elite churches in the heart of Atlanta are prepared to rise up and bite the proverbial hand that feeds them.

PARTNERSHIPS BETWEEN CHURCH AND SOCIETY

An exceptional example of how Atlanta's black churches have formed more constructive partnerships with their neighborhood and government agencies comes from the Vine City Housing Ministry, Inc. The Vine City Community, over one hundred years old, has been described as a historically and commercially important neighborhood. Located on the western edge of the downtown business district—directly across from the Georgia Dome completed in 1992—Vine City was once home to a thriving black middle-class cultural and business community. By the 1960s the community had deteriorated almost beyond recognition; there would soon be more public housing located here than in any other section of the city. Analogous to Sweet Auburn, located on the other side of downtown, the demise of Vine City is easily traceable to decades of neglect and indifference by city officials. By the 1980s plunging living standards, escalating unemployment, disintegrating families, rapacious developers, and especially the threatened loss of homes, churches, and finally the community itself proved catalyst enough for the local faithful to become organized. In 1986 eleven congregations, their pastors, residents, and other community leaders devised a collective action plan against governmental plans to erect a state office building (and shortly after that the Georgia Dome) in the latest incarnation of "urban renewal." After months of organized protests the government plan was defeated and replaced by an alternative project of mixed land use.[22] The successful movement to "Save Vine City" was led by Reverend W. L. Cottrell—the fiery, outspoken pastor of the Beulah Baptist Church. Shortly thereafter, the Vine City Housing Ministry (VCHM) was born. Their mission and purpose were clear as Reverend Cottrell explains:

> The industrial complex was moving from downtown in this direction. I defined it as a monster moving with eyes that could not see, ears that could not hear, a heart that could not feel. And our task then must need be to not keep it from

moving, but to sensitize the monster. Give it some eyes to see us, ears to hear us, and give it some compassion, give it a heart so it could feel that we could work together in the combination of rebuilding our community. In the process we could pull all of the churches together—which is the Vine City Housing Ministry. We got all of the preachers together. Brought in the Concerned Black Clergy, brought in the Atlanta Baptist Ministers Union and got them all angry, got the churches angry.[23]

The Vine City Housing Ministry has been an asset to the community in the most concrete of ways. In the Vineyard, on the corner of Northside Drive and Martin Luther King Jr. Drive, sits a cluster of attractive and affordable pastel-colored townhouses, a result of the work of the VCHM. To date, the ministry has built and/or remodeled in excess of five hundred units of housing, a mixture of small apartment complexes, facilities with three to four units, and single-family homes. For a time the VCHM was also engaged in job training and business support via its Employment Resource Center. The fruit of their labors was instrumental in helping the city successfully compete for a $250 million Federal Empowerment Zone grant awarded in 1994 (Atlanta was one of seven cities receiving such a grant). This made new business investments in a 9.3 square-mile area containing thirty of Atlanta's poorest neighborhoods, including Vine City and Auburn Avenue, eligible for tax incentives, property tax relief, and job tax credits.[24] Yet and still, despite the many successes that the VCHM and other community developers have enjoyed, economic redevelopment, particularly on the commercial side, has happened at a dramatically slower pace than envisioned by the community. Severely circumscribed by a lack of corporate capital and government inertia, Vine City's black poor nonetheless continue their efforts to combat poverty and disempowerment with negligible resources.

Perhaps even more than the building and renovating of affordable housing, as important as these activities are, the most remarkable aspect of the Vine City story has been the degree of cooperation between churches. It comes as something of a surprise to learn that none of the participating houses of worship are physically located in Vine City. Nevertheless these eleven churches, with the support of their denominations, have joined material resources to play a leading role in community organizing for economic change. Their success springs from a myriad of other factors as well. As Billingsley notes, the pooling of resources in the African American community requires imaginative, bold, and able leadership—the leadership in this case coming from a group of visionary clergy and parishioners.[25] Effective mobilization further requires the will to suspend individual (and/or institutional) goals for the collective effort. On the one hand, the success of the VCHM was dependent on the cooperation and participation of its member churches, and on the faithful keeping their eyes on the prize of community empowerment on the other. It bears repeating, the work of the VCHM would have met with far less success had extensive collaboration between the churches and other public and private agencies not occurred.

CLERICAL LEADERSHIP IN THE QUEST FOR ECONOMIC AND POLITICAL EMPOWERMENT

No investigation into the political influence of the black church in Atlanta is complete without due consideration being given to the one organization that has aptly been called "the most important ecumenical thrust of the Black Church in the city of Atlanta, the Concerned Black Clergy of Metropolitan Atlanta, Inc. (CBC)."[26] Unlike most faith-based initiatives in the city, the CBC represents a critical mass of clergy and laity (its active membership includes 125 churches), including not a few whites, who come together on a weekly basis to address critical community issues. The CBC's origins date back to 1983 when Reverend Joseph Lowery, then president of the Southern Christian Leadership Conference, and Reverend Cameron Alexander, president of the Georgia General Missionary Baptist Convention, organized a meeting of about twenty socially conscious ministers and lay persons. The primary focus of the faith-based advocacy group then as now was to address the pressing needs of the homeless and dispossessed in Atlanta, the vast majority of whom were and are black.

Since 1997, the Reverend Timothy McDonald, pastor of the First Iconium Baptist Church, has served as president of the organization. A driving force in city politics, Reverend McDonald's resume includes a stint as deputy campaign manager for Maynard Jackson's successful return to the mayoral office in 1989. The CBC has evolved over the years into an organization that provides grassroots education on legislative policies that threaten the stability of working-class neighborhoods. In addition, CBC has developed a myriad of programs that speak to the needs and concerns of Atlanta's African American population. Rooted in the tradition of the black church and black protest, the CBC has become an unmitigated force in the religiously led movement to challenge racial discrimination throughout the city.

The current assault by the CBC on inequality is two-pronged, focusing on economic and community development, and on discrimination in the workplace. Seeing itself as the "voice for the voiceless," the CBC has become a neighborhood leader in the economic struggle for equality. In East Atlanta, reverse white flight is rapidly changing local demographics and raising political tensions, as black homeowners of more limited means fear being uprooted. The area has become a battleground for Reverend McDonald and Atlanta Councilwoman Sherry Dorsey, who have strategically filled meetings of the area's Neighborhood Planning Unit—government created, neighborhood-based organizations approved to review land use changes, subdivision proposals and public projects—with busloads of black residents for the express purpose of controlling zoning requests to the city council. On Atlanta's Southside, the CBC is partnering with Bank of America and the Fulton County Housing Authority to work on affordable housing and a number of other investment projects. The proposed $14 million, fifty-acre mixed-use housing development in East Point will include more than 200 apartment units and 130 homes, marketed to low- to moderate-income renters and buyers. The CBC's initial $20,000 investment is expected to pay dividends in some of Atlanta's most neglected communities for decades.

The CBC affordable housing initiatives follow earlier successful campaigns by the group that encouraged African Americans to transfer their money from white to black financial institutions in protest against glaring racial disparities in local home mortgage lending practices. The effect of unchecked workplace discrimination can be equally deep, and here the CBC represents a substantial oppositional presence in the effort to permanently transform Atlanta's corporate culture. Subtle exclusions from the upper echelons of management and explicit forms of racial harassment are but the latest examples of discriminatory patterns African Americans have faced in the employ of some of the city's leading companies. For instance, after a series of disturbing incidents at Lockheed Martin, the Equal Employment Opportunity Commission issued nine findings of racial discrimination (and one finding of discrimination against the disabled) against the company. Leadership from the CBC and other prominent advocacy groups met with company executives, demanding compensation for loss of wages to black workers due to missed promotions and that the company find ways to end its culture of bigotry and discrimination.

The most potent weapon the CBC has used as an instrument of economic change has been the electoral process itself. From the onset, the CBC has aggressively worked to mobilize the black community for local, state, and national elections, often to considerable effect. In 1998, blacks were 25 percent of the registered voters in the state yet cast 30 percent of all ballots, an 11 percent increase in just four years' time that provided the margin of victory for Democratic gubernatorial candidate Roy Barnes.[27] By contrast, the same midterm elections showed an overall decline in the number of African Americans voting nationwide.[28] Among the groups leading the political resurgence in Atlanta has been the CBC through their sponsorship of voter awareness programs, registration drives, and other activities. During the 2000 get-out-the-vote campaign, the CBC joined forces with the African American Leadership Council, an offshoot of the People for the American Way Foundation, to prepare a comprehensive forty-page voter's manual to assist local pastors and religious organizations with voter education, registration, and participation.[29] In addition, the CBC held strategy sessions with black pastors to help organize inner-city constituents and energize middle-class African

Americans. Due largely to the organizational strength and influence of black churches and their political action committees, not only did Atlanta's black voter turnout surge, it ran counter to the presidential results statewide for Texas Governor George W. Bush.[30]

CONCLUSION

The African American church in Atlanta is a dynamic force for change. As the principal social institution historically owned and controlled by blacks, it continues to function as the main guarantor of cultural values in African American public discourse and life. In explicit ways, black Atlanta's social and political life exhibits an affinity for the organizational and cultural influences of black religion. For the city's black inhabitants, religious beliefs and practices possess important capacity in the public square. In matters of political moment, the institutional black church can be a profound catalyst for change. The important question we have considered is this: How and to what extent are Atlanta's African American churches responding to the economic struggle for equality? Are they prepared to meet the challenges set before them?

The reputation of the city of Atlanta as a center of the civil rights movement is based largely on the premise, both true and false, that the black faith-based community worked together to bring about social and political change. Now more than then, black sacred institutions are needed to work together to bring the economic revitalization of black communities to fruition. As we have seen, working independently, the churches of Auburn Avenue have been able to make some progress on community development but much more is still needed. Not surprisingly, denominational considerations often serve as a serious impediment to collaboration between neighboring churches. Religious territorialism—ecclesiastical divisions fueled by pressures of pedigree, prestige, and power—can be another inhibiting factor. Regardless, whenever the development of a community is stymied, as is the case along Auburn Avenue, the challenge for sister churches is to help create a new sense of community spirit. Solidarity in public advocacy, between churches and with other organizations, must become the rule rather than the exception.

It goes without saying that black churches cannot possibly meet the economic needs of the African American community on their own. Still, as Georgia Tech economics professor Thomas D. Boston notes, "A large amount of money and income goes into the church, and that money needs to be put to work in the community."[31] Through better organization and management of capital within the community, the church can become the creator of jobs, the provider of credit, and a sacramental source for social justice. By investing in women, children, and men, the church will influence the public sphere, empowering and enabling others to engage the political process.

Finally, the actions of black sacred institutions have made an aggregate positive impact on public policy in the city of Atlanta. However, interviews with community activists leave me with little doubt that progressive black church leadership has been virtually invisible in the fight to save Atlanta's affirmative action program and ineffective in critical public debate. Despite the hundreds of black churches in the Atlanta area, only a handful of ministers were frequently and respectfully cited as politically active: Reverend Timothy McDonald of First Iconium Baptist Church; Dr. Gerald Durley of Providence Baptist Church; Reverend Joseph Lowery, president emeritus of the SCLC; Reverend Cameron Alexander of Antioch Baptist Church North; and, on occasion, Dr. Joseph L. Roberts Jr. of Ebenezer Baptist Church. For sure there are others who, for one reason or another, were overlooked or simply forgotten.[32] But for many churches, the recognition that there has been a shift in the political terrain and that the struggle for freedom has moved from the steps of the courthouse and city hall to the inner chambers of power seems never to have been made.

In the end, the work of community empowerment and liberation in black America requires far more than what institutional black religion alone can hope to accomplish. Still, there is every good reason to conclude that African American communities of faith will continue to be a strong source of solidarity and a potent force for progressive social change in an unjust social order. Here and there, across the Atlanta city skyline, glimpses of the prophetic are to be found that point to the potential of black faith communities as they face the twenty-first century.

NOTES

1. According to the U.S. Census Bureau, the city of Atlanta's population has risen after a twenty-year decline from 397,612 in 1990 to 421,007 in 2000, a 5.5 percent increase. The African American population declined from 264,262 to 255,689, or from 67 percent to 61.4 percent of the city's population. Overall, African Americans account for some 26 percent of the twenty counties designated as Metropolitan Statistical Atlanta (MSA), out of a total population of 4,112,198. See Census 2000, Population Division, U.S. Census Bureau, Washington, D.C. Additional statistical sources for data include the Atlanta Regional Commission's Outlook 2001 and Julie Hairston, "Atlanta Draws White Middle Class," *Atlanta Journal-Constitution*, 22 March 2001.

2. A phrase coined by Mayor William Hartsfield in 1955 to project the image of a city living more or less in racial harmony.

3. While not fully inclusive in the theological sense, "African American churches," in sociological shorthand, applies here to all black sacred institutions.

4. A lawsuit was filed in 1999 by a conservative public interest law firm, the Southeastern Legal Foundation, which has worked to dismantle affirmative action pro-

grams in other cities. The charge is that Atlanta's Equal Business Opportunity (EBO) program, which seeks to award up to 34 percent of city contracts to racial-ethnic and female-owned firms, discriminates against white businesses. The foundation has also filed recent suits against metro Atlanta school systems.

5. Cynthia Hewitt, "Job Segregation, Ethnic Hegemony, and Earnings Inequality," in *The Atlanta Paradox*, ed. D. Sjoquist (New York: Russell Sage Foundation, 2000), 210.

6. Maynard Eaton, "Standing Firm: The Southeastern Legal Foundation vs. The City of Atlanta's Affirmative Action Program," *Atlanta Tribune*, August 1999.

7. Carlos Campos, "Tough Talk Spurs Fear of City Rift Overheated," *Atlanta Journal-Constitution*, 7 July 1999.

8. Andrew Billingsley's important new study, *Mighty Like a River: The Black Church and Social Reform* (1999), draws upon a list of churches provided by the Atlanta Ministerial Alliance that included some three hundred churches. A more recent printout provided this researcher by the ecumenical Christian Council of Metropolitan Atlanta puts the number at around 200. A 1995 study by Ndugu G. B. T'Ofori-Atta tallied similar numbers (198). See his essay, "The Black Church in the City of Atlanta," in *The Status of Black Atlanta 1995*, ed. Bob Holmes, 1–38 (Atlanta: Southern Center for Studies in Public Policy, Clark Atlanta University, 1995). In all three samples, churches affiliations are heavily weighted toward Baptist and Methodist in terms of denomination, with smaller representations from the Church of God in Christ, Pentecostal and independent churches; none of the lists are likely complete.

9. Billingsley does not make a strong distinction between programs of social outreach and social transformation but the data is no less compelling. *Mighty Like A River*, 127.

10. R. Drew Smith and Tamelyn Tucker-Worgs define the minimum threshold for megachurches as two thousand persons in weekly attendance. In Atlanta, as in many communities, it has become commonplace for congregations to hold two or more worship services. See their "Megachurches: African American Churches in Social and Political Context," *The State of Black America* (National Urban League, 2000).

11. "Sweet Auburn" was so named by early civil rights pioneer John Wesley Dobbs because of the opportunities blacks were afforded there during segregation.

12. "Atlanta's King's 'Sweet Auburn' recovering after years of decline," 17 January 1998, http://www.ccn.com/US/9801/17/kings.sweet.auburn.

13. See for instance John Blake, "The New Ebenezer," *Atlanta Journal-Constitution*, 7 March 1999.

14. Ernest Holsendolph, "An Economic Awakening," *Emerge*, September 1999.

15. Citizens Trust Bank of Atlanta, First Southern Bank of Lithonia, Georgia (now merged with Citizen's Trust), City National Bank of New Jersey, and First Tuskegee Bank of Tuskegee, Alabama, pledged $5.5 million for the project.

16. Old Ebenezer Church, presently undergoing extensive renovation, experienced similar financing problems in recent months; once again, local black businesses and individuals rallied to the church's aid.

17. Mary Booth Thomas, "An Obligation to the Inner City," *Atlanta Journal-Constitution*, 18 March 1999.

18. Interview with Dr. Joseph L. Roberts Jr., 22 May 2001.

19. John Blake, "The Black Church Faithful Force for Change Answering Call to Save Cities," *Atlanta Journal-Constitution*, 22 August 1999.

20. S. A. Reid, "Hemmed-in City Churches Growing Outside the Box," *Atlanta Journal-Constitution*, 16 October 1997.

21. Wayne A. Santoro, "Black Politics and Employment Policies: The Determinants of Local Government Affirmative Action," *Social Science Quarterly* 76, no. 4 (December 1995): 801–2.

22. The Georgia Dome project was later implemented but scaled back in response to community demands.

23. Interview with Reverend W. L. Cottrell, 25 April 2000. Both Reverend Cottrell and his son, Reverend Brent Cottrell, were extremely generous with their time and informative in their responses.

24. The Federal Empowerment Zone program is scheduled to end in 2005. The executive director of Atlanta's Empowerment Zone is Joseph Reid, an African American and ordained Presbyterian minister. For a good synopsis see Harold Lamar, "The Atlanta Empowerment Zone Corporation," *Atlanta Tribune*, August 1999.

25. Billingsley, *Mighty Like a River*, 131.

26. T'Ofori-Atta, "The Black Church in the City of Atlanta," 27.

27. Dr. Gerald Durley, pastor of Providence Baptist Church and former CBC president, indicates that one of Governor Barnes's first public acts after winning the election was to attend a worship service at Providence, during which he thanked the black clergy and community for their support. Interview on 17 April 2000.

28. David A. Bositis, "The Black Vote in '98," *Joint Center for Political and Economic Studies* (1999).

29. *A Voter's Manual for African American Ministers* (People for the American Way Foundation, 1999).

30. Atlanta, like much of the rest of the nation, encountered voting irregularities during the 2000 presidential election. Unlike some places, however, the electoral outcome was not appreciably influenced.

31. Vikki Ramsey Conwell, "Credit for a Job Well Done: Black Churches Renew Efforts at Building Wealth," *Atlanta Tribune*, January 1999.

32. In a 1993 article the *Atlanta Journal-Constitution* additionally noted the pastors of the following churches had "significant political clout": Ben Hill United Methodist Church, Cascade United Methodist Church, Hillside Chapel and International Truth Center, and Salem Baptist Church. To this list should be added such notable institutions as the Shrine of the Black Madonna #9, the Atlanta Masjid of Al-Islam, St. Anthony's Catholic Church, the African Hebrew Israelite Community, Muhammad's Mosque #15, and Atlantans Building Leadership for Empowerment or A.B.L.E.

2

Black Clergy and Models of Civil Rights Activism in Miami

Clarence Taylor

Since the 1970s, the level of activism for social justice in the United States has dissipated and the country has moved to the right. The growing backlash against the black freedom struggle, the rise of movements hostile to civil rights such as the neoconservative "New Right" and Christian Right, and the election of reactionary Republicans to national, state, and local offices has resulted in reversals of some of the civil rights gains made in the 1950s and 1960s.

The presidential administrations of Ronald Reagan, George H. W. Bush, and George W. Bush have crusaded against civil rights, affirmative action, and programs benefiting the working class and the poor. To make matters worse, the Democratic Leadership Council and its army of conservative Democratic members have moved away from the commitment to civil rights and the welfare state created by New Deal and Great Society liberalism, and instead many in the Democratic Party advocate an agenda of downplaying race and pushing for more economically conservative programs. Julian Bond of the NAACP noted in a recent speech that the Democratic Party today is too often not an opposition party but an "Amen Corner" for the Right. According to Bond, with few exceptions Democrats have been absent without leave for the battle of the American soul. While the Republican Party is "shameless," the Democratic Party is "spineless."[1]

In this period of hostility to racial justice and the absence of a social protest movement, civic and civil rights groups have taken on greater importance because they try to assist those in need by helping to win needed allocations. This chapter examines two civil rights groups operating in the black communities of Miami, Florida—People United to Lead the Struggle for Equality (PULSE) and the African American Council of Christian Clergy (AACCC).

23

Although considered civil rights organizations, PULSE and the AACCC differ in approaches and objectives. PULSE is a pressure group. Pressure groups promote the interest of their constituents by extending pressure on public officials and institutions of power.[2] Without a doubt, PULSE has adopted a militant approach, engaging in direct economic and political coercion of targeted institutions and those in power. The group relies on an organizing model that embraces confrontational tactics to achieve results, thereby legitimizing it in the communities it serves.

The AACCC, on the other hand, is a moderate, service-oriented organization. It has been more willing than PULSE to compromise with and accommodate those in power, in exchange for receiving goods and services on behalf of black communities in Miami. The AACCC acts as a power broker, relying on the services and resources it extracts to legitimize it among its black constituents. In a state dominated by Republicans, the AACCC's willingness to cultivate close relationships with those in state and local government and its ability to negotiate with those in power for fairer allocation of resources has been its trademark.

PULSE and the AACCC also differ ideologically. On several issues PULSE leans more to the left whereas the AACCC is more conservative. The former advocates that the state contribute resources to the poor and set up mechanisms to assure equal opportunity and an end to racial discrimination. PULSE embraces the public sector as vital to the lives of poor and working-class people. On the other hand, the AACCC stresses individual responsibility and a greater reliance on private entities instead of the state. Nevertheless, this paper contends that both approaches have been effective in bringing attention and support to these organizations and in helping provide needed services to black communities in Miami. Nonetheless, the militant and moderate methods employed by these pressure groups have their drawbacks, as will be discussed.

DEMOGRAPHICS IN MIAMI-DADE

Miami is just one of thirty incorporated municipalities in Dade County. It is the largest city in the county, with a population of 362,470 out of a county population of 2,253,362, as of 2000. According to the 2000 United States Census, there were 1,291,737 Hispanics in Miami-Dade, making up 57.3 percent of the population.[3] The Hispanic population is diverse, with Cubans making up the largest percentage of that group. There were 650,601 Cubans in Dade County in 2000 (28.9 percent of the Hispanic population). The non-Hispanic white or "Anglo" population has steadily declined in Miami-Dade since 1970. The Metro-Dade Planning Department's data point out that the white population decreased from just over 780,000 in 1970 to a little more than 500,000 in 1995. By 2000 there were 473,964 non-Hispanic whites residing in the city. The reason for this decline is largely due to native-born whites moving out of the county and state.

While the white population has decreased, the black population has grown from roughly 65,300 in 1950 to 440,200 by 1995. By 2000 there were 464,800 blacks in Miami-Dade; however, the number of African Americans has decreased due to large numbers migrating to other counties in Florida and moving out of the state. Nevertheless, blacks emigrating from the Caribbean have replaced African Americans. As of 2000, 35 percent of blacks in Dade were foreign born. A little more than 97,790 Haitians reside in Miami-Dade and comprise the largest and fastest-growing group in Miami who are from the African Diaspora.[4] Also, the Jamaican population increased between 1980 and 1990 from 9,200 to 27,204. There are significant numbers of people in Miami-Dade as well from Trinidad, the Bahamas, Cuba, and other parts of the Caribbean.[5]

SOCIAL AND ECONOMIC WOES IN MIAMI-DADE

Like other metropolitan areas, Miami is plagued by a host of social problems. Some of the major problems plaguing Miami include a high crime rate, a large number of people living in poverty, many persons with inadequate health care, a failing school system, and racial strife. But what makes Miami unique from other cities is the extent to which many of these problems have been interwoven with race, class, and Cold War ideologies.

From its incorporation in 1896, Miami was divided into a racially bipolar world. It was a Jim Crow city where blacks were subjected to racial oppression. People of African origin, for the most part, were relegated to the lowest socioeconomic conditions and were denied political power. Many were day laborers and domestics. People from the African Diaspora were consigned to the area known as Colored Town (later to become Overtown), where many lived in overcrowded inferior housing and received less than adequate municipal services. As the black population increased throughout the decades, other black ghettos were created to maintain the black population including Liberty City, the site of the first public housing project, and Opa Locka and Coral City (both of which were north of Liberty City and Brownsville).[6] Besides being relegated to ghettos and locked out of the labor market, blacks were denied equal public accommodations, received a segregated and inferior education, and were terrorized by the Ku Klux Klan and Miami's police department.

Thanks to the civil rights movement, legal discrimination was eradicated in Miami. However, as Jim Crow was being dismantled, the Cuban Revolution and the ascendancy of Fidel Castro sparked a massive exodus from the

Caribbean island, and many Cuban exiles settled in Miami. Between 1959 and 1980, eight hundred thousand Cubans fled to Dade County in order to escape communist rule. Because of the 1966 Cuban Adjustment Act, Cubans were allowed to settle in the United States and given resident status. Many of the earliest arrivals were from Cuba's elite—business people, doctors, lawyers, and other professionals—and they helped establish an economic enclave. Sociologists Guillermo J. Grenier and Max J. Castro define an economic enclave as a "distinctive economic formation characterized by the spatial concentration of immigrants who organize a variety of enterprises to serve their own ethnic market and the general population." By 1990, 42 percent of all enterprises in the County of Dade were owned by Hispanics. Miami had the highest per capita number of Hispanic-owned businesses in the country. Miami's Hispanic population had little interaction with Miami's black population and, in many cases, competed with them for economic resources and employment.[7]

Nonetheless, the black middle class has continued to expand. For the last three decades black median income rose as greater numbers of blacks moved into a variety of professions. The black middle class grew but, unfortunately, so did the ranks of the black poor. The participation of blacks in the labor force declined from 76 to 74 percent during the 1970s. Black unemployment in 1980 was 24 percent, up from 17 percent a decade earlier. The black unemployment rate was triple that of whites and double that of Hispanics. Female-headed households increased. Although there were sixty-eight hundred black businesses, the average sales and receipts were $40,943, or only 5 percent of all sales and receipts for the county. They were half that of Hispanic-owned businesses.

Crime also plundered the black areas of Miami-Dade. The crack-cocaine epidemic of the 1980s that hit Miami hard devastated the black areas. Violent crime drove businesses away and insurance rates soared. As businesses and the black middle class left Overtown, Liberty City, Carol City, and other black areas, they left behind a homogenous community of poor and chronically unemployed and underemployed residents. Although crack use has plummeted nationwide, this is not the case in Miami. Even with a rapidly declining crime rate in the city (the lowest since 1984), a hard-core group of crack addicts still exists as of the early 2000s. Many of these people are young. From 1995 to 1998, 26 percent of youths who were arrested and who were between the ages of fifteen and twenty tested positive for cocaine. Two-thirds of the suspects arrested had crack in their system. According to journalist Art Levine, more men than women seem to use crack. Forty-five percent of men arrested in the South Florida city had cocaine in their system and two-thirds were crack users. The largest number of those testing positive for crack has been blacks. While whites make up 19 percent of those testing positive and Hispanics 29 percent, blacks account for 52 percent. Hence, drugs remain a major problem in black communities. In January 1999 a wave of killings in Liberty City was linked to a drug war. Levine argues that drug use remains high in Miami because unemployment and poverty are rampant. Close to one-third of Miami's residents live in poverty.[8]

Miami experienced a number of race riots in the 1980s, all taking place after police killed blacks. The most devastating riot was in 1980 where eighteen people were killed, close to one thousand people were arrested in Liberty City and Overtown, 283 businesses were burned and looted, and $100 million worth of property was destroyed, making it the most costly riot in the history of the United States. In its report on the 1980 riot titled, "Confronting Racial Isolation in Miami," the United States Commission on Civil Rights claimed that "current conditions in the Nation's cities indicate that discrimination based on race and ethnicity continue to permeate and undermine the lives of the urban poor." It found that black communities in Miami were isolated and excluded "from the economic growth experienced by other communities." The commission found that a "sustained displacement and exclusion from economic opportunity and mobility have resulted in a serious erosion of spirit in the black community where the prospects for success have continuously become dimmer, apathy has replaced drive and ambition among many of Miami's black residents." The report contended that the influx of Cubans and their success and the declining position of blacks created resentment among people of African origin in Miami. After extensive research, interviews of residents in Miami's black communities, and numerous public hearings, the commission concluded that in housing, employment, and education the situation had degenerated.[9]

A decade after the riot, little change had taken place in Miami's black sections. Between 1980 and 1990, the poverty rate in Liberty City increased and between 1990 and 1995 total jobs in the neighborhood decreased by 47.6 percent. The *Miami Times* reported in July 1990 that despite the fact that the Metro Miami Action Plan (set up by the county to help in the recovery effort) received $20 million from the county to help improve education, housing, and health services in Miami, little had improved over an eight-year period. Although $1.8 million or 14 percent of the allocated budget had been spent on educational initiatives, the high school dropout rate increased from 7 percent in 1983 to 10 percent by 1990. These numbers do not include the number of students leaving school to pursue a general education diploma. According to Miami-Dade County Public School figures, by 1993 the dropout rate among blacks was over 12 percent. For Hispanics the rate was over 10 percent compared to 8 percent for Anglos. There was no improvement in health statistics. The infant mortality rate was 15.9 percent, twice that of whites. The percentage of blacks dying from cancer remained higher than whites that died from the disease.

The incidence of black teenage pregnancies remained twice as high as that among whites. As late as March 1990, Miami did not have an official office to deal with the homeless. Delores Dunn, director of the Miami Women and Children Shelter, said that a shortage of affordable housing has made life even more difficult in Miami. She said that the center has turned away four thousand women and children in a three-month period. Jeffrey Hepburn, assistant director of the Department of Development and Housing Conservation for Miami, said there were five thousand people in need of housing. The annual report by Camillus House estimated the homeless population at between ten and fifteen thousand in Miami. In 1990, there were only four hundred emergency shelter beds. The low minimum wage could not pay for housing. Moreover, the closing of businesses made the employment situation worse. A report released in 1989 entitled "Safety Network" declared that the homeless problem in Miami increased by 100 percent in just a little over one year.[10]

In May 1993, the Dade County Commission created a task force on homelessness. In its report, the task force estimated the homeless population at six thousand. Over 50 percent were single men and anywhere from 70 to 90 percent were substance abusers. It also estimated that 15 to 25 percent were HIV positive, 30 to 50 percent were mentally ill, and 40 percent of the homeless were homeless families.[11]

At the dawn of the twenty-first century, South Dade's black communities are still facing great difficulty. Despite the fact that in May 2000 the national unemployment rate was 3.9 percent, the unemployment rate in Liberty City was 9 percent. Nor has the education of black children in Miami gotten any better.[12]

The dismantling of national welfare and the creation of Florida's workfare program, entitled Work and Gain Economic Self-Sufficiency (WAGES), has done little to reduce poverty in Miami. In 1998, there were twenty-eight thousand welfare recipients expected to lose their benefits by the year 2000. While those running WAGES have pointed to its success in the sunshine state, it has been a disaster in Miami. In December 1999, the *Miami Herald* reported that the state has threatened to revoke the operating charter of Miami WAGES. It was forced to return $8 million to the state after a bookkeeping error. After three years of trying to take people off of welfare and finding them employment, it managed to find jobs or job training for twenty thousand people. The paper noted that at any given time Miami WAGES has seventeen thousand clients, which is the largest caseload in the state. Many clients get lost in the system and lose contact with service providers. In early December the program could not account for eleven thousand participants. Many of the clients have few skills and many have a criminal background. The state department of labor recently dumped eighteen thousand cases on the local WAGES without offering assistance. Since WAGES's inception, twenty-one board members and seven managers have resigned.[13]

For the last two decades, Miami's economy has doubled in size. But during that same period, the poverty level has also doubled. The Junior League of Miami pointed out that close to one in three children in the city live in poverty. Over "6,000 homeless people live with only 1,963 spaces to meet their immediate needs (1,800 are children and 40 % are families)." Roughly seventeen hundred children are in foster care and "1,300 others are in the care of relatives other than their immediate family due to neglect, abandonment or abuse where they remain, on the average, 3.7 years." Women have also been hit hard by domestic violence. In 1994, more than eight thousand women filed petitions for restraining orders to flee abusive husbands or partners. Close to sixty-four thousand households in the city are headed by single women with children. Forty-two percent of them live in poverty.[14]

Race and ethnic relations are poor in Miami-Dade, and U.S. immigration policy contributes to increased racial strife in the county. While people escaping communist Cuba were classified as political refugees and welcomed into the country, people fleeing from Haiti did not receive similar treatment. Francis Duvalier ("Papa Doc"), who came to power in 1957, sparked a mass exodus of Haitians in the 1950s with his brutality and with policies that created economic instability. The early waves of Haitians fleeing to the United States first settled in New York City, but by the 1970s large numbers began arriving in Miami. The media called the new Haitian arrivals "boat people" because large numbers were crammed into small vessels making the 730-mile trip from Haiti to Miami. Naming Haitian refugees "boat people" left the public with no description of their political position. But the notion of boat people also connoted that Haitians were nomads with no roots and were coming to Miami to look for handouts. Alex Stepick notes that in the 1970s the Haiti newcomers were falsely accused of having tuberculosis and spreading the disease. Many were fired, especially those working in restaurants and hotels. "The fear proved unfounded, and the hysteria gradually subsided. But the damage had been done. Many Haitians lost their jobs and negative stereotypes and fears of Haitians became firmly embedded in the general South Florida population. Haitians were perceived by many to be not only disease-ridden, but also uneducated, unskilled peasants who could only prove a burden to the community." It did not matter that many of the Haitians who settled in Miami migrated from New York City, that a significant number had arrived by plane and not boat (which indicated a higher socioeconomic position), and that many who came on boats had some education and had skills. With pressure from local politicians to stop the flow of Haitians and to deport those who had settled, the Immigration and Naturalization Service imprisoned new Haitian arrivals and denied work permits to those who were allowed to stay. They were classified as economic refugees and usually detained and sent back. Hundreds of Haitians were confined to Krome Detention Center while Cuban refugees were released to the Cuban community.[15]

Blaming Haitians for spreading tuberculosis was based on racist sentiment. Both the Centers for Disease Control and the Food and Drug Administration banned the use of blood from Haitians and sub-Saharan Africans, la-
beling them as high risk for carrying the AIDS virus. Both agencies based
their action on a rumor that Haitian immigrants were a source of AIDS in
Belle Glades. There was no scientific justification for the ban. The prohibi-
tion first applied to Haitians who came to the United States after 1977 but
was extended to natives of Haiti, sub-Saharan Africa, islands close to sub-
Saharan Africa, and anyone who had a sexual relationship with those
groups. The ban affected more than community health. It had a profound
impact on race relations in South Florida.

Haitians, African Americans, and others pointed out the hypocrisy of the
government, noting that while the government aided Cuban refugees, providing them with economic assistance, tuition to the public university system, and
money to support Cuban businesses, they were detaining Haitian refugees in
overcrowded prisons and sending many of them back to face torture and possible death at the hands of Haitian death squads. It is important to note,
though, that this disparity in immigration policy and social treatment of Cuban
refugees and Haitians was based not only on race, but on Cold War ideology.
The United States has always pointed to people fleeing communist countries
as proof that those countries were totalitarian states that robbed their citizens
of basic human rights. As Cubans flocked to the United States they served to
undermine Castro's government and they justified the United States' embargo
and other policies to help bring down the communist government. The 1966
Cuban Adjustment Act, making Cubans eligible for parole and permanent resident status, was a political act during the Cold War period.[16] Moreover, the
ruthless Haitian dictatorship led by Duvalier was an anticommunist ally of the
United States. The United States aided the government and helped train its military force. When the military and guards tortured and killed Haitian citizens
opposed to the Haitian dictatorship, the United States did nothing to stop it—
not wanting to jeopardize its relationship with an ally of U.S. Cold War politics.

ADDRESSING THE NEEDS OF THE COMMUNITY

A social Christian theology has provided a political framework for black ministers in Miami-Dade, with black churches in the county using cooperative
strategies to address the needs of poor black neighborhoods. Ministers and
churches have pooled their talents and resources in a common effort to address various problems, drawing on ministerial alliances and organizations
created by activist black clergy well before the civil rights movement. Important black ministerial groups organized in Miami include a chapter of the
Southern Christian Leadership Conference, the Baptist Ministers' Council,

and the Miami Christian Improvement Association. More recently, two of the most active ministerial organizations in Miami-Dade have been the People United to Lead the Struggle for Equality (PULSE) and the African-American Council of Christian Clergy (AACCC).

People United to Lead the Struggle for Equality (PULSE)

PULSE was created in 1980, after several days of rioting in response to the acquittal of four police officers that killed a black man by the name of Arthur McDuffie. Black clergy and lay people organized PULSE because they were convinced that the 1980 riot was a symptom of high unemployment, poverty, poor quality schools in the black community, police brutality, and the lack of black political empowerment. These clergy and civic leaders wanted to create an organization that addressed the concerns of working poor and moderate-income persons, giving them an alternative to street rebellion. The group focuses locally (but not nationally) on issues facing disenfranchised, voiceless black communities.

PULSE consists of forty-six churches and religious bodies, including thirty Baptist congregations, two Presbyterian congregations, two Holiness-Pentecostal congregations, two United Methodist congregations, and one African Methodist Episcopal (A.M.E.) congregation. In addition to churches, member organizations include the American Postal Workers, Professional Black Fire Fighters, Progressive Firefighters Association, Federation of Black Employees, Concerned Seniors Group, Mildred and Claude Pepper Tenants Association, Omega Psi Phi, and several other fraternities. PULSE's membership is limited to community organizations and is led by a board of directors, consisting of the president, executive director, and numerous other board officers and members.[17]

Unlike other civil rights groups that rely on individual dues and outside support from grants and fundraising, PULSE relies on its member organizations, most of which are black churches. Because of their political and economic independence, black churches have contributed enough money for the organization to operate two buildings and hire a full-time executive director and secretaries. The main office in North Miami is equipped with telephones and computers and has a large room where community meetings are held. Its relative independence from those outside the black communities of Miami-Dade allows PULSE to take more militant positions than other groups and to directly challenge those in business and governmental leadership. PULSE serves as an example of what sociologist Aldon Morris calls an indigenous model. Building on resource mobilization theory, Morris contends that an indigenous perspective relies on a community's resources, "social-activists with strong ties to mass-based indigenous institutions," and strategies that can be used against those in power.[18]

In order to empower ordinary people PULSE has created area vice presidents whose job it is to identify the major problems ravaging their particular areas. Once they become aware of a problem, it is brought before the board of PULSE who assesses whether the organization should try to solve the problem. PULSE attempts to answer several questions when deciding to respond to a neighborhood problem. Is the issue far reaching? Is it a problem that has an impact on a large segment of the community? Does it have a major impact on the community? How many people are concerned about and willing to work on the issue? If these questions are answered satisfactorily, then the organization adopts the issue and throws its weight behind solving the problem. The cities within Miami-Dade County that have PULSE vice presidents are Brownsville, Carol City, Homestead/Goulds, Liberty City North, Liberty City South, Opa Locka, Overtown, Richmond Heights/Perrine, and Coconut Grove/South Miami.[19]

Although it is a mostly ministerial organization, PULSE has adopted an approach used by the Student Nonviolent Coordinating Committee (SNCC). Instead of controlling a campaign from the start to the finish, PULSE attempts to identify local leaders in a community and then develops a plan of action with those leaders. Leadership and organizational concerns are addressed before a campaign is launched. In addition, it attempts to determine vital questions such as who will chair meetings, how the organization and community can determine whether people will participate in the campaign, what steps should be taken to win the campaign, and who will notify the press.[20]

PULSE has used a number of tactics to solve issues, including protests, lawsuits, negotiations, and collaborations with other organizations and sectors. During its twenty-four-year history, PULSE has claimed a number of successes. It won the support of the late Governor Lawton Chiles for its HOTSPOTS campaign. This crime prevention program allows citizens to report criminal acts anonymously with a "HOTSPOT card." PULSE board members, pastors, and citizens ride into high-crime areas with county police to assure that these areas are being "neutralized of criminal activity." HOTSPOTS is a means for citizens to take action against crime without the fear of retaliation from criminals. It also is a means of forcing the police to take action in high-crime areas. The HOTSPOTS campaign has resulted in hundreds of arrests and the confiscation of three hundred thousand illegal substances.[21]

PULSE has won concessions from the private sector by contending that businesses operating in black communities should be responsible to those communities. It negotiated with First Union Bank of Florida and received a $100 million commitment from the bank to build affordable housing for the poor. In March 1998, members of PULSE met with the president of Royal Caribbean Cruise Lines Ltd. to discuss a lawsuit brought by black employees against the company, complaining of racial discrimination.[22]

But PULSE's major arena has been the public sphere. It fought and won a decision by the Florida Supreme Court banning lawyers from using a peremptory challenge to exclude people from serving on juries because of race or gender. PULSE also secured an ordinance to install eighteen hundred fire hydrants in unincorporated Dade, an area made up mostly of black residents. Also, in 1998 PULSE won a pledge from Miami's City Commission to allocate $25 million in community block-grant funds for Overtown. PULSE claims that it was successful in winning the $25 million because it took large contingents of supporters to commission meetings and organized a rally before the commission met to consider the proposal. PULSE credits direct action and not negotiation for persuading the commission to provide the money.

PULSE targeted Allapattah Middle School because of horrendous conditions, including deteriorating side panels, a dirty kitchen area, and broken water coolers. Roaches were found where food was prepared, feces were smeared on the walls of the school, and it had deteriorating portable classrooms. PULSE was made aware of the horrendous conditions of the school by a homeowners' association who asked for the group's assistance. PULSE representatives visited the school and demanded that the conditions be rectified. As a result of the public awareness campaign, the school was transformed into a viable learning center.[23]

A major issue PULSE has addressed throughout its existence has been police brutality. In fact, it has been the leader in the fight to eradicate police attacks against black people in the county. The civil rights organization uses three methods to address police brutality. The first is an immediate reactive response to individual cases. When police have committed crimes against civilians, including the beating, shooting, or killing of an innocent person, PULSE has sought justice through various means. The response has usually been hiring lawyers to defend or bring charges against abusive officers, demanding meetings with police chiefs, mayors, other city officials, and the Justice Department, and holding rallies and demonstrations. One result of these actions is they have given people an alternative to street rebellion.

PULSE's effort to force cities to hire more black police officers is both an attempt to end racial discrimination in hiring and a means of addressing police brutality. The justification for hiring black police officers is that those sharing a similar culture have a better understanding of the community and are less likely to be involved in violent confrontation. After receiving several complaints from black residents in the city of Hialeah over the city's refusal to hire black police officers and firefighters, PULSE investigated, gathered information, and presented the complaints to the U.S. Justice Department. PULSE found that even when the city hired blacks they were usually fired. Of the two hundred police officers the city employed, only five were black. PULSE asserted that the city's racial discrimination practices could be traced back to 1959. The Justice Department sued the city of Hialeah and in 1998, Hialeah, whose population is 87 percent Hispanic, signed a consent decree agreeing to hire fifteen black police officers and fifteen black firefighters.[24]

PULSE has also tried to convince the city of Miami to create a citizens' investigative panel to curb police abuse against blacks. Miami has a long history of police committing violent acts against black residents. In most cases, the incidents have involved white or Hispanic police officers killing blacks—in several instances resulting in street rebellions. The riots of 1980, 1982, and 1989 were sparked after police confrontations with people of African origin. While there has been no major eruption between police and blacks in Miami in more than a decade, tensions still remain high. PULSE has demanded that the city of Miami establish a citizens' investigative panel that has the power to subpoena police officers.[25]

PULSE has been less successful in its attempt to persuade the city of Miami to create a strong Citizens' Investigative Panel. In 1992, members of the organization met with Metro commissioners to persuade them to expand the present citizens' investigative panel from five to twenty-one members and that it be given the power to investigate cases and subpoena police officers. But the police officers' union opposes the creation of a stronger panel and the commission has agreed with them. However, in 1998, PULSE became a member of the Independent Review Panel. The panel was established to give the people of the county a way to voice problems they may have with any county agency, including the police department. While PULSE has been less successful in its fight for a strong citizens' investigative panel, it did manage to convince Miami to declare a moratorium on the use of the chokehold by police officers. Moreover, it has joined efforts with the ACLU, Miami-Dade NAACP, and a group called Brothers of the Same Mind to call on officials to create a citizen review board with subpoena power.[26]

The fight for black political representation in Miami has been yet another major battle PULSE has led over the years. After the defeat of Reverend Richard Dunn by a Cuban candidate in the fall of 1996, there were no blacks on the city commission for the first time in thirty years. PULSE demanded that the city adopt single-member district voting for commission seats or it would file a lawsuit. Although, then Mayor Joe Carrollo initially agreed to adopt a single member district plan and even appointed a "Blue Ribbon" panel to recommend new districts, he backed out claiming that he could not support PULSE's demand that Miami pay the organization's legal cost in this battle. The civil rights organization was forced to follow through with its lawsuit after it had agreed to drop the demand for payment of its legal bills and the mayor did not respond. PULSE accused the mayor of stonewalling and sued the city. Despite Carollo's request that the city be given a two-month period to respond to the suit, a U.S. district judge ordered the mayor to allow his blue ribbon panel to do its job and create single-member-voting districts. In the fall of 1997, a referendum was passed creating five districts assuring that at least one seat on the commission would go to a black person. The only at-large position was the seat for mayor.[27]

According to its annual 1997–1998 report, PULSE has established several committees to continue its work, including a committee to end discrimination (whose major function is to review the functions of government and corporations), a fair share jobs committee that fights for proportionate employment for the black community, and an education committee that monitors the budgetary process and its impact on schools in black communities.[28]

One of the most disturbing campaigns PULSE has been involved in was the fight to repeal a law protecting gay and lesbian rights. In 1998 the Miami-Dade County Commission passed an amendment to the county's human rights ordinance that prohibited employment and housing discrimination based on sexual orientation. Without a doubt, the most publicly outspoken person on the issue of repealing the amendment to protect gay and lesbian rights was Nathanial Wilcox of PULSE. Wilcox, cochair of Take Back Dade, a coalition of groups working on behalf of the repeal, has lashed out against what he deems as immoral behavior on the part of gays and lesbians. In clearly homophobic rhetoric, the executive director of PULSE blames gays for the spread of AIDS, drugs, and other crimes and argues that homosexuals simply need to change their behavior. He is incensed at any comparison between the suffering of blacks and gays and lesbians. "Gays ain't never had to sit in the back of a bus or were not able to drink water at a water fountain."

Both PULSE and the AACCC supported and defended the use of a flyer created by the coalition that claimed that "Martin Luther King Jr. would be Outraged! If he knew homosexualist extremists were abusing the civil rights movement to get special rights based on their sexual behavior." This is despite Corretta Scott King's statement that her husband, Reverend Martin Luther King Jr., never publicly spoke about gays and lesbians, but privately expressed concern about discrimination of people based on their sexual preference. Undaunted by the words of the widow of the slain civil rights leader, Wilcox argued, "It is the Bible, not King's words that is the last authority on the subject." Although Reverend Bennett claimed he had misgivings about using King's photo on the flyer, "as a Christian organization, we should make a statement that we believe King would have gone against the ordinance."[29]

In the end the repeal campaign failed and many were angry and dismayed at the position PULSE took and were particularly upset over the language used by Wilcox. Reporter Lisa Kennedy raised the question: "Why is it that the language of discrimination always sounds the same no matter who's mouthing it?" Craig Washington, executive director of the Atlanta Gay and Lesbian Center, criticized the campaign by citing King's words: "Injustice anywhere is a threat to justice everywhere." He noted that there is no evidence that "King supported oppressing gays." The *Miami Times*, the city's black weekly, reported that although many members of PULSE were satisfied with the position the organization took on the repeal issue, "some did disagree with the group's stance. . . . Comments of church pastors and members suggest that PULSE didn't have widespread support for the repeal of the Human Rights Ordinance."[30]

To be sure, the image of Martin Luther King Jr. was manipulated by proponents of the repeal, especially since they did not have any evidence that King opposed the protection of the rights of gays and lesbians. To simply claim that King was a minister and therefore would have opposed what they claimed to be "immorality" is conjecture and not evidence.

However, while criticism can be leveled at PULSE as well as other repeal proponents for appropriating the image of King for their cause, trying to curtail the rights of gays and lesbians, and using homophobic language in their pursuit, one should not ignore that in its efforts to repeal the Human Rights Ordinance PULSE remained committed to the approach it has adopted throughout the years. In this campaign the church-based organization challenged state power by trying to mobilize people, relying heavily on its networks, and distributing thousands of pieces of literature.

The African-American Council of Christian Clergy (AACCC)

The AACCC came into existence soon after the William Lozano trial at the urging of an African American city commissioner, named Arthur Teele Jr., who called a group of black clergy together to form a black church-based organization that would address itself to the problems plaguing Miami-Dade. The AACCC is an interdenominational and an intercultural organization made up of pastors and ministers. Unlike PULSE, the membership is open to individual ministers, and, although it is not a prerequisite, they should be connected to churches. Reverend Richard Bennett, the organization's executive director, states that there are three hundred churches "affiliated" with the AACCC. This affiliation means the AACCC has developed a strong network, and these three hundred churches taken collectively have thousands of members. As affiliates of the ministerial alliance, they distribute AACCC literature; agree to use their church bulletins to inform the community of the organization's meetings, events, and services; and publicize AACCC's positions. The organization's leadership consists of a board of directors, a president, first and second vice presidents, an executive director, a director of programs, an administrative support person, a secretary, a financial secretary, a treasurer, and a chaplain. While PULSE receives financial support from its membership dues and black churches, the AACCC relies on local and national grants. It also receives financial assistance from the city's Department of Juveniles. To be sure, its funding makes it more vulnerable to local, state, and national political leadership.[31]

The AACCC calls itself a "pastoral group," not advocating any religious doctrine or political position but, instead, focusing on providing services to the community. Bennett, however, maintains that the AACCC is a "social ministry." While PULSE uses protest and rallies, files lawsuits, and is confrontational, the AACCC is a more moderate organization and has concentrated on molding the behavior of the black poor of Miami-Dade. "Our mission is to aid the elderly, help educate the youth, provide for the homeless, set moral standards for our community and assist our public agencies, including the Miami-Dade police Department, the City of Miami-Dade Police Department, and the Department of Juvenile Justice."

A basic ideological differences between PULSE and AACCC is that the former recognizes and challenges structural inequality while the latter contends that the major problem facing blacks is that they are not prepared to function in a competitive society. "Consequently, we end up with a segment of the population that is unprepared to adequately compete in today's civilization. Because this segment of the population lacks certain skills necessary to compete on an equal level, many drop out in sheer frustration." The AACCC does not see the road to political empowerment through political activism hence it does not encourage enhancing political democracy among the black working class. It sees itself as providing services and morally and socially uplifting the black communities of Dade.

The AACCC did not publicly criticize Congress or President Clinton for ending the national welfare system. Instead it took steps to help welfare recipients adjust to the changes. "The faith community is being called up to pick up the slack," according to the council. The group claims to be connected to various referral agencies that offer job training and placement of former welfare recipients. "Our training will prepare our populace to make a smooth transition to the public sector." The absence of a critique on eradicating the national welfare system on the part of the AACCC points to its politically moderate leaning and its reliance on acting as a service-oriented organization. In fact when other civil rights groups lambasted Clinton and Congress for their action, the AACCC offered a message of hope and asserted that during this period "opportunities are endless."

The ministerial organization has not taken a position on Governor Jeb Bush's decision to end affirmative action and replace it with his controversial plan, One Florida Initiative. A key component of One Florida is the twenty-percent scheme that assures that the top 20 percent of each school in the state will be given a seat at one of the state universities. In fact, Reverend Bennett has made it clear that he personally supports the initiative. His criticism is not of the plan, but of the governor, who he claims should have implemented his plan and slowly dissolved affirmative action. The AACCC also has not taken a position on Bush's A-Plus Education program.[32]

The AACCC's view that individual behavior must be modified to adjust to a competitive society is reflected in its programs for young people. Its Project H.U.G.S. is a juvenile service attempting to increase youth skills "in a positive manner through the elevation of self-esteem and leadership classes." Its Stay in School program is housed at Charles Drew Middle School and encourages teens to stay in school by offering tutoring services and a learning atmosphere in which students can study. At the same time that the AACCC employs strategies of behavior modification, it embraces the view that incarceration and the removal from the community of criminals is a viable resolution. Hence, the ministerial organization participates in the Weed and Seed program. The program attempts to revitalize the areas from NW 7th Avenue to NW 27th Avenue and NW 54 Street in Liberty City by creating a secure refuge from drug activity and crime so that young people and adults can gather to receive needed services and socialize. In order to make the area safe, the AACCC works with the police department in Liberty City by identifying criminals in the community so that they can be "weeded out." According to Reverend Bennett, once the "bad guys" such as drug pushers and violent criminals are removed, churches and other groups plant the seeds to help the community grow. When crime drops, the neighborhood improves and businesses will be more willing to invest and public and private social service agencies will be safe to provide needed services to the community. Although it is difficult to measure exactly how successful the Weed and Seed program has been, crime has dropped dramatically in Liberty City. In fact, in 2002 Liberty City had only fourteen murders, compared to twenty-eight a year earlier. It is Bennett's contention that because of the dramatic drop in the crime rate, faith-based groups, health agencies, and a group called Jobs for Miami (which offers counseling, recruitment, assessment, training, and job placement), have come into Liberty City. Moreover, New Century Development Corp., which offers housing rehabilitation, ownership counseling, and assistance in purchasing homes, is also operating in Liberty City.[33]

In the late 1990s when a drug war erupted in Liberty City and several young people were killed and police increased patrols in the community, the AACCC maintained its view that an increased presence of police in predominantly black communities was not harmful. While not protesting the heavy police presence and what some declared to be harassment of young black men in the neighborhood by police, Reverend Bennett declared that if the police come and catch you on the corner loitering, as long as you're moving, well, you're not really loitering."[34]

True to its service-oriented approach, the AACCC through a federal grant has created a computer lab station. Located directly across from the headquarters of the organization, children in the community who would otherwise not have access to such services make use of the ten computers and the Internet access provided by this center. The center is open after school for a few hours and children are taught how to use the Internet, word processing programs, and database software, as well as learning other computer skills. Each child is limited to two hours a day in order to insure that many children in the community have the opportunity to learn to operate a computer.[35]

The AACCC has not challenged the Republican-dominated state legislature in Florida, rather it has reached out to it for support. An example of its stress on cooperating with power is the organization's request for funding by the state legislature. In the year 2000 the church-based group asked for $150,000 to help provide low-income residents in Dade with information and referrals, employment searches, computer training, and GED referrals. Its appeal was based on benefits to Dade's black and Hispanic poor, and also to the state. It emphasized that the state would benefit from such a loan because the AAACC's program could decrease unemployment, lower crime rates, and reduce illiteracy. This appeal was clearly designed to strike a chord with Governor Jeb Bush and Republican state representatives and state senators in Florida who have emphasized that private organizations in poor communities should address social and economic concerns facing the poor in those communities.[36]

Besides working within the political system and becoming power brokers, the AAACC has also built alliances with private church-based groups to help bring needed services to black and Latino communities. Along with the Jesuits' Gesu Church, Mt. Zion Baptist Church, St. Agnes Episcopal Church, St. Francis Xavier Catholic Church, Temple Israel, Trinity Episcopal Church, the Greater Miami Rabbinical Association, the National Conference of Christians and Jews, United Protestant Appeal, and the Catholic Community Services, the AAACC created an organization called Faith in the City. The group was formed in 1988 by Norma Orovitz, president of Temple Israel in Miami. Faith in the City meets monthly to conduct ecumenical services and plan projects in Miami without trying to promote any particular religious faith. One of its projects has been an annual Spring Celebration. At its ninth annual Spring Celebration gathering, the group emphasized the theme, "Love One Another." Clergy and lay people sang songs, conducted prayers, and presented awards to community leaders who aided the homeless and the elderly.[37]

One of the major projects of Faith in the City is called Congregations Accessing Resources for Employment (CARE), a program that helps the working poor and those on workfare find and retain employment by arranging transportation, day care, and social services. The churches in the coalition also provide social-care workers, counseling, and training for clients of CARE. The member churches of Faith in the City contact businesses associated with Welfare-Transition (formerly known as WAGES) who are searching for workers.[38]

CONCLUSION

Contrary to popular opinion, the black religious community of Miami-Dade is civic minded and politically dynamic, using a variety of approaches to address the growing disparity between rich and poor, intense racial and ethnic division, a failing educational system, homelessness, and a host of other social, economic, and political ills plaguing blacks in the county. This chapter has focused on two church-based groups that have tried to tackle social, political, and economic conditions in Miami's black communities. PULSE and AAACC act as mediating structures providing constituents with what political scientist R. Drew Smith calls a "terrain independent from governmental and business sectors for negotiating political and economic life."[39]

Black churches, ministerial organizations, and ministers have managed to move into black communities and have met with some success. Because of the severity of the problems facing Overtown, Liberty City, Carol City, Brownsville, and other black communities of Dade, the religious communities are faced with a difficult task and cannot do it alone. Greater effort on the part of local, state, and national governments, the business community, and other civic groups across ethnicity and race must be involved in the effort if the goal of racial and economic justice is ever going to be reached in this very diverse and viable community.

NOTES

1. Julian Bond, "Civil Rights Under Attack," Speech to the Unitarian Universalist General Assembly, Boston, Massachusetts.

2. V. O. Key, *Politics, Parties, and Pressure Groups* (Ty Crowell, 1964).

3. U.S. Census Bureau, Census 2000, Table DP-1, *Profile of General Demographic Characteristics 2000.*

4. Between 1980 and 2000 their numbers increased by 84, 930.

5. Guillermo J. Grenier and Max J. Castro, "The Emergence of an Adversarial Relation: Black-Cuban Relations in Miami, 1959–1998," *Research in Urban Policy* 7 (1998): 34–35; Marvin Dunn, *Black Miami in the Twentieth Century* (Gainesville: University Press of Florida, 1997), 335–37.

6. Raymond Mohl, "Black Miamians are Struggling to Overcome Segregation Legacy," *Miami Times*, 14 April 1991; Dunn, *Black Miami*, 156–70. Some of the best articles examining Miami's racial and ethnic divide are Raymond Mohl, "The Pattern of Race Relations in Miami Since the 1920s," in *The African American Heritage in Florida*, ed. David A. Colburn and Jane L. Landers, 326–56 (Gainesville: University Press of Florida, 1995); Mohl, "Shadows in the Sunshine: Race and Ethnicity in Miami," *Tequesta: The Journal of the Historical Association of Southern Florida* 49 (1989): 63–80; Paul S. George, "Colored Town: Miami's Black Community, 1896–1930," *Florida Historical Quarterly* 56, no. 4 (April 1978): 432–47; George,

"Policing Miami's Black Community, 1896–1930," *Florida Historical Quarterly* 57, no. 4 (April 1979): 434–50; Grenier and Castro, "The Emergence of an Adversarial Relation," 33–55. Despite their usefulness, none of these articles pay attention to the black religious community in Miami.

7. Raymond Mohl, "Coming of Cuban Refugees Stalled Progress in Ending Racism," *Miami Times*, 9 May 1991; Grenier and Castro, "Emergence of an Adversarial Relation," 38.

8. Art Levine, "Miami's Vice," Salon.com, 11 May 1999, www.salon.com/news/feature/1999/05/11/crack/index.html.

9. *Confronting Racial Isolation in Miami: A Report of the United States Commission on Civil Rights*, June 1982, v–vi, 22–87; *Miami Herald*, 14 May 2000, 1A, 18A.

10. Butler, "Role of MMAP Again under Spotlight as Conference Opens Today," *Miami Times*, 12 July 1990.

11. Miami Dade County Public Schools Management and Accountability Office of Educational Evaluation and Management Analysis, June 1999; Task Force on Homelessness, "Dade County Community Homeless Plan."

12. *Miami Herald*, 25 June 1999; 2 February.

13. *Miami Herald*, 3 December 1999. Press Release, "Miami-Dade Mayor Alex Penelas Names Sergio Gonzales Director of Office of Job Creation and Welfare-to-Work," www.penelas.com/sergiopr.htm.

14. Junior League of Miami, Inc. "Strategic Plan," www.juniorleagueofmiami.com/strategicplan.html.

15. Alex Stepick, "The Refugees Nobody Wants: Haitians in Miami," in Grenier and Stepick III, *Miami Now* (University Press of Florida, 1992), 58–60.

16. Immigration and Naturalization Service, Press Release, "Clarification of Eligibility for Permanent Residence Under the Cuban Adjustment Act," 26 April 1999, www.ins.usdoj.gov/graphics/publicaffairs/newsrels/CubaRel.htm.

17. Ella Elam to Dear Friend, 22 March 2000; interview with Nathaniel Wilcox, 24 March 2000; *Miami Times,* 6 February 1997; PULSE's 18th Annual Convention Journal, 15 May 1999, 1.

18. Aldon Morris, *The Origins of the Civil Rights Movement* (New York: Free Press, 1984), 282.

19. PULSE's 18th Annual Convention Journal, 1.

20. PULSE leaflet, "Developing an Issue."

21. PULSE leaflet, "PULSE's HOTSPOT Campaign"; interview with Nathaniel Wilcox.

22. Interview with Nathaniel Wilcox; *Miami Herald*, 6 April 1998.

23. Interview with Nathaniel Wilcox; PULSE leaflet, explaining its what the organization is, how it is organized, why it was organized, its goals and accomplishments; *Miami Times*, 19 November 1998 and 16 December 1999; *Miami Herald*, 11 August 1999.

24. Interview with Nathaniel Wilcox; *Miami Times*, 20 February 1997.

25. Demonstrations did take place in the fall of 1999, when a Hispanic police officer shot and killed an unarmed nineteen-year-old black man. In his thirteen years on the police force, this particular police officer had shot and killed four people and had opened fire and wounded a security guard he mistook for a suspect. He also "accidentally" sprayed the inside of an apartment with shotgun pellets. While demonstrations were peaceful, Reverend Victor T. Curry told a crowd of demonstrators outside of police head-

quarters, "Hell, it ain't no black folk shooting Cubans down in the street behind those badges. It's Cubans shooting black people. Check the record." Miami Sun Sentinel.com, 2 October 1999, www.sun-sentinel.com/news/detail/0,1136,24500000000109226,00 .html.

26. Interview with Nathaniel Wilcox; PULSE Annual Report, 1997–1998; ACLU Press Release, 23 April 2002, archive.aclu.org/news/2002/42302html.

27. Districts 1, 3, and 4 have a majority Hispanic population while district 5 has a majority of blacks. District 2 was created to assure that a non-Hispanic white be elected. *Miami Herald*, 5 September 1997.

28. PULSE Annual Report, 1997–1998.

29. *Miami Herald*, 2 August 2002; *Washington Times*, 20 January 2003.

30. *Miami Times Online*, 3 March 2004; Lisa Kennedy, "Channeling MLK in Miami," NiaOnline, www.niaonline.com/CDS_Templates/print_template?1,1018,2296,00.html; "Commercial Use Seen as Taint to King Legacy," *Washington Times*, 20 January 2003.

31. AACCC leaflet, explaining the organization's purpose, programs, services, and names of administrative staff and board of directors.

32. "AACCC Welcomes the NAACP," African-American Council of Christian Clergy, http://weedandseed.com/AACC.htm.

33. *Miami Herald*, 4 January 2000, interview with Reverend Richard Bennett; Weed & Seed Neighborhood Resource Guide, May 1998; African-American Council of Christian Clergy, untitled document, weedandseed.com/AACCC.htm.

34. "Police For Now Hold the Power in the Liberty City Drug Wars," Media Awareness Project, 11 January 1999.

35. Interview with Reverend Bennett.

36. Community Budget Issues Request-Tracking ID # 798, AAACC Community Resource Center, www.leg.state.fl.us/date/session/2000/senate/budget_issues/SENReg798.htm.

37. Delores Fernandez, "Faith in the City," companymagazine.org/v152/faith.html.

38. Fernandez, "Faith in the City."

39. R. Drew Smith, *New Day Begun: African American Churches and Civil Culture in Post-Civil Rights America*, vol. 1 (Durham: Duke University Press, 2003), 2–3.

3

Bennett W. Smith Sr. and Ministerial Influence on Political Life in Buffalo

Sherri Leronda Wallace

This chapter examines the historical and contemporary influence of one minister's relatively singular, yet major influence on local politics in Buffalo, New York, from 1972 to 1999. The Reverend Dr. Bennett W. Smith Sr.'s arrival in Buffalo has been described as the reawakening of Buffalo's African American electorate. Through a myriad of protest-oriented activities, Smith called attention to the plight of Buffalo's African American communities and mobilized African American voters to elect politicians responsive to their communities' needs. His seminal efforts resulted in a historical electoral evolution of black politicians who, for the first time in history, comprised a majority of elected positions in the city. These politicians were routinely endorsed from the pulpit during Smith's Sunday "early-morning" television and radio broadcasts.

In Buffalo, Reverend Smith's reputation was "part preacher, part civil rights leader, [and] part politician."[1] Smith, who passed away in 2001, believed religion and politics were intertwined. Every aspect of life at the church Smith pastored in Buffalo, the St. John Baptist Church (which is the largest and wealthiest black church in the city), was connected to local politics. Members were strongly encouraged to register to vote and to participate in social and political events, and the church routinely held activities at the church designed to facilitate community electoral mobilization. St. John's power base mirrors the leadership structure found in other politically active African American churches. These churches typically include "the heads of civil rights organizations, the heads of business and civic organizations and the press, and perhaps an educator or two."[2] More importantly, as Aldon Morris notes, "The relationship between the minister and the congregation is often one of charismatic leader to followers rather than the formalized levels of command found in large corporations."[3]

The factor of social prestige that attaches to clergy,[4] who are largely economically independent of the larger white society, elevates their political and social position in the exchange networks, which is a major asset individually and collectively for economically destitute and disconnected African American communities. Individually, clergy leaders who benefit from a large and diverse network can utilize the exchange as a resource that can apply to furthering the goals of their own church ministries; but collectively, they can use the exchange as a source of valuable information and entrepreneurial contacts with other clergy and congregants in a position to assist, contribute, or volunteer to work together to achieve social ends for the broader community. When individuals in local communities are bankrupt of these social ties, they most often look to the local clergy and church as the source of information and resources, trusting that the clergyperson can assist them with their needs/problems out of feelings of obligation toward humankind.

It is important to underscore that it was not the black church as an institution per se, but rather "a certain number and type of individual ministers that have provided leadership" for their local African American community who are the messengers for political activism.[5] William Berenson, Kirk Elifson, and Tandy Tollerson's empirical study of political activism among African American clergy found that the level of political activism correlated strongly to the age, education, monetary strength of the church, and "Black identification" of African American ministers.[6] Specifically, "the study concludes that young, highly educated preachers with a strong sense of Black identification and from financially secure congregations are the most politically active."[7]

This chapter examines how individual influence and institutional networking intersect in Bennett Smith's social activism within Buffalo. The discussion draws partly on the concept of "social capital," which "consists of networks and norms that enable participants to act together effectively to pursue shared objectives."[8] For political scientist Robert Putnam, who revived the term, social capital is viewed as the product of social relations composed of the "features of social life—networks, norms and trust—that enable participants to act together more effectively to pursue shared objectives, individually and collectively,"[9] which distinguishes it from physical and human capital. A further distinction within the social capital literature is that social capital is related to both an *internal bonding* dynamic within a group or organization and an *external bridging* dynamic between groups or organizations.[10] The present chapter argues that Smith drew on the former (meaning the influence conferred upon him by his pastoral leadership at St. John Church) in order to develop the latter (meaning his influence within the broader civic and ecclesiastical community). The chapter relies on Smith's personal writings, a series of interviews with Smith and with sixteen other Buffalo-area clergy by the author, and media accounts and secondary literature.

COMMUNITY DEVELOPMENT, POLITICAL
ACTIVISM, AND PERSONAL INFLUENCE

For Bennett Smith, politics and religion have been intrinsically intercon-
nected. He marched from Selma to Montgomery with the Reverend Dr. Martin Luther King Jr. and worked side-by-side with the Reverend Jesse Jackson
in the Operation PUSH organization.[11] Smith's instrumental political foundations were laid, however, in Cincinnati, Ohio, where he served as pastor of
Mt. Auburn Baptist Church, and then as pastor of Lincoln Heights Baptist
Church. In Cincinnati, Smith partnered closely with other activist clergy such
as the Reverends Otis Moss, Fred Shuttlesworth, Clayton Waller, and R. L.
Mitchell in the founding of the Valley Christian Improvement Association
(VCIA), which later became SCLC and Operation PUSH.[12] The VCIA started
as a political organization seeking to educate the African American community about social and economic inequalities and to address school desegre-
gration, among other things.

When Smith moved to Buffalo, an African American community that he
perceived as politically quiescent, it meant formulating a new style of local
protests. It meant developing a church-based programmatic activism that
recognized and challenged the power of the historical local political machine. Reverend Smith characterizes his move to Buffalo, New York, as a
"mixed blessing." Said Smith:

> It was a personal disaster on interpersonal relations because of the fact when I
> came to New York, I came with a reputation as a civil rights fighter. I came with
> a reputation as a revivalist. I came with a reputation as one who is "fire and
> brimstone" [Smith received a Grammy nomination for his popular sermon,
> "Watch Them Dogs"]. . . . I came to an old congregation where again, the peo-
> ple had Southern roots, and they were people that weren't very well educated.
> They had not been exposed to academia on a large scale. There were maybe
> five schoolteachers in the entire congregation and the others were factory
> workers. Buffalo was a factory town. These where people who came to Buffalo
> not to come to work for Kodak and Xerox as the ones in Rochester did, but to
> work in foundry, to work in hot molten steel areas where all you had to do was
> be able to read and write and sign your name.[13]

Historically speaking, the migration of Southern African Americans into
Buffalo during the early twentieth century placed increasing demands on
what was then a small community of migrants in terms of housing, employment, and recreational facilities. Yet, as Williams argues, this tremendous in-
flux of newcomers did not destroy community formation for African American settlers. These migrant Southerners brought with them a history
regarding race relations, but more importantly, a well-developed community
infrastructure. "They left communities in the South where the Black church

and family formed the core of the community along with fraternal societies and a variety of civic and social organizations and Black businesses"; thus, Southern African American migrants infused a "renewed spirit of struggle into Buffalo's Afro-American community, and provided that community with tools to wage a war for equality and human dignity."[14]

Watkins characterizes the early twentieth-century community of African Americans in Buffalo as a dynamic combination of individual pragmatism and instrumentalism. Basically, African American Buffalonians were known to support "at various times and to different degrees of intensity: The Marcus Garvey Movement, The NAACP, The Colored Workmen's League, and The Negro Progressive Club for Racial Uplift."[15] In fact, African American Buffalonians are often inclined to form their own organizations to protest social inequality as can be seen with the latter two being originally founded among Buffalo's African American residents[16] and with the varied and numerous local neighborhood and community organizations that exist today.

Naison implies that an enduring strength of Buffalo's African American community is the vitality of its organizational life. Although the city of Buffalo often ranks last among major cities in terms of economic prospects for African Americans, its "African American neighborhoods are filled with block clubs, churches, and community action groups which provide residents with cultural and social outlets, vehicles to mobilize around community problems, and mechanisms of articulating their needs to city government."[17] Many of these local community-based organizations and/or action groups were founded in the midst of a political upheaval that took place during the early 1960s and continued into the mid-1970s. Nationwide, a widespread call for local grassroots community activism and government policy encouraged broad-based political and community organizational formation. Advocacy and self-help organizations emerged throughout the African American community during this time because many of them obtained government funding independently of the city bureaucracy.[18] Thus, in contrast to some of Reverend Smith's personal reflections, there is evidence to suggest that African American Buffalonians were evolved to some extent in local community economic development activities, although outside the realm of the cohesive and effective voting bloc of the black church.

Naison also points out that "Black Buffalo was caught up in the ferment of the Civil Rights and Black Power movements; local activists participated in Student Nonviolent Coordinating Committee (SNCC), Congress of Racial Equity (CORE) and the Black Panthers, and community residents took part in several civil disorders."[19] Most of this activity took place outside the traditional church-based activism that characterized the civil rights movement in the South and, perhaps, in Cincinnati; but it was realized through a revival of the notions of self-help determinism that has its earliest roots in nineteenth-century black social political thought of African American male leaders, like

Booker T. Washington, Marcus Garvey, and W. E. B. Du Bois, who sought to find constructive responses to institutional economic and social segregation and discrimination policies.[20]

The essentials of this basic concept centered around the return of the sociopolitical community to the center of economic life and the linkage of economic activity to such social objectives as mutual benevolent and religious societies and/or fraternal and sorority clubs. These organizations, in turn, served as the seedbeds for civic participation ranging from emancipation to civil rights through which African Americans used the power of the ballot and protests to rally for more equitable distribution of resources within their communities.[21] By the late 1960s, broadly based political participation philosophies in America embraced strands of utopian and communitarian thought. An advocacy organization called Build, Unity, Independence, Liberty, Dignity (BUILD), formed on the national grassroots campaigns of the innovative organizer Saul Alinsky, emerged in Buffalo, spawning effective political mobilization to improve the school system, the city government, and construction unions.[22]

Peter Pitegoff characterizes the complex history of the rise and decline of the BUILD organization in Buffalo. He argues that

> BUILD was perhaps the most far-reaching community organizing effort in Buffalo's recent history, primarily among African American citizens and organizations. With assistance from Saul Alinsky's Industrial Areas Foundation, local organizers and leaders built a broad-based coalition of organizations on Buffalo's East Side [the predominantly African American community]. Particularly in its early years, BUILD was influential player in the public school system, in private sector affirmative action policies, and to some degree in economic development planning.[23]

However, as Reverend Smith accurately suggests, the emphasis on human services pervades Buffalo's African American community-based organizations and diverts attention and scarce resources from more systemic approaches that involve community organizing and economic development.[24] Given Buffalo's African American community, which consists of a disproportionately large poor and economically marginal population heavily dependent on government funding and other social services, Reverend Smith correctly perceived that the only power base that the African American community truly possesses is political power achieved through the voting franchise.

Although Smith agreed that the NAACP actively fought police and fire department discrimination in the federal courts in Buffalo, it was not until his active Operation PUSH campaign of the early 1970s that Buffalo's African American community came to realize their voting strength: "Nobody was in the streets protesting! Nobody was in the streets marching!

Nobody was in the streets picketing! No one! I was able to get some radio time [for the Operation PUSH program] from the radio station and go on the air and articulate what was going on in the community . . . how black people were being treated, taking advantage of . . . how complacent we were in the plant jobs."[25]

It was Reverend Smith who started the Operation PUSH campaign in Buffalo, New York. Nationwide, Operation Breadbasket became Operation PUSH under the leadership of a new African American visionary, the Reverend Jesse Jackson. A follower of Dr. King, Jesse Jackson's charisma attracted and held the allegiance of many local politically active ministers long enough to build a forceful movement of national and international viability.[26] Reverend Smith was among this national group of ministers. He states emphatically: "I brought Jesse Jackson to Buffalo [during the first two] months I was here. I organized the community. I never got over three ministers in the whole city to agree to work with me . . . many other ministers would not touch it, but I decided to push on and forge on anyway. It was in my blood!"[27]

Reverend Smith aggressively protested discriminatory practices of major companies in the Operation PUSH "Selective Patronage" campaigns: "In the churches and bars, in the beauty parlors and barbecue joints, in the places where words are currency and trading always is brisk—in these places . . . the campaign begins. . . . We are withdrawing patronage from companies that do not cut us in from the boardroom to the boiler room."[28] Reverend Smith recollects that one company, A & P, responded in precisely the same manner in Buffalo as it did in Cincinnati when he and his few community followers picketed in front of their Ohio stores. They closed the stores and moved out. He argued, "They closed three stores in the community at one time and moved rather than to hire blacks."[29] Although Operation PUSH had fifteen national programs that promoted African American entrepreneurship, placed disenfranchised racial veterans in jobs, aided and counseled addicts, and assisted in legal problems for economically poor racial communities, its most renowned program was the campaign for academic excellence underscored with the self-esteem statement "I AM SOMEBODY."

Reverend Smith aggressively advocated for the program dubbed Project EXCEL in Buffalo's public school system, arguing that "Blacks must now stop 'cursing the darkness and light a candle.' We must excel in the institutions of education in this country, so as to be able to effect change for the benefit of Black people."[30] A full discussion on the political and economic failures of the national Project EXCEL program is beyond the scope of this present work; however, one can surmise that the EXCEL campaign became the catalyst for the St. John Christian Academy, a private church-based, state-chartered school, founded by Smith in the mid-1980s. A strong advocate of "Afrocentric" education for upward social mobility, Smith instituted several other related programs held on St. John Baptist Church premises, such as government-funded programs like the HUD job training site designation for welfare-to-work participants, and "Project Gift" for mentally and physically challenged children, among others.

St. John was also awarded a government-sponsored public housing contract by the Department of Housing and Urban Development and needed a pastor with leadership and expertise to facilitate the completion of the 150-unit complex, called McCarley Gardens. At the time, St. John was the only black church in the city involved in housing development. Although Smith was active in the Elliott Community Redevelopment coalition of thirteen black churches that led to the Town Gardens Housing and Commercial Plaza on the East side, as Naison recalls, St. John was the only individual African American congregration with the financial resources in any sizable allocation to sponsor low-income housing for families.[31] After McCarley was erected, Smith indicates his next move was to build housing for senior citizens: "I saw Baptist Manor go up that was directed by Delaware Avenue Baptist church [a white congregration]. I noticed that the Catholic church . . . [had] an application being submitted and approved for a Senior Citizen [complex] . . . but [none for] blacks, nowhere in this city."[32]

Reverend Smith reconvened his team for the McCarley Gardens project and pursued housing for senior citizens in the community. This time, Reverend Smith would encounter a political confrontation with the mayor whom he accused of being racist and whom he refused to support during the 1977 campaign, deciding instead to support the city's leading African American candidate, Arthur O. Eve. Reverend Smith recalls that when HUD announced that St. John would be awarded a 150-unit Senior Citizen Housing contract, later named St. John Tower, the city—as a form of political payback—gave a 90-unit contract to the only African American minister who supported the mayor's campaign. In addition, Reverend Smith opened a church-based federally chartered credit union, St. John Credit Union, to underwrite the church's development projects. Although several African American churches sponsor service programs (food pantries, senior citizen groups, crime watch), only St. John has programmatically applied its resources to economic development or neighborhood revitalization in the overall African American community.[33]

Reverend Smith's success in garnering community economic development projects for St. John encouraged other African American churches to follow suit. Today, some of the fifteen African American individual congregations involved in housing or community development projects in Buffalo recognize that it is Smith's active leadership that opened the door for subsequent black churches. Smith's success with community economic development programs did not distract him, however, from his protest campaigns for racial and economic justice in Buffalo's African American community as a whole.

Smith reflected, "I only wish that I could have enlisted them [the ministers] in my protest movement as they have come on board in the providing of services to the area . . . because protest always precedes service rendering."[34]

Reverend Smith emphatically argued that Buffalo missed the whole civil rights movement. He states, "Buffalo had no one that they could point to that participated in Selma, participated in Montgomery, participated in any of the movement with Dr. King as the civil rights movement unfolded. No one from this town participated. So consequently, they had no history of involvement [with protest against racial injustice]. No sensitivity to what was taking place among African American people throughout the South. No involvement of clergy."[35] In fact, two local African American politicians told Smith that on the one trip that Dr. King made to Buffalo on November 9, 1967, to speak, "no Black minister would go to the airport to meet him."[36] The two politicians had to go alone. Reverend Smith considered it a "special mission by God" to come to Buffalo. He recalls, "God equips us with what we need" because "He [God] had plans for him" to eradicate this political inactivity among Buffalo's African American community.[37]

Smith did enlist a number of ministers in mounting a credible threat to close down the Kensington expressway to protest against the New York State Transportation Department. The Kensington expressway divided the African American "Fruitbelt" community and failed to provide adequate pedestrian passageways from one side of the expressway to the other. Smith's well-organized and ready-to-mobilize community-wide protest resulted in the erection of the Elm-Oak Arterial for pedestrians across the expressway.[38] During the brief period of violence between the city's African American and white school children on school buses, Smith called for all ministers to ride the school buses until the violence was under control.

His reputation as an influential political broker expanded through his membership on the city's subcommittee on Police Community Affairs, which investigated the brutal killings of African American males in the early 1980s. Reverend Smith openly challenged the police department, which historically had been strained in its race relations with the African American community. As the principal spokesman for the Buffalo African American community in the tense period following the .22-caliber killings, Reverend Smith often contradicted official statements that progress was being accomplished in the investigation. He even organized a shopping slowdown in downtown Buffalo to ensure the .22-caliber probe was "not put on the back burner."[39] Smith unapologetically characterized the shootings as racially motivated as all of the shootings were directed at African American males. It is important to underscore that most of Reverend Smith's influence as a political broker came as a result of his demonstrable ability to marshal political votes in the African American electorate at the local and state level.

Prior to a public falling out between Reverend Smith and Arthur O. Eve, the African American deputy speaker in the New York State Assembly, Reverend Smith actively used his pulpit to promote Eve's mayoral campaign in 1977. Smith argued that "[a]lthough the mayoral candidate was not a member of this church, we felt as if we should support him. . . . So our church became involved in voter registration and voter participation. . . . We sent a message that 'you can't be a good citizen in heaven without being a good citizen on earth.'"[40] Stated another way, Smith has argued, "The pulpit is the most natural place in the world to be political. I tell my people who to vote for from the pulpit. I endorse candidates from the pulpit." In fact, at St. John a voter registration card is a requirement for church membership. "If [my parishioners] don't vote, they are not members in good standing." Smith argues that politics are connected to every aspect of life, and "he is not averse to admitting that politics determines the church's present and future: 'When politicians drive by my church on a Sunday morning, they know that 90 percent of the people in there are voters. How can they pass us by?'"[41]

Placed within the overall local political context, Sullivan has characterized African American voting power in Buffalo as being initiated by several factors. First, the proportion of blacks to whites in Buffalo is higher than ever: the 1980 U.S. Census showed that the white population dropped more than 30 percent from 1970 to 1980, but the black population held steady and now makes up close to 30 percent of the city's total of 350,000. Second, a recent voter registration drive signed up five thousand more black persons, adding to a traditionally high black voter registration. Third, blacks had already tested their voting clout: they played the key role in delivering the majority vote Governor Mario Cuomo received in Buffalo in the 1982 election. Finally, a variety of national factors—the anti-Reagan sentiment among blacks, the presidential candidacy of black activist Reverend Jesse Jackson, and the symbolically important victory of black mayor Harold Washington in Chicago—were certain to motivate black voters in Buffalo.[42]

It is customary during the Buffalo campaign season for most of the major local, state, and national candidates to visit and appeal to St. John's congregation for their electoral votes due to Reverend Smith's influential electoral activism and local decision-making authority. Some of the political uneasiness between Reverend Smith and Arthur O. Eve perhaps emanated from Smith's failure to support his mayoral campaign in 1989. In support of Senator Anthony Masiello, Smith argued, "1989 would not be the year for a African American to run for mayor. We should all unite behind a man with a proven record—Sen. Masiello."[43] Some claimed that the strong relationship between Smith and Masiello was due in part to Smith's wife, who then served as a legislative aide in Masiello's office and later served for four years as the second African American treasurer for the city in his administration.[44]

Smith wielded political influence on the national level as well. He met for two hours with Ronald Reagan when he was campaigning in Buffalo during the 1980s.[45] He openly challenged U.S. foreign policy initiatives because, as he puts it, "Blacks came here as a foreign policy decision," therefore, "[w]e have a legitimate right to be involved in foreign policy discussions."[46] Most of Reverend Smith's national prominence resulted from his political and religious involvement in the Progressive National Baptist Convention, Inc. (PNBC), which emanated from the social justice campaigns of the late Reverend Dr. Martin Luther King Jr. It proved to be a natural progression for Reverend Smith to promote his local style of protest-oriented activism at the national and international levels. But it was at the local level where Smith's leadership left an indelible mark. In a city where seven African Americans at one time constituted a majority voting bloc on the city's common council, including the council president, one can well see the result of the persistent effectiveness of this African American political mobilization. Reverend Smith's leadership demonstrates the belief held by many African American clergy that "faith works" when tested through differing venues of challenge and inspiration.

CONCLUSION

After over two decades as pastor of one of Buffalo's largest churches, white or African American, Reverend Smith was viewed within state and local political circles as a man with political clout. In fact, many argue that the only other African American with major influence in the city was his long-time opponent Arthur O. Eve, deputy speaker of the New York State Assembly.[47] Smith recollected that his own local reputation was built on his protest-oriented role and activities as the national vice president and Buffalo chairman of Operation PUSH (People United to Serve Humanity) during the 1970s and wedded to his leadership as the pastor of the progressive St. John Baptist Church.

Most of the African American ministers interviewed agreed that Smith effectively built his social networks with local clergy and politicians through political activism in both local and national campaigns in the African American community.[48] This inevitably led to partnerships and collaboration on new developmental projects with mostly younger and educated clergy eager to participate in and influence the local political arena. In this vein, Smith mobilized black social capital to work together with local and national African American clergy to achieve social ends.[49] He capitalized on the historical experiences of African Americans and the cultural attachments and loyalty to the black church and its internal bonds and networks to build financial wealth for St. John Baptist Church, which was not solely independent of government funding, but certainly not totally reliant upon it. Utilizing intercommunity or "bonding" social ties among congregants and political or "bridging" ties among local politicians and community supporters, which crossed social divides of religion, class, ethnicity, and socioeconomic status, Smith created a broader range of networks that contributed to social capital for the African American community.[50]

As the social capital networks built through the leadership activities of Smith in Buffalo became more diverse, the prominence of St. John Baptist Church increased, as did Smith's reputation among local and national clergy and politicians. The foundation for Smith's community economic development activities was facilitated in his early days through his political protests and activism (Operation PUSH activities; pulpit endorsements/voter registration drives; convention hall activities for local, state, and national political candidates; and Black History Month programs), which built his reputation in the community. This helped him to negotiate for government-sponsored housing and collaborate with other churches on commercial development (McCarley Gardens low-to-moderate-income housing and St. John Tower Senior Citizens Housing). As Smith pursued more and more government-sponsored projects/programs for his congregation, he shifted from collaboration and partnerships with other local clergy toward building linkages to national clergy and broader funding opportunities (the establishment of the St. John Federal Credit Union, the Smith Child Life Foundation Fund, and the annual free income tax preparation services for senior citizens and congregants). In a sense, Smith began to divest himself of local community ties to "find a potentially more diverse network" with more abundant economic opportunities.[51] He did this initially through educational activities (Early Head Start Program, Project EXCEL, Project Gift, and St. John Christian Academy), then later through government-sponsored job-training activities (HUD-sponsored Neighborhood Network Center operated through St. John).

Some argue that a networks approach to social capital has the tendency to minimize the "'public good' nature of social groups, regarding any benefits of group activity as primarily the property of the particular individuals involved," which explains the emphasis on Smith's leadership role as the locus of social capital.[52] Oftentimes, institutional and discriminatory practices can undermine efforts by disenfranchised and disconnected African Americans to act in their collective interest; thus, many rely on courageous leaders who can articulate self-help ideals that promote programs and strategies that are embedded in the African American values and cultural traditions derived from the enslavement period, but also reflect the economic interests of the masses of African Americans found in inner cities.[53] Following in the leadership traditions of DuBois and Dr. King, as the social capital networks expanded for Smith, he attempted to direct his spiritual and political activities to "restore hope" in the African American community in Buffalo.

NOTES

1. P. Fairbanks, "Politics of the Pulpit," *Buffalo News Magazine,* 18 July 1993, 4.

2. M. Holden, *The Politics of the Black "Nation"* (New York: Chandler, 1973); Ronald Walters and Robert C. Smith, *African-American Leadership* (New York: State University of New York Press, 1999), 109.

3. Aldon Morris, *The Origins of the Civil Rights Movement: Black Communities Organizing for Change* (New York: Free Press, 1984), 7.

4. R. Cnaan, M Basta, S. C. Boddie, A. Cnaan, L. Hartocollis, K. Prochezka, and G. Yancey, "Bowling Alone but Serving Together: The Congregational Norm of Community Involvement," report prepared for the Center for Research on Religion and Urban Civil Society, University of Pennsylvania, Philadelphia, 1998.

5. Walters and Smith, *African-American Leadership,* 53; Holden, *Politics,* 12.

6. W. Berenson, K. Elifson, and T. Tollerson, "Preachers in Politics: A Study of Political Activism among the Black Ministry," *Journal of Black Studies* 6 (1976): 373–92.

7. Walters and Smith, *African-American Leadership,* 54.

8. R. Gittell and A. Vidal, *Community Organizing: Building Social Capital as a Development Strategy* (Thousand Oaks, Calif.: Sage Publications, 1998), 15. Moreover, Gittell and Vidal discussed (p. 16) others who have broadened meanings and key elements for "bonding and bridging social capital" such as K. Temkin and W. Rohe, "Social Capital and Neighborhood Stability: An Empirical Investigation," *Housing and Policy Debate* 9, no. 1 (1997): 61–88, who emphasize the sociocultural milieu and institutional infrastructure; X. Briggs, "Brown Kids in White Suburbs: Housing Mobility and the Multiple Faces of Social Capital," *Housing and Policy Debate* 9, no. 1 (1997): 177–221, who focuses on the use of social capital as leverage and social support; L. Keyes, A. Schwartz, A. Vidal, and R. Bratt, "Networks and Nonprofits: Opportunities and Challenges in an Era of Federal Devolution," *Housing and Policy Debate* 7, no. 2 (1996): 21–28, whose work discusses long-term trust and relationships, shared vision, economic incentives to mutual interest, and financial nexus; W. Powell, "Neither Market nor Hierarchy: Network Forms of Organization," in *Research in Organizational Behavior,* vol. 12, ed. B. Straw and L. Cummings, 295–336 (Greenwich, Conn.: 1990); M. Granovetter, *Getting A Job: A Study of Contacts and Careers* (Cambridge: Harvard University Press, 1994), and M. Granovetter, "The Strength of Weak Ties," *American Journal of Sociology* 78, no. 6 (1993): 1360–80; and R. Burt, *Structural Holes: The Social Structure of Competition* (Cambridge: Harvard University Press, 1992), all focus on the strength of weak ties and structural holes in social capital.

9. Robert Putnam, "Tuning In, Tuning Out: The Strange Disappearance of Social Capital in America," The Ithiel de Sola Pool Lecture, *PS: Political Science & Politics* 28, no. 4 (December 1995): 664–65.

10. Robert D. Putnam, *Bowling Alone: The Collapse and Revival of American Community* (New York: Simon & Schuster, 2000); and Gittell and Vidal, *Community Organizing.*

11. Fairbanks, "Politics of the Pulpit," 4.

12. On December 25, 1971, Operation PUSH replaced VCIA/SCLC Operation Breadbasket to advance not only economic development activities but also to increase political participation among Cincinnati's African American community. Also, Smith organized and arranged for the redesignation of Humboldt Park in the heart of

the African American community as the "Martin Luther King Jr. Park," commemorating the assassination. He surmised the genesis of the Martin Luther King Jr. Park started with "this preacher and three or four lay persons."

13. Bennett W. Smith, interview with author, Buffalo, summer 1998.

14. L. Williams, "Afro-Americans in Buffalo, 1900–1930: A Study of Community Formation," *Afro-Americans in N.Y. Life & History* 8, no. 2 (July 1984): 202.

15. R. Watkins, *Black Buffalo 1920–1927* (unpublished dissertation, State University of New York at Buffalo, 1978), 3.

16. Watkins, *Black Buffalo*, 3.

17. M. Naison, "In Quest of Community: The Organizational Structure of Black Buffalo," in *African Americans and the Rise of Buffalo's Post-Industrial City, 1940 to Present,* ed. H. L. Taylor Jr., 207 (Buffalo, N.Y.: Buffalo Urban League, 1990).

18. Naison, "In Quest of Community," 209.

19. Naison, "In Quest of Community," 209.

20. R. Halpern, *Rebuilding the Inner City: A History of Neighborhood Initiatives to Address Poverty in the United States* (New York: Columbia University Press, 1995), 128; S. Shipp, "The Road Not Taken: Alternative Strategies for Black Economic Development in the United States," *Journal of Economic Issues* 30, no. 1 (1996): 79–95; A. Harvey, "A Black Community Development Model: The Universal Negro Improvement Association and African Communities League 1917–1940," *Journal of Sociology and Social Welfare* 21, no. 1 (1994): 113–24.

21. Shipp, "The Road Not Taken"; Halpern. *Rebuilding the Inner City*, 128.

22. Naison, "In Quest of Community."

23. P. Pitegoff, "Buffalo Change & Community," *Buffalo Law Review* 39, no. 2 (1991): 327–28.

24. Pitegoff, "Buffalo Change & Community."

25. Smith interview, 1998.

26. James M. Washington, "Urban Economic Development Strategies of African-American Baptist Clergy during the Cold War Era," in *Churches, Cities, and Human Community: Urban Ministry in the United States, 1945–1985,* ed. C. J. Green, 273. (Grand Rapids, Mich.: William B. Eerdmans. 1996).

27. Smith interview, 1998.

28. F. Bruning, "Big Corporations Getting PUSHed Around," *Buffalo News*, 23 May 1982, B5.

29. Smith interview, 1998.

30. Bennett W. Smith Sr., "Black Americans Urged to Join New Push for Excellence," *Buffalo Courier Express*, 23 July 1976, 1, 16.

31. Naison, "In Quest of Community."

32. Smith interview, 1998.

33. Naison, "In Quest of Community," 211.

34. Smith interview, 1998.

35. Smith interview, 1998.

36. Smith interview, 1998.

37. C. Allen, "Buffalo Mission Called Product of Providence," *Buffalo News*, 3 May 1980, A7.

38. Allen," Buffalo Mission." T. Buckham, "Expressway Sit-in Threat Spurs Search for Funds," *Buffalo News*, 24 August 1979.

39. Bruning, "Big Corporations."

40. Smith interview, 1998.

41. M. Sullivan, "The Reawakening of Buffalo's Black Voters," *Buffalo News Magazine*, 11 September 1983, 8.

42. Sullivan, "Reawakening of Buffalo's Black Voters," 7–15.

43. Borrelli 1988: C1.

44. Fairbanks, "Politics of the Pulpit," 6.

45. Bruning, "Big Corporations."

46. *Buffalo News*, 13 February 1980, 13.

47. Fairbanks, "Politics of the Pulpit," 4.

48. Sherri L. Wallace, "Buffalo's 'Prophet of Protest': The Political Leadership and Activism of Reverend Dr. Bennett W. Smith, Sr.," *Afro-Americans in New York Life and History* 25 (July 2001).

49. M. Orr, *Black Social Capital: The Politics of School Reform in Baltimore, 1986–1998* (Lawrence: University Press of Kansas, 1999), 24.

50. M. Woolcock and D. Narayan, "Social Capital: Implications for Development Theory, Research, and Policy," *World Bank Research Observer* 15, no. 2 (August 2000): 230; and Gittell and Vidal, *Community Organizing*.

51. Woolcock and Narayan, "Social Capital," 233.

52. Woolcock and Narayan, "Social Capital," 234.

53. V. P. Franklin, *Black Self-Determination: A Cultural History of the Faith of the Fathers* (Westport, Conn.: Lawrence Hill & Company, 1984), 203.

4

Black Ministers and the Politics of Personal Influence in Columbus

Yvette Alex-Assensoh

Historically, African Americans have faced the paradox of fighting for inclusion in an American political system that has historically practiced conspicuous exclusion and discrimination of minorities in general. The periodic exceptions to this included the Reconstruction period (1865–76) and the contemporary era since the 1965 Voting Rights Act. Otherwise, African Americans have been continuously excluded from formal and legitimate forms of participation in the American political process.

As a consequence of the significant odds to bring about their political inclusion, the process of black politics is most aptly described, in the words of an old Negro spiritual, as the art of "making a way out of no way." In an effort to "make a way out of no way," the process of black politics has been dependent upon organizations, leadership, and institutions outside the normal realm of electoral politics to gain access to the political process.[1] In that respect, the black church has served as the most important institution in the process and practice of black politics.[2] With respect to suffrage—electoral and other voting rights issues—the black church has invariably served as a virtual incubator of black political leadership, as a vehicle for voter registration, and as the mobilizing force for financial as well as personal resources from times of slavery to the present.

One important implication of historical black exclusion from the American political process is that, prior to the 1970s and the increased election of African American officials, black church politics and black secular politics have seen such a fusion that they have become virtually synonymous. Before blacks could either vote or serve as viable candidates for earmarked public offices, black pastors and their associate ministers were often called upon by the white political establishment to distill and, often, to present the views of the black masses. Invariably, they were also expected to serve as buffers between white elected politicians and the more radical elements of the black community.[3] Toward these ends, the modern phase of the civil rights movement and the Voting Rights Act of 1965 facilitated a dramatic increase in black elected officials and, most importantly, a secular component of black politics that was separate and distinct from black church clergy, although still dependent on the black church for electoral support.[4]

This chapter utilizes ethnographic data from five predominantly black Baptist churches to analyze the process of black church politics in the city of Columbus, Ohio. The data, collected during visits to the interviewing sites, provide the evidence for this study and are taken from structured, person-to-person interviews with five pastors in the Columbus metropolitan area; the interviewees and their church affiliations are Reverend Phale Hale of Union Grove Baptist Church; Reverend A. Wilson Wood of Bethany Baptist Church; Reverend Dr. Keith Troy of New Salem Baptist Church; Reverend Dr. Jesse Wood of Love Zion Baptist Church; and Reverend Leon Troy of Second Baptist Church. Additionally, census data were used to provide contextual information on the socioeconomic and political conditions of the city.

Meanwhile, in linking the process of black church politics in Columbus to the secular aspects of black politics, this chapter explores two specific research questions, namely: what tactics are employed by black church politics to gain a measure of inclusion in the local politics of Columbus, and how do these tactics compare with the strategies typically utilized in the process and practice of secular black politics?

BACKGROUND AND RESEARCH LITERATURE

Much of the existing scholarship on black politics examines the reliance on varied electoral activities, including voting, as mechanisms for political inclusion.[5] This, indeed, is because the vote has historically been considered the primary mechanism in the quest of blacks for political inclusion in an exclusionary and discriminatory system. To some extent, this strategy has netted some important benefits, including increases in black municipal employment, improvement in city services for blacks, benefits for black business elites, some increases in expenditures for social services, especially at the municipal level, and increased representation from the African American citizenry.[6]

In apportioning responsibility for these political gains, researchers have consistently highlighted the important relationship between secular black politics and black church politics. Again, this is particularly so as churches have functioned within the realm of key institutions in the development of black political leadership and important political skills among congregants as well as the mobilization of voters.[7]

Traditional research on the black church has focused on its role in the various phases of the civil rights movement. However, much more recent research has chronicled the church's role in equipping its members with political skills and resources.[8] Researchers have demonstrated that, politically, very active church groups often help in facilitating mobilization among the black masses, which has consequently led to increased levels of voting and in the participation of campaign activities, higher levels of racial identity, psychological impetus for sustained political involvement, and organizational resources for collective action.[9] A crucially important caveat for all of the aforementioned findings is the fact that the social isolation, concentrated poverty, and fragmented family contexts endemic to many aspects of inner-city communities do not, necessarily, undermine the successful transmission by black churches of these political skills and resources.[10]

Notwithstanding the important contributions of the black electoral strategy, research on black politics has also underscored the limited utility of voting and black representation to deliver significant black political power. This is particularly so, as the election of black elected officials has had little effect on the economic inequalities that relegate blacks to the bottom of the American socioeconomic ladder.[11]

Consequently, over the last two decades research on black politics has emphasized the need to move beyond a singular electoral strategy. Additionally, scholars have contended that black politics should balance the priorities of integration with the need to build strong, ideologically informed political organizations, which can develop issue agendas, convert those issues into public policy options, and mobilize support for those options.[12] Research on black politics has also identified the importance of an inclusionary agenda that focuses on economic and political power. To a large extent, research on black politics has focused on the efforts of black secular politics, including those of the Reverend Jesse Jackson and the NAACP to wrestle economic gains for blacks, but little research has assessed the activities of black church politics in issues of economic empowerment and organization building.

Grounded in the research on black political empowerment, it is argued by this study that black church politics is involved in a similar quest for inclusion in an exclusionary and discriminatory political system. In some respects, black church politics also employs tactics that are very similar to those of black secular politics, especially with respect to electoral activities and representational issues. On the other hand, however, this chapter further demonstrates that black church politics in Columbus is moving beyond a reliance on electoral strategies and secular black political leaders as it forges independent initiatives aimed at economic empowerment and organization building.

Meanwhile, the chapter contends that the foregoing efforts complement the process of secular black politics while simultaneously providing alternative and different routes of access to the political process in Columbus. In a nutshell, the analyses of black church politics are suggestive of three patterns of influence: a politics of personal influence, organizational clout, and economic empowerment partnerships. Based on this evidence, the chapter also explores the relevance of black church politics, especially as it moves beyond the pale of electoral strategies to claim new ground in the quest for equality and inclusion among African Americans.

THE POLITICAL AND SOCIOECONOMIC
CONTEXTS OF COLUMBUS

Any attempt to assess the process and practice of black church politics in Columbus must begin with an examination of the municipal governing structure. Columbus is a city with a strong mayoral system, whereby the mayor wields considerable political clout or power. For example, the elected mayor heads the administrative branch of city government, and he or she is responsible for appointing directors to most of the city's departmental offices. In addition to appointive powers, the mayor, as the chief executive officer of Columbus, also has veto power. As a result, he or she has the ability to strike down any ordinance or resolution passed by the city council that runs counter to his or her wishes. A necessary, but not sufficient, step in the quest of influencing Columbus municipal politics, therefore, is having ample access to the reigning mayor.

Prior to 1999—when Columbus elected its first African American mayor—blacks had very little access to the mayor's office and its preeminent influence in municipal politics. That is because all of the previous (pre-1999) mayors had been white and most also had been Republican by political affiliation. As a result, area blacks had extreme challenges in competing against dominant and, obviously, racist ideologies and structures as well as facing the formidable conflicts over contrasting ideological views. That lack of access to the mayor's office was significant when one considers the almost fifty-year span of time from the 1950s, when blacks comprised a significant population in Columbus, until the 1999 election of Michael Coleman as the first elected black mayor.

Interestingly, the pluralist perspective of American politics contends that there are multiple points of entry for political influence, thus suggesting that blacks, who are excluded from the mayor's office, may gain access to political empowerment through the city council directly. While the city council has, traditionally, served as a point of influence in the political process, that has not been the case among blacks of Columbus. Instead, however, all of its seven city council members are elected at-large. Scholarship on black politics has consistently identified at-large electoral systems as a foe to minority empowerment. Unlike district- or ward-based elections that allow council officials to focus on the needs of a particular community, at-large council members are elected citywide. As a result, city council candidates and elected city council members are less likely to devote significant attention to the desires of particular groups, including minority groups. This is because they are seen as representatives of the entire city. Under those circumstances, the special needs of many disadvantaged black Columbus residents have consistently been overlooked, as city council officials, who desire to be reelected, avoid accusations of pandering to the interest of a particular group, especially when general support is needed for reelection bids. Thus, although blacks have been successful in serving as elected members of the Columbus city council, they have done so by deemphasizing a specifically progressive black agenda.

Based on the legacy of black exclusion from the dominant positions of power in the politics of Columbus, Ohio, it is not surprising to observe the gross inequalities that still exist in black and white standards of living. As depicted by table 4.1, African Americans—as a racial group in Columbus—are largely concentrated in five Columbus neighborhoods, namely South Linden, North Central, Milo-Grogan, Near East, and Driving Park. These neighborhoods are located primarily on the east side of the city, many in concentrated poverty neighborhoods, where at least 40 percent of the population lives below the poverty line. Most of the churches included in this study are also located in this area.[13]

Educational attainment among African Americans in Columbus—as depicted by table 4.2—is depressingly low. Much of the research on employment trends among African Americans show that a first academic degree (i.e., B.A., B.S., or B. Ed.) is almost a necessity to succeed economically in today's job market. Yet, in all of the predominantly African American neighborhoods of Columbus, the percentage of individuals with a bachelor's degree hovered below the 10 percent mark. Equally troubling are the relatively high percentages of African Americans who report their overall educational attainment as "some high school," which means that they even lack the fundamental and elementary qualifications like a requisite high school diploma. In the Milo-Grogan neighborhood, for example, 45 percent of the residents report their education as "some high school," while the percentages in South Linden, North Central, Near East, and Driving Park neighborhoods are around 30 percent. Given the people's low levels of education, the obviously high levels of poverty and low median incomes, depicted by table 4.3, are not very surprising.

Columbus, as a Frostbelt city, has experienced massive job loss in the manufacturing sector that once served as the economic backbone for city

Table 4.1. 1998 Population Statistics for Predominantly Black Neighborhoods

Racial Categories	Columbus, City	South Linden	North Central	Milo-Grogan	Near East	Driving Park
Asian, Pacific Islander	3.1%	1%	0.2%	0.7%	1%	0.5%
African American	25%	90%	90%	92%	89%	93%
Native American	0.2%	0.2%	0.2%	0%	0.3%	3%
White	72%	9%	9%	7%	9%	6%
Other	0.5%	0.4%	0.2%	0%	0.6%	0.3%

Source: City of Columbus Planning Office.

Table 4.2. 1990 Educational Attainment in Predominantly Black Neighborhoods

Level of Attainment	Columbus, City	South Linden	North Central	Milo-Grogan	Near East	Driving Park
Below 9th Grade	6%	12%	11%	14%	13%	10%
Some High School	16%	33%	27%	45%	29%	32%
High School Graduate	29%	33%	35%	27%	29%	32%
Some College	20%	15%	17%	10%	16%	17%
Associate Degree	6%	3%	4%	2%	4%	6%
Bachelor's Degree	16%	4%	6%	1%	6%	7%
Graduate/Professional Degree	8%	1%	2%	1%	3%	1%

Source: City of Columbus Planning Office.

Table 4.3. 1998 Income Statistics for Predominantly Black Neighborhoods

Income	Columbus, City	South Linden	North Central	Milo-Grogan	Near East	Driving Park
Family Income < $15,000	19%	37%	25%	51%	50%	28%
Median Household Income	$34,791	$21,625	$33,282	$13,469	$16,000	$23,125
Average Household Income	$17,397	$26,301	$34,612	$18,533	$23,180	$29,285
Per Capita Income	$41,357	$9,069	$13,121	$6,902	$9,898	$11,170

Source: City of Columbus Planning Office.

residents. Unlike many of the readily abundant service-sector jobs, which require formal education and skilled training, the manufacturing jobs offered opportunities for workers with lower levels of education and skill, as they were able to make the minimum or living wage that is accompanied by the much-needed health and retirement benefits. As a result of this deindustrialization, which was accompanied by unemployment and underemployment, the Ohio capital became one of ten major cities that witnessed the largest increase of residents living in concentrated poverty neighborhoods, where at least 40 percent of the residents lived below the poverty line.

Table 4.3 delineates the consequences of deindustrialization for the poverty status in predominantly black neighborhoods. Between 25 and 50 percent of African American residents, in predominantly black neighborhoods, live in poverty. Moreover, with the exception of the North Central neighborhood, which also has the lowest level of individuals with incomes below the poverty level, the median household income for black neighborhoods lags tremendously behind the overall median income of $34,791 for the city of Columbus. Again, for example, in the Milo-Grogan and Near East neighborhoods the median annual incomes for a typical family of three people are $13,469 and $16,000, respectively.

As depicted by table 4.4, in addition to the disparity in low levels of education and income, African Americans also tend to live in housing that is much older and often worth less in property value than those of other residents in the city of Columbus. For example, only 18 percent of Columbus residents generally live in housing units that were built before 1939. In the predominantly African American neighborhoods of Milo-Grogan and Near East, however, almost half of the residents live in housing that was constructed before 1939.

Also, not only are African Americans more likely to live in outdated, dilapidated housing, but they are also less likely to live in neighborhoods with new housing units being built or massive renovations being carried out. Of the 2 percent of new construction that occurred in Columbus since 1989, none is located in the predominantly black neighborhoods of South Linden, Milo-Grogan, and Near East, while a mere 0.2 percent of new housing was sited in the North Central neighborhood. However, it was the neighborhood of Driving Park that was the only predominantly black area that generally received a proportional percentage (i.e., 2 percent) of new housing construction.

Very clearly, evident from the foregoing statistics is the fact that the African American community in Columbus has serious problems in the specific areas of educational attainment, the concentration of poverty, and quality housing. The next section of the chapter identifies the strategies that black church politics in Columbus has utilized to bring about an amelioration of these problems.

Table 4.4. 1990 Housing Units by Year Built for Predominantly Black Neighborhoods

Housing Units by Year Built	Columbus, City	South Linden	North Central	Milo-Grogan	Near East	Driving Park
1989–March 1990	2%	0%	0.2%	0%	0%	2%
1985–1988	9%	0.4%	2%	1%	0.5%	0%
1980–1984	8%	0.4%	5%	2%	2%	1%
1970–1979	20%	5%	13%	3%	9%	5%
1960–1969	19%	11%	28%	10%	12%	7%
1950–1959	16%	28%	25%	24%	13%	23%
1940–1949	10%	32%	16%	15%	16%	29%
before 1940	18%	23%	11%	45%	46%	32%

Source: City of Columbus Planning Office.

THE POLITICS OF PERSONAL INFLUENCE

One of the most common patterns of black church politics, which was operative in Columbus municipal issues, was the so-called politics of personal influence. Under this type of influence, the black clergy used such personal characteristics as technical skills, charisma, and political status of an elected official to influence political actors and/or the political process. Seen as a long-standing tradition among the black clergy, the tactic has been used successfully in electoral and nonelectoral issues. It has generated some gains for blacks in the areas of employment, viable public policy alternatives, and refocusing attention to the areas of black need. Three of the pastors interviewed for this study indicated unabashedly that, as members of the active black clergy, they have used their personal influence in this manner: the three are Pastor Phale Hale, Pastor Jesse Wood, and Pastor Leon Troy.

For fourteen years, Reverend Phale Hale, the pastor of Union Grove Baptist Church, served the community as an elected state representative, whereby he helped to sponsor legislation affecting a number of important areas. The following list, which he spelled out in our interview, gives some indication of the extent of the political power that he wielded as a state representative, coupled with its implications for Columbus residents in general:

> I sponsored bills to end segregation in the cemeteries of the State of Ohio. I retired from the legislature undefeated in 1980 and chose my successor, Otto Beatty. I gave him my seat and swore him in. I put the first black highway patrolmen on the state highway in the State of Ohio. I put the first black tellers in the banks in the city of Columbus. That bank is now one of our tenements down on Mt. Vernon. I was responsible for how Ohio State University got its first black professor, Dr. Charles Ross in sociology.[14]

Reverend Jesse Wood, the current president of the Black Pastors' Conference, has not held any elected political office but, as one of a small number of black Republicans in the city today, he wields some influence in Republican circles. Reverend Wood offers the following assessment of his own involvement in politics:

> I have been extremely active in politics. I helped to form back in 1973, '74 the first black Young Republican Club in the country. So, for the last twenty years I have been extremely active in politics. There was a group of four of us who helped to elect Jim Rhoads governor in 1974. So folk in this town, under most circumstances, in the political arena, know me. They know my political involvement as well as my politics. So in that sense, it is not unusual to find me out front on political issues. I am always taking the position that political parties are vehicles like Fords and Chevrolets and you pick the one you think you can drive the best and will get you where you want to go in the best way. I don't apologize for it at all to anybody. The reason I don't, I say this, that when

Republicans sit in offices then its black Republicans who go to these candidates
to try to make a difference on whatever is going on in our community. So when
there are issues in the community I get the phone call, not my black Democrat
counterpart. And so therefore I never permit black Democrats to feel like they
have all answers. Or that they can make decisions for me. That's why I let my
folk know what my part is. I have no problem with that. I refuse to let them
commit me to Bush because the one thing I have always said, I said this when
I first started out in politics is that I will be black first and Republican second.
I will say it even today. I support the party. But I will say in a moment when
Bush is not representing the best interest of the black folk, or anybody locally
not representing the black folk.[15]

Also, Pastor Emeritus Leon Troy served for eight years as the special assistant to Mayor Dana Rinehart, a white elected mayor. In an interview, he
made it clear that, although he was not an elected political official, he was
still able to provide two examples of how he shaped public policy in ways
that were beneficial to the African American community in Columbus:

I served as special assistant to the mayor for eight years. I was his community
representative. In that capacity, I spoke all over this community and constantly
sat at the table with his cabinetry to remind him what he was doing up there
with his dollars how exactly this impact the intercity policy. For example, the
city decided to do new lighting. Traditionally, in the past, it always started in the
outer boundaries and came inward. By the time you got to the inner city, you
always ended up having little lighting left. So the outer boundary always got
lights first, although the inner city needed lights most. So I persuaded the mayor
to start his program in the inner city first and move out. This was a policy
change. The second policy change is that I convinced him that it would be good
to be more accessible to the community, especially minorities in the community.
So we moved the cabinet meetings around town. We met in the city hall once
or twice a month and then we met in the neighborhoods of each of the area
commissions. It would be broadcast from that. The mayor's cabinet was going
to meet at such and such a place and the people came on Monday at the May-
side Commission and decided for a recreational center. This gave the people a
chance to have access to the mayor, the cabinet and have a concern, to be as-
signed to people. As you move the government around, we didn't have the
Statue of Liberty concept type for example, in my arms—let my knowledge drip
off you as everything goes. That's how I got that parking place. So that will be
two examples of how you shape policy and I invited the entire cabinet to
church services. The cabinet came and I addressed my message that day about
as to how the church and government must come together and work together.[16]

While the politics of personal prestige is very similar to and complimentary of secular black politics, the process of black church politics is also engaged in organization building, an important aspect of black empowerment
in the post–civil rights era.

BLACK BAPTIST PASTORS' CONFERENCE AND
THE ROLE OF ORGANIZATIONAL CLOUT

A consistent lament in the scholarship on black political behavior is the lack of disciplined and effective organizations, which can effectively articulate issues, mobilize support for them, and translate these issues into viable public policy options. The fifty-year-old Columbus Black Baptist Pastors' Conference is an example of an emerging organization that wields significant political clout and is poised for even greater influence in the coming decades.

The Black Baptist Pastors' Conference (BBPC) is the organization of current pastors, former pastors, and retired pastors in the Columbus metropolitan area.[17] The BBPC, which has been in existence for over fifty years, has grown to address housing and educational inequalities as well as spiritual concerns of black Baptist pastors. These two issues have remained at the forefront of the BBPC's agenda. Most important about the BBPC is its support of traditional efforts based on electoral strategies as well as more innovative tactics that engender economic empowerment among the black disadvantaged masses.

In an effort to remain independent, the BBPC operates and thrives solely on the dues of member pastors, and these funds are used to support the activities of the organization. Administratively, the BBPC functions through the work of elected officers, including a president, two vice presidents, three secretaries with specified duties, a treasurer, and a chaplain. There are also committees formed to address political and spiritual issues. Most important in terms of political implications is the BBPC's Political Action Committee, which is responsible for informing the conference of important political issues and crises. Moreover, it is this committee that is often approached by elected officials, candidates, and city organizations that wish to use black pastors as a tool of dissemination and influence.

During the years of formal exclusion from voting and office holding, the conference served as blacks' primary conduit for the transmission of information about municipal politics. Though not consistently done, many of Columbus's former white mayors used the BBPC as a sounding board for policy initiatives and also to disseminate information relevant to the black community. Historically, the BBPC has used the media to articulate its support for issues of importance to the black community. Over the last two decades, however, Columbus mayors have included the BBPC as part of their legitimate policy community, as they have met regularly with the mayor and other elected officials to discuss municipal issues and also to address concerns of the black community, as distilled by black pastors.

When asked about the effectiveness and political clout of the organization, Reverend Dr. Jesse L. Wood, who currently serves as its president, offered the following elucidation: "Some of the clout is real, and some of it is perceived.

I don't think that we have always exercised real clout, but perception is 51 percent of reality. Every time we meet, we have someone knocking on our door, who wants us to be an advocate for something. We try to be selective. Without a doubt, our organizational presence in the city, and our presence in certain matters have changed the politics of Columbus for the better."

As an organization, the BBPC has lent support to black elected officials and candidates, supporting the traditional black electoral quest for inclusion. For most of its fifty-year history, the BBPC did not extend its organizational endorsement to individual candidates. That is because such endorsements could facilitate infighting and strife over candidate selection. However, in 1999 the BBPC broke with this long-standing tradition, as it extended its first candidate endorsement to Michael Coleman, the city's first viable African American candidate for mayor. That support was due to the overwhelming contention among BBPC members that Coleman had paid his dues (as president of the city council) and that he was eminently qualified to serve as the city's mayor.

The BBPC endorsement went a long way to enlist the mayor's attention for and response to issues affecting black Baptist churches in Columbus and also provided an internal point of access for black church politics in mainstream Columbus politics. Among Mayor Coleman's first administrative creations was the establishment of an Office of Community Affairs.[18] One of the chief policy advisors on community affairs is Reverend Larry Price, a former state representative who is also an ordained minister. Not only did the mayor create this office, but he also established it as part of the mayor's office, which provides the black community, black churches, neighborhood groups, and such organized groups as the Black Pastors' Conference with direct access to the seat of municipal governance and power.

There is also ample evidence that the mayor's Office of Community Affairs is bringing about much-needed positive change in the status of inner-city neighborhoods. Through an instituted program known as "Neighborhood Pride," the mayor has enlisted the services of park, sanitation, fire, and code departments as well as neighborhood groups and residents to improve the conditions of Columbus neighborhoods. Now in its second year, this program has completed refurbishing efforts in sixteen of the city's neighborhoods. Additionally, Mayor Coleman has facilitated grant and loan programs to provide money for home improvements, especially for senior citizens and individuals with limited or fixed incomes. To some extent, the conference's early endorsement of Michael Coleman's mayoral candidacy has helped tremendously in providing access to the mayor's office and positive, tangible benefits to black residents in the city. The policy changes that Mayor Coleman has made in Columbus are consistent with the research scholarship on black politics, as he has increased funds for social services, increased municipal employment among blacks, and increased representation of blacks and others in municipal politics. Additionally, due in part to the efforts of the BBPC, he has provided black clergy with access to the inner corridors of municipal policy making in Columbus, which will be beneficial to the secular process of black politics in general. As a result, the conference has contributed to the struggle for black political authority and affected the process by which public policy is made in Columbus.

In addition to its supportive role in black electoral activities, the BBPC has played a pivotal role in articulating and generating responses to issues that negatively affect the black community. A recent example of their organizational prowess as a megaphone for the articulation of black interests is their effort to redress issues of lending discrimination vis-à-vis black churches and black residents in Columbus. Indeed, in the late 1990s, three members of the Pastors' Conference initiated efforts to redress the racist tendency of banks to deny loans to black churches or to extend loans only under the provision of heavy collateral. The initial response of these three BBPC members was to move all church funds, in the amount of hundreds of thousands of dollars, from banks that were known to have refused loans to banks that were more equitable in their lending practices. The BBPC served as a site for the dissemination and implementation of this plan, in which member pastors also participated actively. Ultimately, it resulted in a partnership with Huntington National Bank, which opened up banking opportunities across the United States for black churches and black residents.

Soon, the concept was dubbed "Community-Centered Banking" (CCB) and it was also extended to individual homeowners and their efforts to get equitable financing from credit institutions. Reverend Dr. Keith Troy of New Salem Baptist Church explained the concept and how it was used to enhance the lives of blacks in the Columbus area.[19] He offered the following detailed explanation:

> Community Center Banking is the result of a partnership with Huntington National Bank and rectifies peoples' credit issues in our community. And we developed a no-abusive policy for the bank, which allowed us to put folk in houses, who made as little as $13,000 a year, based upon certain benchmarks that they had to hit and go through. Credit counseling and credit cleanup was a part of that. If you had been bankrupt, the longer it would take you, would be twenty-four months. Anybody inside of that we could get you in through that. We were able to literally transform renters into homeowners, which, we maintained, changes the community. If I own my house, I'm going to take care of it a whole lot differently than if I rented. And if you really want to change the neighborhood, look at who owns the home in those neighborhoods. So that was a passion of mine. I had seen so many folks in generational welfare in terms of apartment after apartment after apartment never owning anything of significance by them. So we were able to design that program with a cut off of $67,000. It is amazing, how much house you could get for $67,000 in Columbus.

The programs, I forget how many millions of dollars—I can always get that figure for you—*60 Minutes* came in and did a special on it sometime ago. We
are now in dialogue with Fannie Mae to deliver the same kind of program for
moderate-income folk. The ceiling has been set now for $215,000 to take the
same program and bump it up beyond low income to what they call moderate
income. Well, $215,000 in Columbus can buy you a whole heck a lot of house
in this town. And what we discovered was the same issues that low-income
folks had—moderate income folks had. They are what we call the rich-poor in
terms of those kinds of things. So, to us that became a very key issue in terms
of dealing with something to me that just was almost criminal. How folk could
determine where certain folk could live, and not have access to the better
school systems or all of those kinds of issues and concerns. So I think it is one
of our proudest achievements.[20]

Emerging out of the organizational structure of the Pastors' Conference are
several initiatives, partnerships, and working groups. Most politically relevant among them is the economic empowerment partnership, which seeks
to provide economic opportunities to black America's forgotten sector: the
unemployed, welfare mothers, and working poor.

PARTNERSHIPS FOR ECONOMIC EMPOWERMENT

In the invariable quest for political power, research on black politics has
chronicled dramatic increases in black office holding coupled with the persistence of and, in some instances, increases in black poverty and black unemployment and increased gaps in the socioeconomic status of blacks and
whites. These ironic and unfortunate predicaments have prompted the call
for a dual empowerment strategy that focuses jointly on economics and politics. Secular black politics has been slow to embrace this agenda, fettered
unduly by the constraints of the American political system. However, black
church politics has always contained an element of economic empowerment, and the analysis of black church politics in Columbus highlights important contributions to those efforts. What is especially important about the
efforts in Columbus is that they are targeted toward the economically disadvantaged segment of the black population, which is in direct contrast to the
benefits of black electoral representation, which largely accrue to the black
elite. In Columbus, the economic empowerment partnership includes Reverend Troy of New Salem Baptist Church, Reverend Dr. Jesse Wood of the
Love Zion Baptist Church, Dr. B. J. Washington of Mount Herman Baptist
Church, and Reverend Dr. Timothy Clarke of First Church of God. Reverend
Troy offered the following comment about the economic empowerment
partnership.

We began to ask ourselves: What is it that the churches do together? That is because we believe churches have great resources individually but even more so collectively. So, three of my colleagues and myself formed what we call a unity partnership and were able to fulfill Franklin County Human Services Request for Proposal. The interesting concept about this partnership is that we are four close friends. Two of us pastor in the Northeast quadrant and at the time we started it the other two lived in it. So it gave us two big solid perspectives for folks who live in it how the church would affect them with the vocal pastors in it. It has worked well for us. We built a 4.5 million dollar facility. It houses the welfare-to-work program. Our concept was different, because in the past churches always wanted to do programs. Some programs do better than we do and that is what they get paid to do. Our concept, however, is to own the resource in the community because we were tired of people building the stuff in our community and then when the program was over, we were left with those eyesore, huge, government buildings that were not complimentary to our community. We were able to do that. The building is not quite three years old now and is first part of a three-point phase for us. We are now in discussion and negotiation with Grant Riverside Hospital to build a health facility the same size. We hope there will be an educational piece for that community with Columbus State, Ohio State, and Columbus public schools coming together and being able to provide all kinds of advanced educational courses. Usually when people take courses from college they have to go to that place or it is a suburban location. Very few of those are located in the heart of the inner city where we think there's tremendous opportunity for folks to advance themselves if it's fairly close. So, therefore, it carves out what we call the Unity Campus. That's part of our interfacing with those kinds of educational and employment entities that share with them the extreme amount of wealth in the community—it is human wealth—and be able to look at that from that vantage point.[21]

CONCLUSION

Against the backdrop of a discussion of secular black politics and the perpetual quest for black inclusion in America's obvious exclusionary political system, this chapter has explored the process of black church politics in Columbus, Ohio. In summation, one can underscore that the data are suggestive of three patterns of black church influence, namely: (1) the politics of personal influence, (2) organizational clout, and (3) economic empowerment partnerships. In many respects, the study's findings extend beyond the specific case of Columbus to impart important theoretical and substantive information about the process and relevance of black church politics in the twenty-first century, and indeed in the post-twentieth-century civil rights era.

First, the processes of black church politics and secular black politics may be deemed as partners in the quest for black incorporation in America's historically discriminatory political system, especially so as they have been complementary in their pursuit of a workable electoral strategy. As demonstrated throughout the chapter, past research on the black church did show that the findings of the current study amply reconfirm the importance of black church politics in providing crucial resources needed to support black political candidates; this is also particularly so in the most recent election of Columbus's first black mayor.

Additionally, this study has also identified ways in which black church politics has garnered resources and access to municipal policy making as a result of this support. Again, these findings are consistent with the scholarship on the implications of black empowerment, which shows that black mayors have been adept at providing various benefits to the black community. At the same time, this reliance on an electoral strategy is seen as limited in its ability to radically reform the distribution of key socioeconomic resources that are crucial for the economic and political empowerment of African Americans in Columbus and other American cities.

Second, a related strategy of influence, which has been unearthed by this study, is the "politics of personal influence," whereby black ministers used personal characteristics and resources to influence political actors and the political process. In the study of Columbus, we demonstrated the benefits of this pattern of influence with respect to the provision of alternative policy choices, increasing black representation, and providing isolated benefits to specific members of the black community. Like the electoral aspect of black church politics, this pattern of influence mirrors certain aspects of secular black politics. Such notable past black political and social leaders as Adam Clayton Powell, Harold Washington, Martin Luther King, and Malcolm X have valiantly used the "politics of personal influence" in the interests of and, indeed, on behalf of the African American masses to generate significant benefits.

However, the significant and unredeemable downside of the "politics of personal influence" is that the benefits are often short-term and linked inextricably to an individual personality. When the individual, therefore, passes or is removed from the political scene, so does black access to the inner corridors of political power. Consequently, as shown by the study, "politics of personal influence" is the least beneficial pattern of black church politics identified, especially when it operates without the support of a leadership cadre and disciplined black organizations.

Third, the chapter identified two positive ways in which black church politics in Columbus differs from and can serve as a viable model for secular black politics. For example, in the past fifty years, black pastors in Columbus have used the Pastors' Conference as a vehicle of influence in the municipal policy-making process. As a financially independent organization, it is viewed by Columbus political officials as the legitimate voice of the black community and is consulted regularly about municipal issues. Most importantly, the conference serves as an organizational structure and the backbone for the articulation of black interests and also for the formulation of economic empowerment issues. As a result of the organizational network provided by the Pastors' Conference, black church politics has engaged in an economic empowerment partnership, which has succeeded in providing banking, housing, and welfare-to-work initiatives for disadvantaged members of the African American community in the Columbus area. As a result of their efforts, black clergy in approximately thirty cities across America are engaged in similar activities, which testifies to the significance of their efforts beyond the Columbus community.[22]

In the areas of organizational resources and economic empowerment, black church politics in Columbus has extended beyond the confines of electoral activities. Unfettered by the institutional constraints of secular black politics, clergy involved in the process of black church politics are charting new territory that addresses directly the dire economic conditions of the black community. In this respect, black church politics in Columbus is succeeding in reaching the most disadvantaged element of the black community, a group that has benefited the least, as compared with the black middle class, from black mayoral representation. As a result, the latter two patterns of black church politics—namely organizational clout and economic empowerment—are the most promising for black church politics and its secular component, as they provide independent bases of black political power, which is unfettered by partisan and political loyalties that often diminish the potency of black political influence.

Theoretically, the study's findings, in sum, underscore the importance of making conceptual distinctions between black church politics and black secular politics. When viewed merely through the realm of secular black politics, with its singular focus on electoral activities and black representation, the important and politically relevant activities of the black church can easily be overlooked. This, indeed, is especially so when church politics is focused on nonelectoral (or nonpartisan) activities that are directed toward organization building and economic empowerment, in which secular elements of black politics are not traditionally engaged.

Additionally, conceptual distinctions between black secular politics and black church politics also make clear the important contributions that the black church continues to perform in the electoral arena, by instilling parishioners with political skills and mobilizing them for participation in elections. In this way, the formidable and relevant contributions of black church politics—as both independent and complementary forces in the struggle for black political empowerment—can be clearly evident and acknowledged.

NOTES

1. Hanes Walton, *Invisible Politics* (Albany: State University of New York Press, 1985).

2. Manning Marable, *How Capitalism Underdeveloped Black America* (Boston: South End Press, 1983); C. Eric Lincoln and Lawrence H. Mamiya, *The Black Church in the African-American Experience* (Durham: Duke University Press, 1990).

3. William E. Nelson Jr., *Black Atlantic Politics* (Albany: State University of New York Press, 2000).

4. James W. Button, *Blacks and Social Change: Impact of the Civil Rights Movement in Southern Communities* (Princeton: Princeton University Press, 1989).

5. Some important works on the topic include Lucius Barker, "Black Electoral Politics," *National Political Science Review* 2 (1990); Rufus Browning, Dale Rogers Marshall, and David Tabb, *Protest Is Not Enough* (Berkeley: University of California Press, 1984); Richard Keiser, *Subordination or Empowerment? African-American Leadership and the Struggle for Political Power* (New York: Oxford University Press, 1997); Robert C. Smith, *We Have No Leader: African Americans in the Post-Civil Rights Era* (Albany: State University of New York Press, 1996).

6. Nelson, *Black Atlantic Politcs.*

7. Walton, *Invisible Politics.*

8. See Douglas McAdams, *Political Process and the Development of Black Insurgency, 1930–1970* (Chicago: University of Chicago Press, 1982); and Aldon Morris, *The Origins of the Civil Rights Movement* (New York: Free Press, 1984).

9. Some important research articles in this area include: Laura Reese and Ronald Brown, "The Effects of Religious Messages on Racial Identity and System Blame among African Americans," *Journal of Politics* 57, no. 1: 24–43; Allison Calhoun-Brown, "African-American Churches and Political Mobilization: The Psychological Impact of Organizational Resources," *Journal of Politics* 58, no. 4: 935–53; Fredrick Harris, "Something Within: Religion as a Mobilizer of African American Politics," *Journal of Politics* 56, no. 1: 42–68.

10. Yvette Alex-Assensoh and A. B. Assensoh, "Inner-City Contexts, Church Attendance, and African-American Political Participation," *Journal of Politics* 63, no. 3: 886–901.

11. Smith, *We Have No Leader.*

12. Lucius Barker, Mack H. Jones, and Katherine Tate, *African-Americans and the American Political System* (Upper Saddle River, N.J.: Prentice Hall, 1999).

13. Data for tables 4.1–4.4 come from the 1990 Census and City of Columbus Planning Office.

14. Interview with Reverend Phale Hale of Union Grove Baptist Church, Columbus, Ohio, October 1992.

15. Interview with Reverend Dr. Jesse Wood of Love Zion Baptist Church, Columbus, Ohio, October 1992.

16. Interview with Reverend Leon Troy, pastor emeritus, Second Baptist Church, Columbus, Ohio, July 2000.

17. Interview with Reverend Dr. Jesse Wood of Love Zion Baptist Church, Columbus, Ohio, September 2001.

18. Interview with Reverend Larry Price, policy advisor on community affairs, Office of the Mayor, Columbus, Ohio, July 2000.

19. Interview with Reverend Dr. Keith Troy in Columbus, Ohio, July 2000.

20. Interview with Reverend Dr. Keith Troy.

21. Interview with Reverend Dr. Keith Troy.

22. Interview with Reverend Dr. Jesse L. Wood, president of the Black Pastors' Conference, Columbus, Ohio, September 2001.

5

Black Faith-Based Coalitions in Boston: Civic Advantages and Challenges

James Jennings

This chapter examines the emergence of two major black coalitions of faith-based organizations in the city of Boston: the Black Ministerial Alliance and the Ten Point Coalition. These two organizations represent a new civic tool used by activist ministers and congregations to express the preferences of the black religious sector in the city of Boston. The networks are a mechanism for facilitating the participatory role of faith-based organizations in initiatives such as job training, public safety, and youth development and for supporting black political leadership in the city. The information for the study is based on interviews and meetings with a small group of ministers and community activists between 1999 and 2000.

This analysis begins with an explanation regarding the significance of assessing the work of faith-based coalitions in Boston politics. It is important to remember that the black church has a long history of civic and political involvement in the city. What is novel about the Black Ministerial Alliance and the Ten Point Coalition is *not* that they are involved in civic life, but rather that these two coalitions represent a different mechanism for civic participation than activist black churches and clergy have used in the past. A brief overview of both coalitions is provided followed by a description of select political and community activities pursued by these groups. Following this overview the chapter examines two political controversies that found the Ten Point Coalition and the Black Ministerial Alliance on opposing sides. The chapter concludes by describing advantages that these coalitions have in civic and political activities, as well as the challenges that the coalitions face in terms of Boston politics.

SIGNIFICANCE OF FAITH-BASED COALITIONS

There are only a few studies examining coalitions among black churches. A groundbreaking one is Robert A. Clemetson and Roger Coates's *Restoring Broken Places and Rebuilding Communities: A Casebook on African-American Church Involvement in Community Economic Development.*[1] As the authors argue, faith-based networks are emerging as prominent civic actors and distributors of government services. As noted by one observer, "Network structures are being used in the area of community development to empower communities and to try to solve problems previously reserved for government intervention. . . . They are vehicles for tapping into dominant community resources and creating synergy and trust among otherwise independent actors. They encourage building community involvement and innovative solutions to complex problems."[2]

A majority of black religious institutions in Boston are located in the predominantly black neighborhoods of Roxbury, Dorchester, and Mattapan. Other than small businesses, churches represent the most numerous kinds of institutions in Boston's black communities. Churches outnumber community-based agencies, community development corporations, and human service agencies. These religious institutions represent both Christian and Islamic faiths as well as places of worship that provide worship services in various languages, reflecting African, Caribbean, and Latino cultures. While the ministers of these churches tend to be male, there are a significant number of churches headed by women pastors, making Boston's rate of women religious leaders higher than national figures.[3] The two coalitions discussed here cover a wide range of the religious institutions as members in Boston's black neighborhoods, reflecting diversity in terms of denomination, leadership, and the size of congregations.

There are several reasons that justify the selection of these kinds of coalitions for understanding the dynamics of activist black congregations and clergy in Boston. First, as is the case nationally, the black church in this city is increasingly being turned to as an actor in the provision of social and human services in low-income communities. This is partially due to the way the federal government is becoming involved with the states and social welfare provision. Devolution, a term summarizing this development regarding federal and state relations, is a call for less government interference or influence at the national level in matters related to social welfare. But along with devolution comes reduction in fiscal commitments and resources in many areas that are of major interest to local communities. As devolution occurs, faith-based organizations that have long been involved in social welfare issues become more salient as arenas for the delivery of services that are traditionally handled by government welfare agencies and the non-profit sector. There are increasing reports documenting the recruitment and utilization of black religious institutions and their leadership for participation in a range of community and economic development activities in urban neighborhoods.[4]

A second reason for pursuing this study is the fact that churches and religious institutions do have organizational characteristics that can be translated into civic resources. Black churches enjoy social and community legitimacy and have a tradition of community involvement. These institutions are highly organized, have a committed and spiritually bonded membership, and have the potential and capacity to raise funds independent of government or businesses. They can mobilize volunteers effectively. As Fredrick C. Harris notes, black churches can disseminate information quickly and with efficiency for purposes of political mobilization.[5] Another valuable resource is activist ministers who represent an educated group in the black community. Many ministers have acquired organizing skills that can be applied towards the mobilization of both congregants and community residents on behalf of civic and political affairs. This is a key resource in encouraging people to work on behalf of issues and political candidates who are perceived as important to their community's well-being. Related to leadership resources is the capacity of faith-based organizations to provide space and arenas for public and civic discourse regarding issues facing the community.

Black religious institutions can also communicate effectively with their congregations on a range of issues. Consequently, congregations can be mobilized rapidly for various causes when and if the need arises. Harris also notes that black churches can facilitate the learning of organizing skills among congregants who learn these skills in church work. These organizing skills are easily transferable to the civic arena. And, adds Harris, this sector of civic life represents potential supporters and voters who can be solicited on behalf of electoral candidates or political issues.[6] These kinds of church-based resources have allowed black ministers to be key participants in the city's civic and political affairs. A question to be asked for this analysis is, how are church-based political resources utilized by the two coalitions?

A focus on advocacy networks nurtured by black churches is a commentary, in part, on the state of the institutional infrastructure in Boston's black communities. In a research report issued by the Trotter Institute on the state of black community affairs in 1985, educator Hubie Jones wrote,

> The status of institutions in Boston's Black community cannot be understood or assessed outside the context of this community's relationship to the larger white community. This fact is illustrated by the elements that shape the existing social dynamic: numerical minority status, limited political clout, embryonic black business development, outward drainage of financial resources, the poverty of most of its residents, and blocked channels to opportunities and resources in the external community.[7]

Except for reference to numerical minority status, this assessment remains applicable today. So a key question is, can black religious-based networks make a difference in the city of Boston?

CONTINUING CIVIC AND POLITICAL INVOLVEMENT

The civic involvement of black churches is not new in Boston.[8] Unfortunately, a few articles published about this topic suggest that black churches had little or insignificant involvement in community and political affairs before the late 1990s.[9] A review of Boston's civic life in the decades of the 1960s, 1970s, 1980s, and 1990s would show an active involvement of black churches that included significant political breakthroughs, the provision of social and human services, the establishment of independent black schools, and collaborative efforts with other sectors in Boston's civic life. Throughout the 1950s and 1960s black faith-based organizations in the city worked extensively in the areas of youth services, public safety, housing, education, and economic development. As Jones described in his essay, "Black churches provide social services, employment assistance and educational programs. Today, the only educational alternatives to the public schools in the black community are church-operated: St. Joseph's School, Berea Academy (Seventh Day Adventist), Owens-Roberts Educational Center (People's Baptist Church), and Clara Muhammad School (American Muslim Mission)."[10] Jones comments that while some efforts have a mixed history of success and failure, "collaborative religious services have been inspirational, vibrant events, reflecting the potential power of collective action."[11] This author gives several examples of such collaborative activities: the establishment of an international famine relief effort under the "African American Churches for African Support" in 1985; the Baptist Minister's Conference of Greater Boston, an organization that met to discuss religious and social concerns; and the establishment of the Black Ecumenical Commission in the later 1960s, whose mission was "to work with Black churches to assist them in responding to the problems of poverty and disenfranchisement experienced by Blacks and other minorities in Massachusetts."[12] There are numerous examples of this earlier work throughout the 1970s and 1980s.[13]

Black ministers and churches have also entered the political thicket of Boston. Issues that have motivated involvement on the part of black ministers include education, youth, and public safety. Activist ministers have sought electoral office and have been active in mayoral races, as well as contests for the Boston City Council and School Committee. Black ministers played a key role, for instance, in the debate during the early and mid-1990s about whether or not the Boston School Committee should be appointed or elected. The Interfaith Ministerial Alliance, a precursor to the Black Ministerial Alliance of Greater Boston, endorsed and worked on behalf of an appointed school committee in cooperation with Mayor Raymond Flynn's administration.[14] Black ministers have been involved in political and policy debates in the area of economic development. They have also served in many government and policy-making positions in the city. For example, Reverend Joseph E. Washington of the Wesley United Methodist Church in Dorchester served as senior advisor on equal rights under the mayoral administration of Ray Flynn. In the mid- and late 1980s, Minister Don Muhammad of the Nation of Islam developed a relationship with the mayor and then police deputy superintendent, William Celester. This relationship was widely perceived as helpful in responding to high crime rates in the Grove Hall section of Roxbury.[15] Reverend Ray Hammond of the Bethel A.M.E. Church was appointed to head the Boston Education Reform Committee to lobby for retention of the appointed school committee.[16]

Black ministers have created ad-hoc alliances for purposes of endorsing or running candidates for office and for supporting ballot initiatives. They have also planned cooperative political strategies and actions on various civic matters. In 1983 more than thirty black ministers collectively endorsed Mel King for mayor and helped to propel him into the final runoff election. This was the first and only instance in Boston's history in which a black person obtained enough votes to earn a spot in the runoff election for mayor.[17] In 1991 Reverend Ellis Hagler of the First Church of Roxbury ran for the office of mayor and was able to garner several thousand votes, albeit in a losing effort. Activist black ministers were instrumental in assisting the administration of Mayor Flynn to change the Boston School Committee from an elected to an appointed body in 1992. This was a racially and politically divisive issue in the city, especially in the black community. While an overwhelming number of black voters rejected the call for an appointed school committee, a group of black ministers supporting Mayor Flynn on this issue were key in the success of the campaign.

There are other examples of individual activists influencing the public sphere in Boston. Reverend Michael E. Haynes of the Twelfth Baptist Church in Roxbury, with the active support of his congregation, has a long list of community accomplishments, including his legendary work with youth in Roxbury.[18] Reverend Haynes was elected as a state representative in the Massachusetts legislature for three terms, between 1965 and 1970. He was appointed to the State Parole Board and the Board of Pardons for sixteen years, serving under three governors. He also was appointed to Boston's Fair Housing Commission under Mayor Flynn in 1989.[19]

Another activist minister who enjoys a strong reputation in Boston is Minister Don Muhammad, who is the spiritual leader of the Nation of Islam's mosque in Roxbury. Affectionately known as "Minister Don" by many in the black community, this activist minister has focused his civic work on minority youth. He is recognized for his participation in education and youth issues in Boston as well as for his interest in the economic development of the Roxbury neighborhood. One example of his recognition as a civic leader in Boston is the awarding of the city's Paul Revere Bowl given for outstanding public service on the part of an individual citizen. The work of Mosque #11 and "Minister Don" in the area of economic development was also touted in a study published by the Federal Reserve Bank of Boston.[20]

In summary, and as discussed in other chapters of this volume, the involvement of black ministers and religious organizations in civic life is characterized by participation in an array of political activities.[21] Activist black clergy have utilized a range of roles to influence decisions related to community and economic development, including (1) advising politicians, (2) directing involvement in human and social services, (3) supporting and participating in political campaigns, and (4) participating in coalition-based advocacy strategies. There are many resources that black ministers can utilize in their political roles. These include community-based legitimacy that facilitates involvement in political and civic affairs.

TWO FAITH-BASED STRATEGIC COALITIONS: TEN POINT COALITION AND THE BLACK MINISTERIAL ALLIANCE OF GREATER BOSTON

The faith-based coalitions discussed in this chapter are not the only ones based in Boston and the Greater Boston region. The Greater Boston Interfaith Organization is a relatively large organization affiliated with the Industrial Areas Foundation. It is composed of approximately eighty-five congregations and community organizations that concentrate on housing issues. The organization has been effective in organizing many supporters across racial and ethnic lines in an effort to lobby or campaign on behalf of affordable housing. Other organizations that are formed through coalitions of religious institutions include the City Mission Society, the Massachusetts Council of Churches, and Mattapan-Dorchester Churches in Action.

These faith-based coalitions suggest a different institutional framework for civic involvement on the part of the religious community than past church-based activism. Although different in terms of organizational structure and leadership, the Black Ministerial Alliance and Ten Point Coalition have overlapping memberships. The evolution of the networks reflects the changing role of government and attitudes about the involvement of faith-based organizations in public life as well as a different posture on the part of foundations interested in working in low-income and economically distressed communities. The organizational missions of the Black Ministerial Alliance and the Ten Point Coalition include several components: (a) a concern for organizing the faith community on behalf of civic issues deemed important for the social and economic well-being of marginal neighborhoods; (b) an understanding that there are important resources within the faith community that could be transferred to the civic arena; (c) a sense of obligation that faith-based organizations must help to improve living conditions as part of a spiritual mission; and (d) a history and strong tradition of civic participation at various levels.

The leadership of the two coalitions believes that the faith-based sector in Boston's black communities has key—and perhaps unique—resources that can be identified and applied strategically to improve living conditions for residents. A review of the work and official statements of each organization shows that the ministers involved do not see a contradiction between spiritual salvation and involvement in civic and political affairs of the state. There is a general sense, furthermore, that differences in faith and denominations should not serve to obstruct the building of coalitions and collaborative strategies with other sectors concerned about civic issues. Each network is led by religious leaders who believe that there is a spiritual mandate for civic participation and moral obligation to support and advocate on behalf of the community's social and economic well-being. What follows is a description of the aims of the two coalitions.

The Ten Point Coalition

The Ten Point Coalition is a group of Christian clergy and lay leaders working to mobilize the Christian community around issues affecting black and Latino youth, especially those at risk for violence and drug abuse. The coalition was established following a gang shooting of a victim at a black church in the neighborhood of Mattapan in May 1992.[22] This incident helped to mobilize many religious leaders in the black community. Clergy collectively developed a pastoral letter and pledged a street-level crusade to help youth, especially those involved with gangs and drugs. As explained by one of the leading spokespersons of the pastoral letter, a major purpose of the call to action is to help move faith-based organizations to include "the salvation of our communities" as they work toward the "salvation of souls."[23]

According to the coalition's document, "A Ten Point Coalition Plan for a National Church Mobilization to Combat Black on Black Violence," this organization is based on membership that seeks to "generate serious discussion regarding the specific ways in which the Christian community can bring the peace of God to the violent world of our youth. We therefore call upon churches, church agencies, and the academic theological community throughout the nation to consider, discuss, debate and implement, singly or in collaboration, any one or more of the ten points." According to Reverend Ray Hammond, the chairman of the coalition and one of its founders, this organization "is an ecumenical group of Christian clergy and lay leaders working to mobilize the greater Boston community, and especially the Christian local church community, around issues affecting Black and Latino youth—especially those at-risk for violence, drug abuse, and other destructive behaviors."

The Reverend Hammond expresses the guiding philosophy of the coalition when he states:

> Somehow we must get beyond the blame game and the sterile either/or debate that makes this crisis either as some conservatives would have it the simple result of a decline in personal and family values or as some liberals would have it the simple result of larger social and political forces. We must acknowledge that there are forces at work both at the personal, family and community level, and at the political, policy and macroeconomic level; that both personal decision and public policies play a role in making our communities safer and stronger. We must move to an emphasis on what I like to call the 3 R's of community and spiritual revitalization: renewal, responsibility, and reconnection—renewal of our faith in the fact that we can make a difference in every aspect of the lives of our youth, their families, and their communities; a willingness to take full responsibility for our respective roles in meeting the needs of our youth, and a commitment to reconnecting and working in collaboration with other individuals and institutions.[24]

The coalition engages in many community activities, but the primary mission of this organization is to mobilize churches to reach out to at-risk youth.

This coalition was incorporated as a formal nonprofit organization in the spring of 1996. There are fifteen board members, eight of whom are clergy. A sample of the activities sponsored by the group includes a training workshop series called "Resurrecting Our Future." The series provides information on domestic violence, community organizing, training for night street patrols as well as activities such as computer and summer camps for youth, information seminars on homeownership, and a microenterprise development project that provides support and information about capital acquisition for emerging entrepreneurs. The coalition receives funding from foundations, an annual fundraising dinner, and local, state, and federal grants, which account for 10 to 15 percent of the organization's budget. The coalition also receives direct or in-kind support from local churches and has developed many inter-organizational relationships with public agencies and community organizations. These relationships involve work with the police department, schools, the probation department, youth-oriented organizations, community health agencies, and community development organizations. The group is attempting to build relationships with other ethnic-based organizations as well. The leadership recognizes that in addition to the African American and European American communities, there are other communities with at-risk youth.

The Black Ministerial Alliance of Greater Boston

The Black Ministerial Alliance of Greater Boston is an association of clergy serving black churches and other minority congregations and individuals representing denominational agencies and ministries. The alliance is the older of the two networks of faith-based coalitions. It is the largest as well, representing a broad base of member churches and religious associations. This coalition has evolved over four decades. Prior to becoming known as the Black Ministerial Alliance of Greater Boston, the organization was called the Interfaith Ministerial Alliance, and before that, it was called the Interdenominational Ministerial Alliance. By the year 2000 approximately fifty member pastors or their representatives were attending monthly breakfast meetings. Reverend Wesley Roberts, the president of the Black Ministerial Alliance and pastor of People's Baptist Church, posits that the alliance is one of the strongest black organizations in Boston as evident in its strong networks and its capacity to organize and mobilize many church members. The mission of this association of faith-based organizations is to provide advocacy for the black community in the areas of political affairs, human services, education, housing, economic development, youth services, and spiritual life. Most of the member churches are located in the predominantly black communities of Roxbury, Dorchester, and Mattapan. The alliance is composed of several advocacy committees reflecting a wide range of leaders in the black church sector.

Shortly after accepting the presidency of this organization in 1994, Reverend Roberts proposed organizational changes that made the coalition more inclusive and allowed it to better coordinate its activities among member congregations and associations. He changed the name of the organization, which was originally called the Interfaith Ministerial Alliance. This name was chosen because the Nation of Islam was a founding member of the organization and members wanted to ensure that the name allowed for the inclusion of the Nation of Islam. Reverend Roberts proposed the name, Black Ministerial Alliance of Greater Boston, which was accepted by the membership and reflected the growing influence of the coalition outside of the predominately black communities of Roxbury, Dorchester and Mattapan. Reverend Roberts also changed the organizational structure so that activities of the alliance are decentralized. The Black Ministerial Alliance of Greater Boston has a president, vice president, secretary, treasurer, and chairpersons for nine advocacy committees. This group of people constitutes the executive committee, which meets on a monthly basis. Committees chaired by individuals are directly responsible for the committee activities. The nine committees, each chaired by a member pastor, are education, spiritual life, criminal justice, housing, economic affairs, human services, political affairs, youth, and inter-church relations. Today, the alliance is a dues-paying member organization. Membership in the alliance is not limited to churches, nor is it limited to African Americans exclusively.

The alliance has developed extensive participation and leadership in many civic issues in Boston. For example, semi-annual meetings with the Boston Police Commissioner and focusing on the reduction of juvenile crime in the black community have been sponsored under the auspices of the Black Ministerial Alliance. The alliance has sponsored workshops on domestic violence awareness for black clergy and has organized workshops and information sessions on the problem of asthma and heart disease. In the area of economic development, representatives from the coalition served as planning committee members for a regional conference on African American clergy and economic development, which was convened by the Federal Reserve Bank. Recognizing the potential influence and work of this organization, the mayor of Boston appointed the president of the alliance to the advisory board of the Boston Empowerment Zone in order that the black religious community would have a voice in policy issues related to the zone and the communities that would be impacted by targeted development.

In 1998, the alliance's board, led by Reverend Leroy Attles of St. Paul's Church in Cambridge, the late Reverend Ozzie Edwards of Elliot Street Church, Reverend Jossie E. Owens of the Second Church of Dorchester, and the Reverend Charlotte Pridgen-Randolph of Wesley United Methodist Church, decided to undertake a major programmatic initiative in education. While the organization continues advocacy work with other issues, its leadership believes that the quality of public education is one of the most critical issues facing the city of Boston. With funding from the Hyams Foundation and the United Way, the alliance developed a proposal to establish the "Victory Generation" after-school program. A major goal of this program is to develop forty licensed after-school programs in member churches as a strategy to increase the academic performance of two thousand middle and high school students throughout the city. The alliance has also received significant funding from foundations to support the planning and implementation of an educational action campaign to empower parents and community residents.

In addition to developing church-based programs, the alliance encourages its members to express their opinions at the ballot box and has not hesitated to adopt public positions on civic issues. As a result, and due to its broad base and extensive activities, the alliance has emerged as an important political player in the black community. In 1995 this organization distributed a controversial memo critical of Mayor Thomas Menino. The memo included complaints about the privatization of elderly housing developments, the mayor's affirmative action stand, and the mayor's seeming lack of commitment to economic development in black neighborhoods during that period. The memo stirred intense public discussions about the mayor's role in responding to the needs of the black community. The alliance also organized and provided testimony against the restoration of the death penalty at the Massachusetts state legislature hearings. It has cosponsored, with organizations such as the NAACP, numerous voter registration drives and strategies to encourage voter participation in elections. And it has lobbied the Boston Housing Authority regarding racial incidents in the city's public housing developments.

POLITICAL CONTROVERSIES

There has been some political conflict between the two coalitions as well as tensions within each of the organizations. A few years ago, divisive statements by some ministers about black elected officials led to the issuance of a public letter on the part of the Ten Point Coalition clarifying who actually speaks on behalf of the organization. In a letter to the *Boston Globe* asserting existing divisions and conflict among black clergy, the leadership of the Ten Point Coalition endorsed a call for unity.[25] Signed by Reverends Jeffrey L. Brown, Ray Hammond, and Samuel C. Wood, the letter noted, "While individual members have differed publicly with other members, the organization has never made any critical statements. Indeed, we are thankful for the support of black elected officials who have worked with us to address common concerns." Further, it reminded readers, "The executive committee consists of Reverends Ray Hammond, Jeffrey Brown, Samuel Wood, and Eugene Rivers. While Reverend Rivers is a respected and committed member, he is not the spokesperson for or the leader of the coalition."[26] There is concern about the negative fallout from the conflict and some ministers have started to develop better relationships and alliances as a result of the tensions.

One political controversy in Boston in 1999 involved the public defense by a few black ministers regarding a local magazine that used a pejorative term about a black individual on the front cover feature article. In its April 1998 issue the *Boston Magazine* published a critical story focusing on Professor Henry Louis Gates of Harvard University titled, "Head Negro in Charge."[27] Quite a few black leaders, including religious leaders, were offended at the journal's use of this term, arguing that it reflected poor judgment, racial arrogance, and disrespect and that it perpetuated racist stereotypes in Boston. The magazine's editors argued that it had license to use this term based on its increasing use in popular culture, as well as the fact that two black ministers, Reverend Eugene Rivers of the Azusa Community Church and Reverend Jeffrey Brown of Union Baptist Church in Cambridge did not object to the term being used in this manner.

Upon hearing that a group of black leaders planned to visit the editor and protest the use of the phrase, the editors contacted Reverends Rivers and

Brown who intercepted the protesters in order to defend the *Boston Magazine* at the same press conference. Reverend Brown asserted in defense of the magazine, "I've been called a head Negro in charge by people in the Black community. . . . It's not a derogatory term, not as it's used now."[28] Many people were also upset at the tone of what was perceived as personal attacks on highly respected leaders who were among the protestors, including Reverend Charles Stith of Union United Methodist Church; Dr. Joan Wallace-Benjamin, the president of the Urban League of Eastern Massachusetts; and Mr. Lenny Alkins, president of the NAACP Boston Branch. As a result of this episode the Urban League of Eastern Massachusetts expelled Reverend Rivers from its board.[29]

Another divisive episode was the response to the indictment of State Senator Dianne Wilkerson, the only black woman state senator in the history of Massachusetts. This controversy occurred just a few months after the "Head Negro in Charge" incident and also involved the public pronouncements of Reverends Rivers, Brown, and Hammond regarding the indictment of Senator Wilkerson. Although making what some considered some tactical mistakes early in her legislative career (such as challenging the leadership of Senate President William Bulger), Senator Wilkerson built a reputation as a strong advocate of women and family rights. Her impressive legislative record included strong advocacy for economic development policies beneficial to poor and working-class neighborhoods. Moreover, Senator Wilkerson was emerging as one of the strongest critics of the powerful insurance industry in Massachusetts. In fact, she held the position of chair of the Joint Committee on Insurance (1996–98) when she was indicted on misdemeanor charges for failing to file federal income tax returns over a period of several years.

Senator Wilkerson pleaded guilty and agreed to pay the taxes she owed in addition to the penalties. Nevertheless, she was placed under house arrest and probation by a state court judge. To many, this action seemed to be an excessive judicial response. Her legislative colleagues, many of whom she combated regarding key social and economic issues, called for her ouster from the Senate. The Republican governor at that time, Paul Cellucci, proclaimed that she should resign or be removed for irresponsible behavior as an elected official. However, the black community and other supporters mobilized on behalf of the senator. Blacks were generally outraged that the media, in particular the *Boston Globe* and *Boston Herald*, were unfair and racially paternalistic in their coverage. Except for the *Bay State Banner,* the *Boston Globe* and *Boston Herald* seemed possessed in presenting the senator's detractors, in particular Reverends Rivers, Brown, and Hammond, as spokespersons of the black community.

Black ministers organized a prayer service at Charles Street A.M.E. Church in support of Senator Wilkerson and in opposition to the negative editorials and press releases. These activist ministers included members of the Black Ministerial Alliance, specifically Reverend Roberts, Reverend Michael E. Haynes, and Minister Don Muhammad. More than a thousand individuals attended the rally to offer support to the senator. As described in a *Boston Globe* story, "The prayer service at Charles Street AME church was like a purification ritual: Minister after minister from Boston's largest Black churches embraced the transgressor and, as if through a laying on of hands, restored her power. When the city's Black clergy last week rallied around embattled State Sen. Dianne Wilkerson, one prominent minister was missing—the Reverend Eugene Rivers, who now stands accused of trying to kick the city's leading Black politician when she was down, after she pleaded guilty to failing to pay taxes for four years."[30]

The Black Ministerial Alliance of Greater Boston supported Senator Wilkerson. Reverend Roberts, in his role as president of coalition, announced that money would be raised on behalf of the senator in order to help her pay the back taxes. As he stated, "We are aware of the nature of her problem and acknowledge the importance of adherence to law. . . . We are also aware of the importance of grace and forgiveness in the face of human error. We are not among those who believe it is right to shoot our wounded."[31] As a result of the actions of this faith-based coalition, the state senator emerged from this episode as yet a more influential player and progressive leader in the politics of Boston and Massachusetts. The overwhelming community support she received during this travail, which was led by activist black ministers, served as a show of political force that was noted by many. Although stories in the *Boston Globe* consistently reported major splits in the black community regarding whether or not the senator should resign, the senator had overwhelming support among her constituents. In fact, in her next electoral bid in 1998 she easily won reelection with overwhelming voter support, receiving 74 percent of all votes cast in her state senatorial district. In the predominantly black wards of her district she garnered a near-unanimous 84 percent. This victory also reflected and represented an endorsement of the work of the Black Ministerial Alliance of Greater Boston as a major political player in the black community.

As a result of these episodes of mobilization there have been attempts to develop greater collaboration and communication within the alliance. Reverend Roberts proposed the idea for a four-point covenant signed by all members of the alliance. This covenant, which was adopted at the Charles Street A.M.E. Church in 2000, includes four proposals for guiding the statements and actions of ministers: (1) speaking well of other churches; (2) agreeing to pray for other churches in a show of solidarity and support; (3) communicating with each other about potential transfers of church members; and (4) consistently meeting to share information and resources that would strengthen interfaith partnerships. The position of the alliance and its leadership is that the message contained in this covenant is key in helping faith-based organizations in the black community work together and that it stands as a model for other community-based organizations to follow.

CIVIC ADVANTAGES OF FAITH-BASED COALITIONS

Both coalitions have served to increase the civic capacity of the black faith-based sector in Boston. There are a number of civic advantages that the Black Ministerial Alliance and the Ten Point Coalition utilize in the political arena. One advantage is that these organizations can attract greater amounts of external funding due to the fact that the institutional infrastructure is not a church-based one. Many foundations may be hesitant to fund faith-based organizations directly but not resistant to fund separate organizations established by a group of churches. One example of this approach is the Black Church Capacity Building Program, initially established by the Hyams Foundation. The purpose of this effort is the provision of technical assistance to churches interested in becoming involved in human service and community revitalization programs. Under this initiative, technical assistance and training includes developing strategic planning, financial management, leadership development, business empowerment, and information technology. But the services are distributed through an institutional conduit rather than directly to individual churches.[32]

Another advantage of faith-based coalitions is that their work and impact ultimately has to be built on some degree of consensus and legitimacy. There is a degree of "built-in" accountability in the work of the two networks in representing the interests of the black community because the legitimacy of the organizations ultimately is dependent on how groups of ministers work together and how they are received in the entire black community. Accountability can be overlooked if civic involvement is based only on the work of individual ministers or churches. In the latter case, civic involvement is based on the work of an individual minister acting upon his or her own initiative rather than on a community agenda that has to enjoy some support beyond one church or minister. Furthermore, the framework represented by faith-based coalitions is less dependent on the charisma of individual ministers or the particular civic orientation of individual churches. Thus, formal networks that require cooperation for decision making allow for the expression of a greater variety of opinions in the black community.

Additionally, the faith-based networks described here can also serve as buffers that allow individual churches to participate in civic issues considered controversial by congregants. For example, the Black Ministerial Alliance has participated in many efforts to raise awareness about the problem of HIV/AIDS in Boston's black community. It was a cosponsor of the "Week of HIV/AIDS and the Black Church" with the "Who Touched Me Ministry" in 1998. The coalition has organized numerous educational activities regarding the problem of HIV/AIDS, which allows many black churches with hesitancy to participate as a coalition partner. Another important civic advantage presented by the two coalitions is a mechanism for incorporating new African-descent groups into African American religious networks. There are increasing numbers of immigrants from Central America, the Caribbean, and African nations who can be welcomed and served by these coalitions, perhaps in more effective ways than by individual congregations. This is important because of the increasing "ethnicization" of the black community in Boston. The non–African American black population is increasing.

These groups include Haitians, Nigerians, and people from other parts of Africa and the Caribbean, as well as some Latino groups from Panama and the Dominican Republic. These newer immigrant groups in Boston's traditional black community are establishing their own churches or joining more established and older black churches. There are some religious institutions, including the Nation of Islam's Mosque #11, that have made efforts to respond to this increasing ethnic diversity. Mosque #11, for example, broadcasts its weekly program, "Hour of Power," in Spanish. One of the points in the Ten Point Coalition, as another example of its outreach, is to develop curriculum for schools that reflects both black and Latino cultures. The kinds of formal networks and strategic coalitions described here can be an effective way for incorporating and giving voice to this increasing ethnic diversity in Boston's black community.

Finally, a major advantage of these networks is the potential of strengthening considerably the political clout of black elected leadership. Although the possibility of factionalism with established leadership is possible, there is also the possibility of an enhanced collective leadership. While the black community has realized political breakthroughs in the 1980s and 1990s, many feel that the political potential has not been actualized. Boston's city hall is composed of a strong mayoral form of government, with thirteen members on the city council. This council is composed of four at-large members and nine district representatives. The school committee is appointed by the mayor. Although the black, Latino, and Asian population of the city now represents the majority of the population, there are only two black city councilors and one Latino member of the city council. Except for the mayoral run of Melvin King in 1983, the only black candidate to win an at-large city council seat during the last two decades was Bruce Bolling. The relative weakness of black political influence has meant that local government and other sectors have leeway in deciding whom they wish to work with in the black community. The coalitions do represent resources that if utilized collaboratively with other sectors and leaders could considerably enhance the political influence of the black community.

94 *James Jennings*

Along with these challenges, and with the political disagreements between activist ministers as described above, this study points toward a need for the two coalitions to (a) generate greater levels of communication and collaboration between the groups; (b) pursue a greater level of programmatic and even financial independence; and (c) expand systematic attempts to work with other sectors, including elected officials and community-based organization representatives. As proposed in the beginning of this chapter, faith-based coalitions can represent a new political tool for enhancing the political and economic well-being of Boston's black community. These networks can be arenas for developing and debating policy and political issues. Such arenas can have the weight of collective decision making based on input from institutions that enjoy legitimacy and command potentially effective resources for political mobilization.

The faith-based advocacy networks described in Boston have evolved into another intermediary institution in the black community. Like many community-based organizations they provide human services, manage programs, represent newcomers, seek funding and resources, and interact with political processes and infrastructures. It is critical for the well-being of the black community but also for Boston that faith-based coalitions seek collaboration on a range of political and economic issues and that the coalitions also reflect accountability in the work they do on behalf of the black community. Teamwork based on public policy agendas that strengthen the black community socially and economically is a major responsibility cast upon these two coalitions.

NOTES

1. Roger A. Clemetson and Roger Coates, *Restoring Broken Places and Rebuilding Communities: A Casebook on African-American Church Involvement in Community Economic Development* (Washington, D.C.: National Congress for Community Economic Development, 1993).
2. Myrna P. Mandell, "Community Collaborations: Working Through Network Structures," *Policy Studies Review* 16, no. 1 (1999): 44.
3. Based on their national survey Lincoln and Mamiya estimated that there were probably less than 5 percent black women clergy in the black denominations; see C. Eric Lincoln and Lawrence Mamiya, *The Black Church in the African American Experience* (Durham: Duke University Press, 1990), 289.
4. See Marjorie B. Lewis, "Public Sector and the Black Church Partnerships: A New Public Policy Tool," *Trotter Review* 10, no. 2 (Spring 1997): 27.
5. Fredrick C. Harris, "Religious Institutions and African American Political Mobilization," in Classifying by Race, ed. Paul E. Peterson (Princeton, NJ: Princeton University Press, 1995).
6. Harris, "Religious Institutions and African American Political Mobilization."

7. Hubert Jones, "The Status of Institutions in Boston's Black Community," in *The Emerging Black Community*, ed. Phil Clay et al., 269 (Boston: William Monroe Trotter Institute, 1985).

8. One of the most informative reports describing the civic history of the black church in Boston is written by Robert C. Hayden and was published by the Boston branch of the NAACP in 1983. Hayden compiled a comprehensive institutional history of ten prominent black churches established in Boston between 1805 and 1913. The author shows that these black churches were major providers of education and youth services to its congregations in earlier periods. See Robert C. Hayden, *Faith, Culture, and Leadership: A History of the Black Church in Boston* (Boston: Boston Branch of the NAACP, 1983). See also George E. Haynes, "The Church and Negro Progress," *The Annals* 140, no. 229 (November 1928); Arthur E. Paris, *Black Pentecostalism: Southern Religion in an Urban World* (Amherst: University of Massachusetts Press, 1982); and James Oliver Horton, *Black Bostonians: Family Life and Community Struggle in the Antebellum North* (New York: Holmes and Meier, 1999).

9. The following articles, while informative, suggest that the black church's involvement in Boston civic and political issues is new. See Jenny Berrien and Christopher Winship, *Should We Have Faith in the Churches? Ten-Point Coalition's Effect on Boston's Youth Violence* (Cambridge: Harvard University, 1999); and Michael Jonas, "The Street Ministers," *Commonwealth: Politics, Ideas and Civic Life in Massachusetts,* Fall 1997, 37. See journalist James Walsh's claim in the *Star Tribune* (2 July 1997): "Just when did Boston's neighborhood activists and Black churches take an aggressive role in fighting gang violence? It wasn't 1989 . . . it wasn't 1990 . . . it was the Morning Star [Baptist Church] incident of May 14, 1992." And despite many articles praising the work of black churches with the Boston police department throughout the 1980s and 1990s, see, "New Partners for the Police" (editorial), *Boston Globe*, 18 February 1998.

10. Jones, "Status of Institutions," 303.

11. Jones, "Status of Institutions."

12. Jones, "Status of Institutions," 304.

13. For reviews of the earlier community work of black churches see Betsey A. Lehman, "Marchers Rap Crime in Black Community," *Boston Globe*, 29 May 1983; Ethan Bronner, "Boston Churches Tackle Community Issues Again," *Boston Globe*, 22 December 1985; Jonathan Kaufman, "Roxbury Man Ministers to Teenagers," *Boston Globe*, 7 February 1989; Don Aucoin, "Tobacco Road Under Siege: Boston's Black Pulpits Join Crusade Against Cigarettes," *Boston Globe*, 25 April 1994; Diego Ribadeneira, "Hands Together Against Aids: Black Clergy Unite in Service of Healing," *Boston Globe*, 24 February 1997; "Aids Awareness in Black Churches" (editorial), *Boston Globe*, 1 March 1997.

14. Richard Chacon, "Black Ministers Group Says Panel Should Remain Appointed," *Boston Globe*, 26 September 1996.

15. Adrian Walker, "Minister Don Draws on Islam to Fight Boston Street Crime," *Boston Globe*, 22 July 1989; see also Robert A. Jordan, "An Unusual Friendship," *Boston Globe*, 18 April 1987.

16. "Former School committee Head to Lobby for Appointed Panel," *Boston Globe*, 9 March 1996.

17. "70 Religious leaders, including 30 Black ministers, endorse Mel King for Mayor," *Boston Globe*, 5 August 1983.

18. See Carol Pearson, "There is No One in the Minority Community Who Has Done More for Young People," *Boston Globe*, 9 December 1985; also, Patricia A. Smith, "From Roxbury with Love: Mike Haynes Exquisite Hand Pulled At-Risk Young Men out of the Maelstrom," *Boston Globe*, 7 July 1992; and a brief biography of his work in Kimberly R. Moffitt, "A Profile of the Reverend Michael E. Haynes of Twelfth Baptist Church in Roxbury Massachusetts," *Trotter Review* 10, no. 2 (Spring 1997).

19. Richard Higgins, "Salute for a Shepard Restored" *Boston Globe*, 6 November 1990.

20. "Faith-Based Economic Development Initiatives in New England," *Communities and Banking*, Fall 1999.

21. In *The Black Preacher in America* (New York: Morrow, 1972), Charles Hamilton focused on historical and contemporary aspects of the black preacher's life, with particular emphasis on leadership in the black church and black communities. In a chapter titled "Preachers and Political Action," he identified three types of preacher roles of political activism at the local level, including the church-based local activist who serves in this capacity on the basis of being a leader of a prominent or large church; the community-based local activist. Religious leaders in this capacity take an active part in local electoral politics as well as in mass-oriented pressure-group politics; the third type of preacher activist uses the church as a specific base to launch and conduct civic programs of various sorts. This type of preacher is much more public and mass-oriented in his approach than the first type and, unlike the community-based activist, combines church organization with the specific program of action. While not being opposed to electoral politics, the church-based programmatic activist focuses on using the church structure to achieve secular goals such as jobs, housing, health care, and educational facilities.

22. Herbert H. Toler, "Rivers of Babylon: A Harvard Man Brings the Gospel to the Crack House," *Policy Review* 4 (Fall 1994): 68.

23. Don Aucoin, "Boston Clergy Urge Crusade on Violence," *Boston Globe*, 25 May 1992.

24. "Raising Responsible Youth in Troubled Times: The Promise and Challenge of Church Involvement, a Boston Perspective" (1999).

25. Adrian Walker, "Black Leaders Battle Over Influence: Clergy, Wilkerson Each Strain to Lead Voters to Kennedy," *Boston Globe*, 17 October 1994.

26. Letters, "Black Group Stresses Shared Views, Not Rivalries," *Boston Globe*, 29 October 1994.

27. Cheryl Bentsen, "Head Negro in Charge," *Boston Magazine*, 27 April 1998.

28. Mark Jurkowitz, "Without Apology the Boston Battle Goes On," *Boston Globe*, 4 April 1998.

29. Charles A. Radin, "Rivers Expelled by Group: Urban League Cites Criticism by Him," *Boston Globe*, 27 June 1998.

30. Peter S. Canellos, "Uproar Over Rivers Runs Deep," *Boston Globe*, 8 October 1997.

31. Adrian Walker, "Group of Ministers Support Wilkerson," *Boston Globe*, 26 September 1997.

32. Alisa Valdes-Rodriguez, "Black Churches Teaming Up with Philanthropies Funds Fight Common Causes," *Boston Globe*, 11 October 1998.

II

BLACK CHURCHES AND ELECTORAL POLITICS

6

Black Churches and Electoral Engagement in the Nation's Capital

Ronald Walters and Tamelyn Tucker-Worgs

In some ways Washington, D.C., is typical of many majority black metropolitan areas in the United States. Demographically it is among a group of cities that is experiencing an out-migration of middle-class blacks and an in-migration of middle-class whites. When it comes to political representation, the District is atypical. The elected city government is over twenty-five years old but Congress has oversight over the city's governance. The District has limited representation in Congress, and the District's representative, Eleanor Holmes-Norton, has limited voting rights in the House of Representatives, a situation that represents a crisis of democracy for District residents.

The public influence of activist black churches in the District is intensified by the peculiarity of being situated in the nation's capital and residing in a city that is home to a number of national political organizations. This makes the District a magnet for all types of political activities, including protests and demonstrations. With an intense level of political activity in the city, activist black churches in the District are often utilized as political platforms. Indeed, they have served as a training ground and refuge for the protesters attending campaigns that range from the 1963 March on Washington to the 1995 Million Man March.

Given this legacy of the black church as a staging facility for social movements, this chapter traces the broader tradition of black church public influence in the District. We take a look at churches that presently exhibit public influence in the District by analyzing clerical leadership. This approach allows us to discover the areas of influence that contemporary black churches exercise, as well as to look at the mechanisms that these churches have in place to allow them to exhibit public influence. We review the activities of a set of exemplary activist black churches as indicated by their activities in the public record. We then utilize interviews of ministers from those activist black churches to deepen our understanding of the motivation and nature of their public influence. We first profile a group of activist churches in the District to consider variations in the history and nature of their activism in community empowerment and electoral activism. We follow with a look specifically at the relationship between activist clergy and churches and the mayoral administrations of Marion Barry, who dominated District politics during the 1980s and 1990s, and whose reelection to the city council in 2004 continues to make him a prominent figure in District politics. We conclude by returning to the activist churches we profile by analyzing the leadership styles and theological commitments that drive activist clergy and congregations in the District.

PROFILES OF ACTIVIST BLACK CHURCHES IN THE DISTRICT

Many black churches in the District have a tradition of participating in politics and community development. They were instrumental in the fight against segregation in the 1950s and the fight for civil rights in the 1960s. Some activist ministers have served in elected office and many more have supported political candidates. Additionally, activist congregations in the District offer social safety nets for poor and working-class residents by establishing shelters, counseling for drug abuse, and providing affordable day-care centers, youth programs, and low- and moderate-income housing. Our examination of black churches in the political landscape of the District finds that many black churches are indeed active in social and political endeavors. They are particularly active in providing information pertaining to issues that affect the black community, by hosting candidate and issue forums and voter registration and education campaigns for congregants and the community at large. The activist ministers of influential black churches encourage civic participation from the pulpit via sermons and announcements. They also encourage civic participation through position statements and personal contact with their members. Furthermore, several of the churches have standing committees that deal with political, social, and community concerns.

We identify some important factors that impact church activism by analyzing five black activist churches in the District that vary by denomination, social class, size, and neighborhood. These churches were identified through two black newspapers, the *Washington Afro American* and the *Informer,* as well as through the *Washington Post.* We also identified activist black churches through discussions with several community leaders knowledgeable about the church/politics scene in the District. From there we generated a list of churches that were deemed publicly influential. For this analysis we chose People's Congregational United Church of Christ, Union Temple Baptist Church, Israel Baptist Church, Nineteenth Street Baptist Church, and Shiloh Baptist Church. We also supplemented our analysis with other activist congregations to illustrate types of activism within black congregations. We interviewed senior or associate ministers at the churches to understand their missions and ministries.

We discovered that the activism of these congregations runs deep. People's Congregational United Church of Christ was founded in 1891. As a black church in a majority white denomination, People's Congregational places a strong emphasis on social justice. The congregation is primarily comprised of middle-class and highly educated black Washingtonians. In fact, a large number of its congregants hold doctoral degrees. People's Congregational averages about 550 members per Sunday and is located in a residential area in Northwest Washington. Union Temple Baptist Church was founded in 1967 and has been led by Reverend Willie Wilson since 1978. The church is located in Anacostia, one of the poorest communities in the District. However, its membership comprises all social classes. Union Temple averages about two thousand members per week and at least 40 percent of the members live in Southeast D.C. The congregation is relatively young, with a majority of its members ranging between the ages of eighteen and thirty-five. Its community activism has garnered national attention. In 1997, Union Temple received the Presidential Service Award from President William Clinton for its service to the Washington community. The congregation is known for its Afrocentric theology, which parallels its commitment to community and electoral activism.

Israel Baptist Church was founded in 1880 and has been pastored by the Reverend Morris Shearin since 1988. The church is located in a mixed-income community in Northeast Washington, in a residential area with a combination of single-family homes and public housing projects. Israel Baptist averages about five hundred worshipers each Sunday and has members from all social classes. However, a disproportionate number of members are middle class and are comparatively older than congregants at Union Temple Baptist Church. Only a small number of members from Israel Baptist are between eighteen and thirty-five years of age.

Nineteenth Street Baptist Church was founded in 1839 and has been led by the Reverend Derrick Harkins since the 1990s. Nineteenth Street is located in an affluent section of Northwest Washington, and the predominantly middle-class congregation has a mixture of older, middle-age, and younger members. Nineteenth Street is involved in an array of outreach ministries, including economic development, job training, and health counseling, and actively participates in the "One Church One Child" child adoption campaign. Shiloh Baptist Church was founded in 1863 and has been pastored by the Reverend Charles Wallace Smith since 1991. Shiloh is a historic black church, having one of the oldest community outreach centers in the District. The church averages about two thousand people per Sunday and has over four thousand (mostly middle-class) members. It is located in Northwest Washington in a predominately working-class black community that is rapidly gentrifying.

ACTIVIST CHURCHES, ADVOCACY, AND COMMUNITY EMPOWERMENT

The activist congregations we profile participate in issue advocacy, covering an array of concerns from education, pollution, and health care to labor, crime, and affordable housing. Issues particular to the District, such as Home Rule and the lack of congressional representation, are also pursued by the aforementioned activist congregations. Again, these churches advocate on behalf of issues by holding information seminars or forums and by hosting rallies, protest campaigns, or a combination of these activities. A case in point is Union Temple Baptist Church. The congregation was vocal against the Washington, D.C. Control Board, which was put in place by Congress in 1995 to weaken the authority of the mayor and city council. Reverend Wilson led a protest march to the homes of members of the control board in opposition to the antidemocratic nature of the nonelected governing board.

Activist black churches have also protested business establishments on behalf of the community. For example, the Reverend Ellis Hagler of Plymouth Congregational United Church in Christ led a protest in 2000 against the Washington Hospital Center over the charge that it failed to provide adequate care for all residents. Reverend Hagler's protests also led to the closing of a liquor store that resided in the church's neighborhood. Similarly, Israel Baptist Church has pursued litigation against a regional sanitation company because of concerns over environmental hazards.

Issue advocacy also takes the form of information seminars. Israel Baptist Church has hosted forums on charter schools, and Union Temple has hosted several forums on the closing of D.C. General Hospital, the leading healthcare facility for uninsured patients in the metropolitan area. In a town hall meeting held at Union Temple, in which current mayor Anthony Williams explained the particulars of the plan, the mayor was heavily criticized and lambasted by the audience, city council members, and Reverend Wilson. They all accused Mayor Williams of not caring about poor people and not keeping his promises to provide adequate health care for Southwest Washington residents. Reverend Wilson, who was an ardent supporter of the Marion Barry administration, was once a supporter of Mayor Williams, but the closing of D.C. General Hospital drew battle lines between the two. The mayor's office refused to renew Wilson's prestigious, low-numbered license plate; such plates are issued to supporters of the administration. "I think

(Wilson) made it clear when we visited with him that he's not a friend of this administration."[1] Wilson's former tag was numbered "16," a leftover perk from his relationship with former Mayor Marion Barry.

In addition to issue advocacy, black churches are also participating in social service provision and community development, using these activities to address problems facing their communities. This is a part of the "holistic approach" that many activist churches in the District embody. Both Shiloh Baptist Church and Union Temple Baptist Church have very extensive social service programs. Four of the churches we analyzed have developed housing programs, and others, such as Union Temple Baptist, have provided jobs to community residents. Israel Baptist Church has an extensive social outreach program that includes day care, a daily senior center, and a community development corporation. These churches utilize the talents of their congregations by successfully carrying out church-based community development.

One church that is particularly strong in community development is Mt. Calvary Holy Church in Northeast Washington. Mt. Calvary has several community-centered ministries along Rhode Island Avenue. The church participates in job training and computer training services and has a food bank that is open daily. Other activist congregations have food and clothing banks, but Mt. Calvary's efforts are different because of the regularity in its operations and the large number of people being served. The church also runs a nursery school and a community center for youth in the surrounding area, which is complete with a game room and computers for educational enrichment.

These community development and social service efforts by activist black churches are especially interesting in light of the recent debates surrounding President George W. Bush's faith-based initiative, a policy initiative designed to remove barriers for religious institutions seeking government grants to support the social service arm of their ministries. Several activist churches in District already receive government grants that help to support their various programs for community revitalization. And many of these churches have formed separate community development corporations (CDCs) as vehicles for much of their community work. This way the church directly remains autonomous from government while receiving government and foundation funds to subsidize community development efforts. Several of the churches that have established CDCs utilize them as organizations to address community, social, as well as political needs.

ELECTORAL POLITICS

The most visible way that activist black churches in the District wield public influence is through their participation in electoral politics. Black activist ministers in the District engage in electoral activities by getting candidates elected to public office. They may campaign or endorse candidates or support particular candidates by holding candidate forums and voter registration campaigns. In terms of campaigning for or supporting a particular candidate for public office there is perhaps no better example of clergy and congregational support than former Mayor Marion Barry's 1994 reelection campaign, which was spearheaded by Reverend Wilson and Union Temple Baptist Church. This campaign will be described in greater detail shortly.

Campaigning for political candidates is not the only way that activist ministers and congregants become involved in electoral politics. Another way is through church leaders' endorsement of political candidates without directly participating in their campaign. One minister stated that he endorsed political candidates through the media but not from the pulpit. "I will support a candidate in the news. I am a citizen of D.C. However, I will not support [candidates] from the pulpit," the minister stated. "I won't because I feel that this is unfair to the other candidates." This minister states further: "When candidates come to my church during election season, I introduce and acknowledge all of them and ask them if they would like to say a few words from their seat. But they do not come up to this church's pulpit."[2] This particular minister will, however, share his view of issues and candidates if people solicit it personally. As he notes, "When people come up to me individually, whether after church or whatever, I will share my opinion. They have given me permission."[3]

As another form of electoral engagement, activist black churches in the District participate in periodic voter registration drives and civic education projects. The 2000 campaign season demonstrated how important a voter education campaign is to informing congregants in activist congregations. Several churches hosted forums where candidates were allowed to share their views with the public and District residents were able to ask them questions about issues. The popularity of these forums for candidates reveals the importance that they carry in giving candidates access to potential voters. As then Mayor Marion Barry remarked at a candidate forum held at Israel Baptist Church in 1998, "The fact that every mayoral candidate is here ought to tell you how important it is to be here."[4]

Perhaps more important than the access to voters that the forums give the candidates is the access to the candidates that the forums provide the public. They are held as public events, not only for the sake of the members of the particular church, but for the public at large. In this way they are a classic example of the church serving as a "public sphere" and as a "discursive arena" for political information sharing. In many cases these forums are an important programmatic area that carries the churches' missions regarding social justice and social action. For example, Shiloh Baptist Church frequently hosts such forums, which spring from their social justice ministry. At Shiloh social justice is an important part of the church's mission and ministry.

In fact Shiloh has both an associate pastor of "social justice" and an associate pastor for "community development." Engaging in this type of civic mobilization is one way that some scholars suggest that nonactivist black churches can and should become active.[5]

ACTIVIST CHURCHES AND THE MARION BARRY YEARS

Black activist clergy and congregations were instrumental in supporting the candidacy and administrations of former Mayor Marion Barry. Barry became mayor of the District of Columbia on January 2, 1979. He immediately began to court some of the most powerful black ministers in the city, specifically Bishop Smallwood Williams of Bibleway Baptist Church, Bishop Walter McCullough of the United House of Prayer, and the Reverend Henry Gregory of Shiloh Baptist Church. Using symbolic and material resources at his disposal as the chief executive of the District, Barry wooed these ministers with "special license plates, invited them to high-profile meetings at the District-building and showcased them at an annual citywide prayer breakfast. Most important, Barry put millions of dollars at the disposal of ministers to fund church-based day-care centers, senior-citizens meal programs, and job-training efforts. He freed city land and low-cost loans for them to build subsidized housing and food stores."[6]

Mayor Barry was exceptionally deferential to ministers who possessed large followings, especially to Bishop McCullough, who became head of the United House of Prayer's empire. The denomination has several millions members throughout the country and, as far back as the 1970s, had assets totaling $34 million.[7] In the 1978 election for mayor, Bishop McCullough's enormous political power was symbolized by a newspaper headline that read, "Politicians Await Bishop's Word," indicating that the bishop was considering whether to endorse front-runner candidates Walter Washington or Sterling Tucker.[8] Although Marion Barry won the election with white liberal support, with the two leading candidates having split the black vote, Barry soon after the election sought support from Bishop McCullough. The source of the bishop's power was the fact that he built considerable housing along the 7th Street corridor, near the heart of the city. The church's real-estate holdings include the Canaanland Apartments, the McCullough Paradise Gardens, and the McCullough Senior Citizens Home. Bishop McCullough paid for the housing developments in cash rather than from District or direct federal support, giving him considerable financial independence from the local political establishment. The church could sustain its own community development efforts without help from local politicians.[9] In time, the United House of Prayer community became a reliable component of Marion Barry's electoral base in several low-income black neighborhoods, one of which was dominated by the House of Prayer housing empire.

However, Marion Barry's own church was the Union Temple Baptist Church, headed by Reverend Willie Wilson. Located in Ward Eight, Union Temple is surrounded by a majority black low-income community. Reverend Wilson developed the church into a massive $4.2 million institution, largely through the attraction of its social and political activism, which combined a pan-Africanist ethos with a traditional Baptist style of worshiping. His personal philosophy is, "to say that the church is the most powerful institution in the black community is an indictment" since the black church should increase, from a psychological standpoint, black empowerment in the secular world.[10]

The activist and nationalist theology of Union Temple was compatible with Mayor Barry's own background as a civil rights and black power advocate; consequently, the congregation served as an important component of the mayor's political base. The church also benefited from the relationship. Union Baptist needed linkages to the city to begin the renovation of an apartment complex, Wayne Terrace, which was completed in 1984, after Barry had begun his second term in office.[11] As one observer notes of the expansive projects of Union Temple during the 1990s, the church's "social safety net is so expansive that the church seems to resemble a sort of mini-government, operating its own community welfare system. In fact, much of the work was begun with taxpayer money in the form of federal and city grants. Agape Town Square (housing complex) initially was renovated with $1.8 million in city and federal funds; the Soul Bowl (feeding program for the needy) got more than $80,000 per year in public money in the mid-1990s; and Harambee House (homeless shelter) continues to receive more than $200,000 a year from the city."[12]

CHURCH MOBILIZATION AND THE DISTRICT'S DRUG CRISIS

In addition to community development and issue advocacy, church-based activism also emerged in the late 1980s around the District's drug crisis. This mobilization was encouraged by the Barry administration. It was, therefore, one of the more surprising discoveries during his second term that Mayor Barry himself had been accused of using illegal drugs. In 1988, Mayor Barry asked churches to become involved in his antidrug campaign that was established through the city's Office on Religious Affairs, a program headed by the Reverend Bernard Lee. The campaign had mixed results. Largely because of the lack of direction and a weak conceptual focus on what exactly the role of church should be in response to the drug epidemic, the campaign failed. Many black ministers in the District felt that the crisis was complicated by the origins of the epidemic, as well as the depth of the penetration of drugs in communities and denominational bickering and leadership posturing that engulfed the effort. Reverend George C. Gilbert of the 130-member Baptists Minister's Conference noted other limitations: "Preaching is our expertise; we don't claim to be doctors or counselors; the problem is so astronomical you feel powerless to do anything."[13] This sentiment, however, did not keep the Congress of National Black Churches from hosting forums in the city nor the Washington Metropolitan Council of Churches, headed by Reverend Ernest Gibson of First Rising Mt. Zion Baptist Church, from proposing solutions to engage churches. Reverend Gibson observed that funds for drug treatment in the city budget had not been distributed to community organizations and institutions, due to an essential conservatism of churches on the issue. Many of the churches had opposed drug legalization policies, considering drug abuse as a moral issue rather an illness.

The lack of direction by area churches did not keep activist churches such as Union Temple from initiating drug-related services. The church ran the Prison Project at Lorton Reformatory, which provided education and other social service linkages to families who had incarcerated relatives who were involved in the drug trade. An important alliance formed between Union Temple and the Nation of Islam (NOI), which was similarly active in prisons and, like Union Temple, became the recipient of city contracts. The local branch of the NOI adopted a drug-infested apartment complex called Mayfair Mansions to rid it of drug dealing by deploying the group's well-regarded security force. Mayor Marion Barry welcomed the assistance of the NOI, which had curtailed drug activity in the Bedford-Stuyvesant area of Brooklyn, New York.[14] Although the deployment of the NOI team was strongly embraced by residents of Mayfair Mansion, the security forces' intensive patrolling and strong physical tactics drew the attention of the local police and the media.

The District's drug crisis became symbolized through Mayor Barry's arrest in an FBI sting operation for drug possession in 1991. The mayor was incarcerated for six months. At this low point in his life, Barry drew support from a dozen black ministers who gave him spiritual support through this ordeal. Their moral authority gave legitimacy to the Mayor's post-prison political career through the theological concept of "redemption."[15] These activist ministers played a significant role when Barry came back after his incarceration to win election to a seat on the city council in 1992 and in his run for mayor again in 1994 where he won a fourth term.[16] Reverend Wilson spearheaded Barry's campaign and served as Marion Barry's spiritual advisor. When Barry was released from prison, Wilson sent eight busloads of members to welcome him and return him home. Wilson described Marion Barry's reelection as "the greatest political comeback in the history of American politics."[17] The depth of Barry's use of religious metaphor was supremely evident in his speech at Union Temple Baptist Church before a crowd of two thousand: "God has blessed me. I feel the power of God's work in me. I feel the God force. I start the day with prayer. There is always prayer."[18]

Although he ran for mayor seeking support from the religious community, the core of Barry's supporters beyond a small group of activist congregations were troubled by the moral dilemma presented by his deeds and the use of redemption to promote his mayoral campaign. On the one hand, there was the feeling voiced by some that "Barry's story of redemption is the stuff of Bible study and Sunday sermons—inspirational lessons about persevering. Those ministers say he deserves forgiveness as much as any parishioner who comes to them repentant and ashamed of drug and alcohol abuse."[19] On the other hand, ministers like Reverend A. Knighton Stanley of the People's Congregational Church noted that although personal redemption is warranted, "the church does not always support the redeemed politically, nor should that be the expectation."[20]

Barry won the mayoral election and his new administration created a considerable platform and political opportunity for Reverend Wilson of Union Temple Baptist Church. When Republicans won control over both houses of U.S. Congress in 1994 and the District's fiscal crisis led to the control board, Reverend Wilson led grassroots opposition against the board. The board, headed by Dr. Andrew Brimmer, a noted black economist and former member of the Federal Reserve Board, trumped the power of the mayor, the city council, and the District's school board. Reverend Wilson led protest demonstrations against the control board in front of Dr. Brimmer's home, opposing the board's usurpation of the power in personnel and policy decisions.[21] Reverend Wilson raised many issues directly that Barry could only indirectly challenge.

Reverend Wilson would even challenge Mayor Barry. When the mayor and Republican Councilwoman Carol Schwartz sponsored a bill that would give jurors the option of ordering the death sentence to anyone convicted of killing a public safety officer, Reverend Wilson, who opposes the death penalty, exhibited his independence by appearing at city hall to protest the measure. He informed the mayor and the council: "I am here to encourage this government to move in a more ethical, moral and divine direction."[22] Signs that Wilson's independence was respected were evident when later that year, Barry appointed the activist minister to a twenty-six-member citizens' committee to find potential candidates for the District's new chief of police.[23] Reverend Wilson's influence on the mayor was illustrated decisively when Barry considered running for a fifth term as mayor in 1998. Barry visited Wilson to seek advice and Wilson, resentful of the fact that Barry had borne the responsibility for most of the perceived ills of the city and considerate of Barry's need to restore his health, told the beleaguered mayor that "enough is enough."[24] In the end, Barry decided in accord with Reverend Wilson's wishes.

DETERMINANTS OF ACTIVIST BLACK
CHURCHES IN THE DISTRICT

We return to our analysis of the five activist churches we identified at the start of this chapter in order to examine the factors that influence their activism in social service provision, community development, and electoral politics. Although activist black churches in the District have traditionally and do currently engage in civic life, scholars of Afro-American religion should move away from painting "the black church" with one broad brush. As was stated at the outset, the tradition of activism is carried on *by a group of churches from among many* in the District. Clearly, many black churches in Washington do not have a tradition of activism in local politics or advocacy on broad economic and social issues. Black churches, including those in the District, are lauded for being at forefront of the civil rights movement of the 1950s and 1960s; they provided organizational resources that sustained the movement.[25] The movement's strategy of nonviolence itself was framed through the edifices of black churches, and religious leaders helped the strategy gain acceptance beyond the church.[26] Although it can be argued that black churches were at the forefront of the civil rights struggle, most black churches did not take part in the movement.

The classic scholarly debate surrounding this issue looks at black churches as either mobilizers of political action or as a hindrance to social activism. And when trying to determine the essential nature of "the black church" scholars fall on both sides of this debate. For example, when looking at black churches and politics, Fredrick Harris finds that religion serves as a resource for black political mobilization.[27] On the other hand, Adolph Reed criticizes the role of black churches as "intrinsically apolitical agency."[28] Given the rich tradition of activist black churches in Washington and since most churches in the district *do not* seek to participate in politics and community empowerment efforts, what characterizes "publicly influential" black churches? Previous research shows that large, urban, middle-class churches that are part of mainline denominations are more likely to be involved in social outreach and political activism than churches that do not exhibit those characteristics. An examination of the five activist churches that we identified allowed us to isolate some characteristics in common. Two key factors that emerged are ministerial leadership and the theological orientation of the church.

Ministerial Leadership

Because of the hierarchical leadership styles in black churches, ministers are the key figures. The "will of the minister" is a key variable that determines whether a church participates in community empowerment activities and electoral politics. In fact activist ministers that have become elected officials such as Floyd Flake in New York (see chapter 9) and Walter Faun-troy, former district delegate in Congress, relied on churches and church net-works as their basis for support. Examining the activist ministers' back-grounds reveals interesting commonalities in our analysis. These ministers tend to be highly educated and active in ministerial alliances. Interviews for this study reveal that activist ministers expressed a prophetic theology, that is, a belief that churches should be concerned with social and political issues, and a liberation theology, a commitment to an aspect of Afro-Christianity that emphasizes liberation from social oppression. These theo-logical orientations are not confined to pastoral leadership, they also reflect the churches' overall theological orientation. These orientations predispose these activist ministers and congregations to political and social activism. Not only are they "activist" preachers, they are drawn to congregations that are activist-oriented. This especially appears to be the case for churches such as Shiloh Baptist and Nineteenth Street Baptist, congregations that had an ac-tivist tradition prior to the leadership of their current pastors.

Formal education is also a critical component of activist leadership. All of the ministers in the study have postgraduate seminary education. Four of them have doctorate degrees and a fifth received a Masters of Divinity de-gree from Howard University. C. Eric Lincoln and Lawrence Mamiya found in their survey of black ministers that clergy who received seminary educa-tion are more likely to practice a theology of black liberation. The relation-ship between seminary education, black theology, and activism was so strong in their survey that Lincoln and Mamiya concluded that black theolo-gians had not done enough to move the concepts of black theology from the academy to the parish. Because the majority of black ministers are not sem-inary educated, black liberation theology failed, according to Lincoln and Mamiya, to transform black communities.[29]

Activist ministers in the District are also involved in ministerial alliances. For example, Reverend Shearin at Israel Baptist Church works with the Washington Interfaith Network (WIN), and many of the candidate forums at his church are cohosted with this group. WIN's parent organization is the In-dustrial Areas Foundation (IAF), the oldest and largest community-oriented organizing network in the United States. Founded fifty years ago by Saul Alinsky, the IAF works with more than sixty congregation-based community organizations across the nation. Reverend Shearin is also the president of the Washington chapter of the NAACP. Reverend Wallace Charles Smith, the min-ister of Shiloh Baptist Church, has been the president of the Progressive Bap-tist National Convention,[30] a national denomination of politically active black Baptists, and was the founding president of the Washington Ministerium, a local ministerial alliance.[31] The Washington Ministerium was founded in part to allow Baptist ministers in the city a vehicle to be more active in political and community affairs.

Reverend Derrick Harkins of Nineteenth Street Baptist is also a member of the Washington Ministerium. Prior to his leadership at Nineteenth Street, he worked with the IAF when he pastored a church in Dallas, Texas. He also served as an assistant pastor at Abyssinian Baptist Church in Harlem, a congregation known for its political activism and community outreach. His formal training in the ministry is indicative of his interest in social causes. He wrote his doctoral dissertation—"A Comparative Analysis of the Social Ministries of Father Divine and Adam Clayton Powell, Sr."—on two black activist ministers during the 1930s, a topic that reflects his interest in church-based community and political activism.

Reverend A. Knighton Stanley of People's Congregational Church was active in the civil rights movement in Greensboro, North Carolina. He was the chaplain at North Carolina A & T during the Greensboro student movement. Reverend Stanley is a board member of the Interfaith Alliance, a progressive interfaith group whose mission is to "promote the positive and healing role of religion in public life through encouraging civic participation, facilitating community activism, and challenging religious political extremism." He is also active in social justice issues on a national level through the United Church of Christ.

Reverend Willie Wilson of Union Temple Baptist is a member of several civil rights organizations and he has worked with leaders of other faiths, specifically the Nation of Islam. He worked with Minister Louis Farrakhan on the Million Man March, when many other Christian ministers refused to collaborate with the Muslim leader on the campaign. He has expressed a willingness to work with black leaders across the religious and political spectrum. This willingness is symbolized by a mural of the Last Supper at Union Temple, which depicts various historical black figures such as Rosa Parks, Harriet Tubman, Malcolm X, and Elijah Muhammad sharing the supper with a black Jesus.

Theological Orientation

These activist ministers or their ministerial assistants expressed a prophetic theological orientation as motivation for their activism. Their prophetic orientation is holistic and reflects the belief that churches should be concerned with all aspects of people's lives. These ministers favored participation in electoral politics and used biblical scripture to support their public pronouncements. They also expressed concern for the District as a community and felt that their mission is to improve the lives of the residents in Washington. The holistic and prophetic theological orientation of the five activist churches whose ministers were interviewed for this study can be summarized by a quote by Reverend Alice Davis, a minister of Shiloh Baptist Church: "We try not to draw a strict line between sacred and secular because all of God's creation is sacred. Those aspects of life that are 'secular' may not be controlled by the church but does not mean they are not sacred."[32] In these activist churches speaking about politics from the pulpit was not a controversial idea—especially about political and social issues. Reverend Harkins noted, "From the pulpit it is important to critique society's social ills such as racism and to remind people of economic realities such as economic injustice. The pulpit is a forum for me to keep the membership appraised of the current social and political issues. Church leadership should be a part of social action and social change." Reverend Davis, an assistant pastor at Shiloh Baptist, explained that during the time of Christ, the church was actively involved in politics. Consequently, ministers should not hesitate to speak of politics from the pulpit. "Politics is just how we govern ourselves. It is part of our religious belief to talk about what is wrong in the community."[33]

Reverend Wilson of Union Temple Baptist Church explained that the holistic theology practiced at his church is based on an African worldview that looks at life holistically and does not compartmentalize various aspects of life. This theology does not separate political, economic, and social aspects of life from spiritual life because "God is concerned with not only soul salvation but also economic, social and political salvation." Reverend Shearin of Israel Baptist Church expressed similar sentiments, "For everybody who is black," he argues, "the whole notion of separation of church and state doesn't exist."[34]

These churches are biblically guided in their understanding of the church's relationship to the secular world. For example, Reverend Harkins indicated that "the Gospel calls for us to advocate things that are right and just," and that Christians should use the "Bible as platform rather than the Bible as cover." This means that the Bible should not be interpreted as instructing Christians to isolate themselves from the rest of the world but rather to propel them to social and political action that will help to improve world conditions. In these churches, the life and teachings of Jesus Christ provide a model for social activism and community involvement. "It is in these prophetic teachings that the prophetic voice of Christ speaks about social justice issues and what a true community that is led by a spirit of God should be like," explains Reverend Davis. Focusing on issues of social justice and a deep concern for economic injustice is important as well. Reverend Stanley pointed out that his church is "a Christian church motivated by the life and teachings of Jesus Christ who largely talks to the lost, the last, and the least."

To these activist churches, following Jesus' example of social activism allows them to fulfill their missions. Reverend Wilson explains, "A proper rendering of what Jesus was about is empowerment. Jesus' teachings were about the kingdom of God and awakening the power of God that resides in the individual—not something that resides outside of self. His mission was to bring good news to the poor, set at liberty the captive, heal the wounded and broken hearted." Reverend Wilson said that following the model set by Jesus as seen from an Afrocentric perspective, "teaches us that you have to deal with all aspects of people's lives. For example political decisions are decisions that are going to affect your people, how they will live and their means of livelihood." In some cases the stated missions of these black activist churches reveal a holistic and prophetic theology. Reverend Harkins explained that the goal of Nineteenth Street as expressed by its mission statement: "To make the gospel relevant and impactful to people's lives. We see it as a part of proclaiming God's transformative power." At Shiloh Baptist Church the mission statement is also revealing in this regard:

> As the SHILOH BAPTIST CHURCH (Washington), we are a part of the Family of God—a vital entity in the Shaw Community—believing in Jesus Christ, spreading the Good News, worshiping, teaching, growing, caring, sharing, cultivating Christian lifestyles, promoting justice, ministering to the needy, the oppressed and physically challenged and people of all ages and nationalities, locally, and internationally. We do this because we are led by the Holy Spirit, and taught by Scriptures to obey the Great Commission: "Go ye therefore, and teach all nations, baptizing them in the name of the Father, and of the Son and the Holy Ghost." (Matthew 28:19)[35]

Shiloh's mission statement is particularly interesting because it reveals another aspect of the holistic, prophetic outlook of these activist churches. The activist ministers that we interviewed all expressed a deep commitment toward encouraging civic involvement and promoting community revitalization in black communities in general but on the local level in particular. Likewise, Reverend Harkins stated that one of the reasons that Nineteenth Street is successful in its community outreach efforts and in encouraging civic participation is because of their activist legacy in local affairs. As Harkins explains, "We are known in the D.C. community and our longevity provides the community with stability. It shows that we have a stake in the community."

The ministers or assistant ministers of these activist churches stated that references to black liberation theology were often made in their sermons. Additionally, biblical characters such as Jesus Christ are represented as black in these churches. One interesting example of symbols of black theology is the artistic designs in the sanctuaries of these churches. For example, at Shiloh Baptist Church stained-glass windows depict aspects of black theology and the significance of the designs are explained in church bulletins. One window depicts the church's "vision of family, ministry and our commitment to our culture, identity and heritage . . . the faces in the windows have been redone to reflect our African backgrounds." Another window reflects the Middle Passage. People's Congregational also has a stained-glass window in their sanctuary that reflects the cultural symbolism of black theology. These symbolic artifacts represent a sense of connection to black communities and recognition of a particular black experience.

There are limitations to our analysis. The churches in our sample are mostly middle class, leaving out nonmainline churches and congregations with larger numbers of working-class congregants. For example, two churches that have strong civic traditions are Bible Way Church and United House of Prayer. A relatively recent congregation, the Mt. Calvary Holy Church of America is part of the Pentecostal tradition and also has a predominately working-class membership. This is not to say that churches with a particular socioeconomic class and denominational characteristic are less or more likely to participate in certain activities. It might be that the resources that members of middle-class churches have at their disposal make it easier for middle-class black churches to take on more social outreach activities. For example, one minister in our study, whose congregation includes a large number of judges, elected officials, and government agency heads, remarked that he often bent the ears of these congregants to express his views and concerns and "get them to do the right thing."

CONCLUSION

Despite the fact that the interviews clearly express the view that there is no separation between the sacred and the secular within the traditional mission of activist black churches in the District, we find that the civic context is important to highlight in determining the peculiar character of black church influence in the city. This context begins with the location of the church in a city located in the nation's capital. Just as important to church-based activism of black churches in the District is the dominance of former Mayor Marion Barry. His candidacies and mayoral administration induced many activist clergy and congregations into electoral politics. Like the election of black mayors in other cities during the 1980s, Barry's ascendancy in District politics occurred in the flash of the first generation of black mayors who depended in almost every instance on the power of activist black churches. With his most recent ascendancy as a council member elected in 2004 from the city's Ward Eight, Barry continues to use his personal faith and his religious connections as a basis for his electoral support. Honed with a tradition of activist leadership and theological proclivities, activist black clergy and congregations will continue to shape the political dynamics of the District of Columbia.

NOTES

1. Yolanda Woodlee, "Criticism of Williams Costs Pastor a Perk," *Washington Post,* 4 April 2001.

2. Interview with Reverend Stanley, 3 October 2000.

3. Interview with Reverend Stanley, 3 October 2000.

4. Michael Powell and Hamil Harris, "The Mayoral Race Goes to Church," *Washington Post*, 14 May 1998.

5. Michael Leo Owens, "Political Action and Black Church Associated Community Development Corporations," (paper presented for the Urban Affairs Association Conference, Los Angeles, California, 3–6 May 2000).

6. Harry A. Jaffe and Tom Sherwood, *Dream City: Race, Power and the Decline of Washington, D. C.* (New York: Simon and Schuster, 1994), 141.

7. Phil Thomas, "Bishop Grace Litigation Thickens as Third Group Enters Case," *Washington Star,* 31 August 1961, Washingtoniana Division, Martin Luther King, Jr. Library, District Government, Washington, D.C.

8. Courtland Milloy, "Politicians Await Bishop's Word," *Washington Post*, 5 September 1978, A1, Washingtoniana Division, Martin Luther King, Jr. Library, District Government.

9. "The United House of Prayer," Urban League Newsletter, Twenty-second Annual Whitney M. Young Jr. Memorial Dinner, Washingtoniana Division, Martin Luther King, Jr. Library, District Government.

10. Dorothy Gilliam, "The Thrust of Church Power," *Washington Post*, 17 February 1986, B3.

11. Katheleen Deveraux, "City, Church Leaders Inaugurate Renovated Wayne Terrace Today," *Washington Times*, 27 October 1985, Washingtoniana Division, Martin Luther King, Jr. Library, District Government.

12. Hamil Harris, "Black Pride and Politics from a Southeast Pulpit," *Washington Post,* 7 July 1996, A1.

13. Harris, "Black Pride and Politics."

14. Patrice Gaines-Carter, "Muslims Gain Barry's Support and Find Services in Demand," *Washington Post*, 22 April 1988, C1.

15. Yolanda Woodlee, "Redemption Becomes Barry's Rallying Cry," *Washington Post*, 5 September 1994, A1.

16. Rene Sanchez, "Barry Rides Home on Wave of Support, Ex-Mayor Borne from Prison by Small but Vocal Group of Backers," *Washington Post*, 24 April 1992, A1; Rene Sanchez, "Preparing for Power, Barry Fine-Tunes a New Machine," *Washington Post*, 22 November 1992, A1.

17. Interview with Reverend Wilson, 8 September 2000.

18. Linda Wheeler, "The Faith in Barry, Mayor's Religious Tone Meets with Belief, Doubt," *Washington Post*, 5 January 1995, J1.

19. James Ragland, "Faith in Barry Becomes Issue for Clergy, Ministers Ponder Checkered Past amid Campaign to Recapture Mayor's Office," *Washington Post*, 31 May 1994, D1.

20. Ragland, "Faith in Barry Becomes Issue for Clergy."

21. Hamil K. Harris and Lonae O'Neal Parker, "Protests Target Members of Control Board, Demonstrators in District Sing, Clap and Pray outside Homes of Officials on Panel," *Washington Post*, 11 June 1996, B3.

22. Cheryl W. Thompson, "D.C. Residents Pack Council's hearing on a Death Penalty Bill," *Washington Post,* 26 June 1997, B5.

23. Cheryl W. Thompson, "Search Begins for Soulsby Replacement, 26 Residents to Help Barry Choose Nominee for New Police Chief," *Washington Post*, 4 December 1997, B6.

24. David A. Vise and Hamil R. Harris, "Praying, Wavering toward a Decision, Inner Circle Urged Barry Not to Run, Inner Circle's Prayers and Advice Helped Barry Decide Not to Run," *Washington Post*, 24 May 1998, A1.

25. In "Men Led, but Women Organized: Movement Participation of Women in the Mississippi Delta," in *Women in the Civil Rights Movement: Trailblazers and Torchbearers, 1941–1965* (Brooklyn: Carlson Publishing, 1990), Charles Payne argues that black church attendance was particularly important for women who engaged in movement activities. Women who attended churches were more likely to participate in the civil rights movement, and they served as the organizational backbone of the movement, through fundraising and other organizational contributions, through the church.

26. Allison Calhoun-Brown, "Upon This Rock: The Black Church, Nonviolence, and the Civil Rights Movement," *PS: Political Science and Politics*, June 2000.

27. Fredrick Harris, *Something Within: Religion in African-American Political Activism* (Oxford: Oxford University Press, 1999).

28. Adolph Reed Jr., *The Jesse Jackson Phenomenon: The Crisis of Purpose in Afro-American Politics.* (New Haven: Yale University Press, 1986), 57.

29. C. Eric Lincoln and Lawrence Mamiya. *The Black Church in the African American Experience* (Durham: Duke University Press, 1990).

30. The organization was formed when a group of ministers broke from the National Baptist Convention, USA, because of their more progressive civil rights strategies.

31. The Washington Ministerium was founded after several local D.C. pastors were ousted from the largest black Baptist ministerial alliance because they favored the ordination of women. Reverend Shearin was one of the ministers ousted. The ordination ceremony was held in Israel Baptist Church where he was the pastor. Pastor Harkins is also a member of the Washington Ministerium.

32. Interview, Reverend Alice Davis, 4 October 2000.

33. Interview, Reverend Alice Davis, 4 October 2000; Interview, Reverend Harkins, 13 September 2000.

34. Michael Powell, Pam Constable, and Hamil R. Harris, "Control Boards That Dwarf D.C.'s Giant," *Washington Post*, 18 June 1998.

35. The mission statement of Shiloh Baptist church can be found on their website: www.shilohbaptist.org.

7

Black Churches and Machine Politics in Chicago

Fredrick C. Harris

As a city encompassing one of the largest and most contiguous black communities in the United States, Chicago has long established itself as a center of African American religious life. The city was one of the greatest beneficiaries of black migration north during the interwar and the post–World War II eras, leading to the development of over one thousand black churches across the city. Those religious institutions would have both positive and negative consequences on the political development of blacks in Chicago. Accompanying the evolution of black churches in the interwar period was the introduction of blacks to Chicago's unique political culture, a culture dominated by patronage-driven politics in which awards and sanctions were implemented for or against political actors who defied or supported the "machine." These two historical forces converged to produce a form of clerical-oriented civic action that would, in various historical moments, clash with reform-oriented movements in Chicago's black communities.

This chapter examines the historical development of African American churches in Chicago from the Great Migration through the election of the current mayor, Richard M. Daley, through the context of patronage-style politics. It highlights how the city's mayors have used government-funded social programs to nurture and solidify political links to black clergy. Paradoxically, while city-funded social service programs encouraged the civic engagement of ministers and churches, they also strengthened the power of patronage-style politics in black communities and, in many instances, undermined efforts to elect reform-oriented candidates as well as to lend support to movements in black communities that addressed inequalities.

This chapter is divided into four sections. First, I explore the mutual benefits that activist clergy gain from politicians and the potential benefit that politicians gain from activist clergy. I argue that the incentives for both sets of elites are to gain the cooperation of the other in order to extract symbolic, material, and altruistic benefits. I then show how material and symbolic incentives that politicians have at their disposal to woo activist clergy developed in the early stages of black politics in Chicago, influencing the relationship between politicians and black clergy for more than a generation. Second, the chapter explores the consequences of the machine–ministerial alliance by showing how that relationship undermined the success of the 1966 Chicago Freedom Movement, a campaign led by the Southern Christian Leadership Conference (SCLC) to address issues of poverty and open-housing in Chicago. Evidence points to how the machine, led by Richard J. Daley, used a combination of incentives and sanctions to keep activist black ministers in line. Third, the chapter explores the factionalism that developed among activist black clergy during the 1983 mayoral campaign to elect Harold Washington, who eventually became Chicago's first black mayor. The analysis demonstrates how lay members opened their churches to the Washington campaign, despite the initial soft support of many black activist clergy in the city. Fourth, the chapter concludes with an analysis of how Richard M. Daley, the city's current mayor, is consolidating support among both patronage-minded and reform-oriented black clergy through his use of symbolic and material rewards.

ESTABLISHING LINKS: MINISTERS AND POLITICIANS AS POLITICAL ENTREPRENEURS

The political relationships that form between ministers and politicians are rooted in what can be described as norms or practices of reciprocity. Such norms assume that two or more parties will receive mutual support from the other. Within the context of black politics in Chicago both activist ministers and politicians have strong incentives to support the other since both have resources that the other needs. For ministers these benefits can either be material, altruistic, or symbolic. Urban political elites have an array of material incentives to induce ministers into civic action—they can supplement the funding of churches through "donations," subsidize church revenues by hosting government-sponsored programs in churches, or, on some rare occasions, hire ministers as city employees. Ministers, of course, can also be altruistically motivated by the desire to provide social services for needy congregants and community residents. Similarly, ministers may have interest in public service. If there is interest, urban regimes have symbolic incentives at their disposal to cultivate relations by appointing ministers to municipal boards or commissions, or using other symbolic gestures, such as renaming a street in a minister's honor.

Ministers, on the other hand, have political resources at their disposal to woo the interest of political elites. Like most elected officials, political elites are primarily interested in getting elected, reelected, or gaining support for policy initiatives. For mayors, especially those who have to maintain the support of diverse constituencies, electoral strategies may entail maintaining or expanding electoral coalitions. Activist black clergy can assist mayors or mayoral candidates in capturing or sustaining the black electorate through individual or group endorsements or candidacies or policies. Given the powerful impact of the social and communication networks in black churches, candidates can, for example, benefit from Sunday visits to churches during an election season or ministers can demonstrate their support of a candidate during regular Sunday services. As previous scholars have shown, political discussions and candidate visits to churches considerably boost the political participation of religious blacks.[1]

In Chicago, the intensity of church-based electoral activism varies by social class; however, the relatively high levels of activism reveal potential electoral resources that can be exploited by political elites who seek black support for votes and policy initiatives. According to findings from the 1991 Chicago Area Survey, more than half of black respondents reported that their ministers encourage members to vote (65 percent) and slightly over half (57 percent) reported that their church "regularly" or "sometimes" hosted political candidates. Only 20 percent of black respondents reported that their minister discussed politics nearly all the time or frequently. However, about a third of respondents (30 percent) reported that their church leaders discussed politics "sometimes."

These church-based levels of electoral engagement, which exceed the nature and intensity of electoral activities in majority-white religious institutions, serve as an additional incentive for political elites to entice activist black clergy. As I have mentioned, political elites nurture ties with activist clergy by providing funding for their social service programs, lobbying city and state agencies on the behalf of ministers, making direct financial contributions to the church or minister, appointing ministers to boards or commissions, and, on some occasions, hiring ministers in salaried positions in city agencies.

In Chicago, the incentives for activist clergy and politicians seeking black support have been complicated by the city's tradition of machine-style politics. Often the activities that have engaged activist clergy have been marred by the exchange of church-based electoral support for political patronage from the machine. Indeed, this exchange is a part of black Chicago's political development and extends well beyond the politics of the pulpit to encompass almost every aspect of the city's civic life. Although this exchange has allowed many black churches to provide social services to needy congregants and neighborhood residents, the relationship has undermined the efforts of reform-minded political candidates and movements that have challenged the machine over a range of public policy issues, specifically open housing, equal educational opportunities, police brutality, inequalities in employment opportunities in city government, and the general inclusion of blacks in Chicago's political, social, and cultural life.

In the post–World War I era, when black Southerners flooded Chicago's South Side, many black ministers began to align themselves with politicians and political machines. These relationships evolved out of the financial precariousness of many black churches, which began to expand in size to accommodate newly arrived migrants. Party competition for migrant votes also inspired the ministers' involvement in politics. Operating as strategic actors, activist clergy accepted fees for backing candidates, often from candidates running for the same office. This strategy insured that they received as much money for their activism as possible since they or their congregation would benefit from the outcome no matter which candidate won. In his book *Negro Politicians*, Harold Gosnell explains clearly the material incentives behind the exchanges that took place between Chicago's black activist clergy and machine politicians during that period.

> Negro ministers have more reasons for going into politics than white ministers. A large proportion of the Negro churches are in debt and the congregations are almost always poor. In Chicago the purchase or the building of the church edifices to house large memberships has called on extraordinary efforts on the part of ministers. In a few cases the white politicians have come to the rescue of the Negro clergymen with large gifts or loans. . . . When these same white politicians are seeking support for their favorite candidates it is natural that they should turn to the ministers who have accepted aid at their hands. These ministers can speak at regular political meetings, they can rally their congregations together on special occasions, and they can open their pulpits to the particular candidates concerned.[2]

An editorial from the *Chicago Whip*, one of Chicago's black radical newspapers during the 1920s, illustrates the strategic actions of activist clergy. Such strategies would lay the ground for future generations of civic-minded black ministers in Chicago. The editorial informed its readers that "as the city of Chicago gets ready for its primary and election of public officials, the political hustlers are getting their old gags polished and ready for action." The editorial further observes that "nondiscripts seek to pawn themselves off as influential characters, and others, who draw no water, claim they carry thousands of votes in their vest pockets. Strange as it seems, but stranger it is true, many of our ministers play this confidence game with deftness and dispatch. They take money from all candidates and all sides."[3]

By the post–World War II era, just as the Democratic party solidified its grip on Chicago's political life, another force would influence the political nexus between activist clergy and politicians: the development in the 1950s of Richard J. Daley's powerful Cook Country Democratic machine and its black submachine led by Congressman William Dawson. The Daley machine's dominance would influence the outcome of Chicago's civil rights campaigns in the 1960s and 1970s. While blacks contributed to Daley's successful electoral coalition, his support softened as black insurgents challenged Daley on school segregation, open housing, slum housing, and police brutality. These reform-minded insurgents, which included few black ministers among their ranks, clashed with machine-backed political and religious elites who worked to thwart reform-oriented movements that emerged out of Chicago's black communities in the 1960s and 1970s.

James Q. Wilson notes in his research on black leadership in Chicago during the 1950s that most black ministers avoided participation in civic affairs altogether. However, clergy who were engaged in civic life were divided in their support for the machine. Wilson noted that "several prominent Negro ministers who have large congregations never fail to support the Dawson organization and are personally close to him." The social-class dynamics influenced ministerial support for the machine: "These ministers are characteristically Baptist or Pentecostal, with large followings among lower-income Negroes," while those who were suspicious of Dawson and the machine were "often better educated and with wealthier congregations."[4]

The incentives and sanctions the Daley machine and the Dawson submachine used to consolidate the support of black political elites are legendary and are beyond the scope of this study. However, the tactics that Daley used to gain support from activist clergy during the 1950s through the 1970s were the same ones employed by politicians during the 1920s. Political reporter Vernon Jarrett of the *Chicago Sun-Times* recalled the actions of a gubernatorial candidate in the early 1950s during a primary election season of Sunday campaigning.

> The candidate had beside him a roster of selected churches and ministers with the recommended amount of cash to be donated to each of them. The candidate also had beside him a box filled with $10, $20, $50, and $100 bills. A black political consultant read off the preach's name and amount of cash. The churches and ministers had been chosen by a legendary political maverick who called himself Billy Goat Brown. Brown was a street-corner orator who headed a civil rights "organization" he titled the "National Negro Conference" or "Council."[5]

One activist clergy learned early about the potential benefits and sanctions that could be distributed by the machine. After unsuccessfully challenging the machine's black incumbent congressman, William Dawson, Reverend Wilber Daniels, pastor of the Antioch Missionary Baptist Church and then president of the local NAACP, quickly made overtures to Daley. Reverend

Daniels, who ran against Dawson as a Republican, operated as a strategic actor, avoiding possible sanctions from the machine while also extracting symbolic and material resources in exchange for his loyalty to the mayor. As Daniels recounts: "I went into his office and won him over. That was not easy, because usually if you crossed Daley you were in the doghouse for the rest of your life. But I realized that I lived in a city that Daley was running, and I wanted to be with him because he could help me with what I wanted to do. From the day we met until the day he died, he was strictly a good friend, all the way down the pike."[6]

As a symbolic reward for supporting the machine Daley appointed Reverend Daniels to the civilian police board in 1972; he later served as the president of the board under Jane Byrne's mayoral administration in the late 1970s. The board is responsible for monitoring police misconduct, among several other responsibilities. However, the board, and Daniels, refused to challenge the policies of the mayor or the police chief, both of whom disregarded civilian complaints about police misconduct. Police brutality in Chicago during the 1960s and 1970s was a serious problem, symbolized by police violence against protesters during the 1968 National Democratic Party Convention and the police murder of Black Panther activists Fred Hampton and Mark Clark in 1969. As one reporter described Reverend Daniels's performance as a "reformer" in 1980: "He served a limp stint as president of the Chicago NAACP during the height of the civil rights movement; he sat as a member of the old Police Board for many years without raising a ruckus; and now he speaks ill of citizens' groups that monitor the board and some board members who would bring change."[7]

Although not considered a reformer, Reverend Daniels's support of the Daley machine netted material benefits to his church that not only benefited the minister's congregants but also helped residents of Englewood, the poor and working-class neighborhood that surrounded Daniels's church. Indeed, during the late 1960s and early 1970s Richard Daley assisted Reverend Daniels with securing funding from city and federal agencies to build low- and moderate-income housing in that neighborhood. By 1979 the church had an annual budget near $1 million with real-estate holdings totaling $9 million.

Reverend Daniels's strategy of working within the contours of patronage-style politics symbolizes the tradition of one dimension of clergy-oriented civic action in Chicago. That tradition, which has its secular counterparts among black political and economic elites in Chicago, barters away opposition against political, economic, and social inequalities in exchange for personal and, to a lesser degree, community-oriented benefits.

In response to his critics Reverend Daniels noted that his support for the machine had policy payoffs. As he explained, "There are people who receive credit for being great black leaders, and then there are those who are doing the leadership that counts. I talk across a desk and get housing built, rather than stand on a street corner with a sign. Now tell me, what's more fruitful for people? I'm called an Uncle Tom, but if I am an Uncle Tom, then show me what Chicagoans who aren't Uncle Toms have done."[8]

As I will discuss below, in the context of the Chicago Freedom Movement and the reform-oriented mayoral candidacy of Harold Washington, this patronage-style civic action among many black clergy has worked to undermine political forces that attempted to address racial inequality in the city. The machine not only had the power to withhold symbolic and material benefits from activists who opposed the machine, it could also impose sanctions against activist clergy who defied the machine.

THE CHICAGO FREEDOM MOVEMENT
AND MINISTERIAL FACTIONALISM

When Martin Luther King Jr. and the SCLC moved the civil rights movement north to Chicago, they assumed that local black ministers and churches would open their doors to a movement. After all, black ministers and churches provided the organizational resources that anchored the Southern civil rights movement. Although most ministers in local communities throughout the South were reluctant to join the movement, mainly because of the physical and material sanctions that white supremacists leveled against activists, black ministers and churches in Chicago were free from those sorts of risks.

To dramatize the existence of slum housing in the city King moved into an apartment in the Lawndale district, a poor neighborhood on the near West Side of Chicago. In addition to SCLC staff, the campaign worked in cooperation with the Coordinating Council of Community Organizations (CCCO), a local civil rights organization that evolved out of a campaign to remove the city's superintendent of education from office. The superintendent maintained overcrowed schools in order to keep the school system racially segregated.

In addition to ministers on the SCLC staff, including James Bevel, Jesse Jackson, and Al Sampson, other clergy directly involved in the Chicago campaign were Alvin Pitcher, a divinity student at the University of Chicago, and Addie Wyatt, a union activist. Among the churches that opened their doors to host mass rallies for the movement were the New Friendship Baptist Church (South Side), the Shiloh Baptist Church (West Side), Stone Temple Baptist Church (West Side), the Fellowship Missionary Baptist Church (South Side), the Greater Mount Hope Baptist Church (South Side), and the Warren Avenue Congregational Church (West Side), then a predominately white church.

Those churches and their ministers were exceptions. By supporting King's crusade they defied Mayor Richard J. Daley, who worked against the movement because it threatened real-estate interests in the city and alienated white ethnics, who were a part of the mayor's electoral coalition. Some black ministers, like the Reverend Joseph H. Jackson, then the powerful president of the National Baptist Convention, urged King to call off the demonstrations. Other activist ministers such as Reverend Wilber Daniels and Reverend Louis Ford, a Daley ally who pastored a local congregation of the Church of God in Christ (COGIC), were silent during the campaign. In his study of the Chicago Movement, James Ralph notes the difficulty getting activist clergy to support the movement:

> Chicago activists knew that the support of local black clergy would provide an important link to black Chicagoans and ultimately to thousands of additional followers. Yet many black ministers were cool to the freedom movement. Some saw no point in the civil rights campaign in Chicago; others worried that charismatic southern outsiders might diminish their prestige; and still others feared reprisals (by the machine) if they worked too closely with Chicago activists.[9]

With the silent opposition of Daley-backed ministers and the sanctions that Daley had at his disposal to punish activist clergy, church-based resources were ineffective in mobilizing Chicago blacks. Indeed, one analyst attributed King's defeat in Chicago to the lack of support from many black ministers and churches. "With the Reverend J. H. Jackson publicly lambasting the crusade and with many ministers fearful of reprisals by the Daley regime, activists struggled to find pastors who would even host civil rights rallies in their churches. Like their ministers, black Chicagoans on the whole had not stampeded into the movement."[10] One minister who supported King and the freedom movement was Reverend Clay Evans, pastor of the Fellowship Missionary Baptist Church and mentor to the young SCLC activist, the Reverend Jesse Jackson. In recounting the events of the movement years later, Reverend Evans revealed the sanctions that the machine used to punish ministers like him who joined the movement: "Many ministers who were with us had to back off because they didn't want their buildings to be condemned or given citations for electrical work, faulty plumbing, or fire code violations."[11]

For Reverend Evans punishment for joining the movement went beyond building code violations. He and his church paid a serious price for their support of the Chicago Freedom Movement by being denied a bank loan for a new church. It took seven years for Reverend Evans and his congregation to finish building, receiving financing only after a group of clergy came together to guarantee the bank loan.

I was trying to build an edifice at 45th Place and Princeton Avenue. The basement foundation had been laid, the steel structure was up, insurance companies and banks had agreed to come together to make a loan, and the contractor was prepared to move forward. . . . I introduced Dr. King to the mortgage broker, and he looked across the table at King and Jesse (Jackson) and me and said "Reverend Evans, I have cautioned you about getting involved. Dr. King, you might mean well but if Dr. Evans stays involved in the movement, people have said to me they are not going to let you have the money. I know you must be well aware that Mayor Daley can stop any structure in Chicago that he wants to."[12]

When asked what separated the ministers who supported the movement from those who did not, Reverend A. Patterson Jackson, the late senior pastor of Liberty Baptist Church, pointed to the financial independence of clergy as a factor. His assessment reveals how important it is for activist black ministers in Chicago to be financially independent, so that they will not be corrupted by political patronage. Reverend Jackson notes this difficulty when commenting on the problems recruiting ministers to the movement: "It is a known fact that a number of our black preachers eat at the mayor's table. You don't eat at the mayor's table and fight the mayor. Quite naturally had they allowed Dr. King in their pulpit they were not an ally to the mayor."[13]

Describing his own situation, Reverend Jackson, whose church built housing for the elderly without the support of city funding, noted, "We have never received a dime from any politician in this church, in its construction, in its program, in anything. The church made sure that I was freed from any wants, so I never had to ask any politician for anything. . . . Give to Caesar what's Caesar and to God what's God. We feel that if you accept a favor from a politician one day you will have to pay it back. I know that."

The Chicago Freedom Movement did not win concessions from the Daley regime. As the most racially segregated city in the United States, black insurgents could not mobilize enough support to defeat policies and practices that maintained residential segregation and poverty. Many ministers who opposed the movement or kept silent were rewarded. The mayor used the largess of federal monies designated for Johnson's War on Poverty and the city's department of Human Services to coopt clerical dissent. As historian Melvin Holli explains, "Federal anti-poverty money was used to keep black churches pro-administration, or at least to keep them from becoming forums for Daley's opponents."[14]

Patronage for black clergy would continue to undermine black opposition to the machine well after the demise of the movement. When Harold Washington was chosen by black progressives to run as an independent candidate for mayor in 1977, to fill the seat after Daley's death, activist black clergy continued to operate under the constraints of the machine. Although the number of black ministers on the payroll dwindled under Mayor Michael Bilandic, his successor as mayor, Mayor Jane Byrne, created Churches United, a social service program that hired black ministers to conduct vocational training and educational programs through inner-city churches. According the Reverend Morris Tynes of the Mount Moriah Baptist Church, one of the organizers of the Churches United, the program was also responsible for "advising the mayors on issues relating to the black community."[15]

Activist clergy who defied the machine were still vulnerable to threats from political actors, even as the machine began to lose its power. Reverend Claude Wyatt supported the independent candidacy of Harold Washington in 1977 and, like Reverend Clay Evans during the Chicago Freedom Movement, was punished by the machine for his support of Washington's candidacy. As he would recount years later, "In my own case I know I had some political problems, and our (church building) foundation laid there for seven years. No bank would touch us. A lot of things happened to us there. We spent a lot of money. We were in court every month for seven years, up until 1985. That happened in 1978."[16] The election of Harold Washington in 1983 would successfully challenge the power of the machine, and, as happened during the Chicago Freedom Movement, activist black ministers were deeply divided over a movement that pushed for racial equality and the dismantling of machine politics.

RELIGION AT THE GRASSROOTS: WASHINGTON'S ELECTORAL INSURGENCY AND CHURCH-BASED ACTIVISM

The 1983 race for mayor pitted incumbent Jane Byrne against States Attorney Richard M. Daley, son of former mayor Richard J. Daley, and Harold Washington, the reform candidate and the first black serious mayoral contender. Each of the three candidates was supported by a cadre of activist black clergy. Most of the ministers who supported Daley or Byrne either symbolically or materially benefited from the Byrne regime, while those who supported Daley hoped to benefit from the patronage ties they had formed under his father. As black voters began to throw their support fully behind Washington's candidacy, the factionalism that had existed among activist black clergy during the Daley years publicly surfaced.

For example, the Reverend Odell White, who pastors the Spirit of Love Baptist Church, favored Richard M. Daley over Harold Washington. He was among the 150 ministers who endorsed Daley. Reverend White felt that the election of black mayors in other cities had caused economic devastation and the election of Washington would do the same for Chicago. "We know what happened in Cleveland, Gary and Detroit. When Mayor Richard Hatcher was elected, the white officials took all the money to Merrillville, Indiana. Gary is now a ghost town." He insisted that Daley would "pull to-gether businesses to generate jobs."

Another Daley supporter, Reverend E. J. Jones of the First Unity Baptist Church, rationalized the group's decision by way of divine guidance: "It is our spiritual insight and my better judgement—and I am not an Uncle Tom, but I believe the homework should be done [on Washington's potential election as mayor]. I guess we got too excited with the extra few thousand voter registration."[17]

The ministerial endorsements for Byrne and Daley did not go unan-swered. In a paid political advertisement in the *Chicago Sun-Times, Chicago Defender,* and the *Westside Journal,* 250 black ministers signed a petition in support of Washington. Referring to other activist ministers as the "splinter group which backs the 'Daley regime' who opposed Dr. [Martin Luther] King" and the "other splinter group which rolls over and plays dead in the face of insult after insult to the Black community from the 'Byrne regime,'" activist clergy for Washington proclaimed that they were "not looking for 'political favors' or plums from the patronage orchard."[18]

Not only did activist ministers for Washington challenge other activist min-isters about their decision to support other candidates, but they also criti-cized those ministers in their Sunday sermons. For example, Reverend Jere-miah Wright, who pastors the Trinity United Church of Christ, preached a sermon titled, "Prophets for Profit," which offered an explanation of what some thought to be the naked self-interest of ministers who endorsed Byrne and Daley:

> There is a predicament common to the profession of preaching and that predicament is the constant recurrence of predators who call themselves prophets. Using the guides of Godliness, the rules of religion and the costume of clergy, they are forever on the prowl and sometimes on the payroll, with their overriding goal of their so-called ministry being how much can I personally get out of it. What is in it for me? In short and in substance, these predators are noth-ing more than prophets for profit. Preachers who got their priorities all mixed up. Professionals who are wired up to the system. Hooked up to the status quo and priests who have lost their capacity for being God's spokesperson because they are tied into money and eating meat from the King's table. They are prophets for profit. They can't hear what God has to say because they are too closely connected with government. Prophets for profits. They can't speak a word of divine judgement against an unjust regime because their salaries are paid by that same regime.[19]

Ministerial support for Washington developed in various ways, and many churches allowed all three candidates to speak before their congregations. For instance, the Westside Ministers' Coalition and Westside Baptist Ministers' Conference sponsored a forum "for scrutiny of candidates in the Mayoral race" where candidates were sent fourteen questions "posed by various Ministers and their Parishioners" that would be covered during the event.[20] Questions covered issues as diverse as affirmative action, neighborhood redevelopment, funding for education, election fraud, and support for lower utility rates. A letter inviting mayoral candidate Harold Washington explained the purpose of the event and specific instructions regarding the structure of the forum: "Our desire is to be informed by your statement of intent as Chief Officer of this City. We are in hope that you will address these questions as fully as possible. We anticipate an attendance of 500. Each candidate will have 15 minutes to make their presentation. After each candidate will have spoken, there will be an additional 15 minutes for the candidates to receive and answer questions."

Similarly, the A.M.E. Ministerial Alliance of Chicago and the Chicago Conference Lay Organization sponsored a forum that included both Democratic and Republican candidates. After a twenty-minute presentation, candidates were asked to take questions from the audience concerning the "school system, delivery of health services, deposits of money in black banks, and the hiring and promotion of blacks in more meaningful jobs and a variety of other social and economic issues."[21]

Ministerial groups were not the only active religious groups backing Washington. Indeed, in many instances church members themselves pushed their ministers to participate in Washington's campaign, as many Southern activists had done during the civil rights movement. In the 1983 mayoral campaign lay organizations independently sponsored candidate forums, providing an opportunity for all three candidates to present their platform to local congregations. One A.M.E. lay organization sponsored a candidates' forum, noting that the event was "not a debate but an opportunity for each candidate to present his/her views."[22] At the Southlawn United Methodist Church on the city's South Side, a candidates' forum became a part of the church's monthly community forum. Sponsored by a lay organization called "church and society," all three of the Democratic primary candidates were invited to "come and share in a ten minute statement and answer questions from concerned voters."[23]

The Reverend Paul Hall invited Washington to speak during his weekly live radio broadcast, stating in a letter to Washington, "The Honorable Mayor Jane Byrne has accepted and we would like to extend this courtesy to you also," adding that if Washington could not make the broadcast, "the invitation is for any Sunday that your schedule will permit."[24] The church and society committee of the Ingleside-Whitfield Church invited Washington to speak during an evening program and noted that a committee member was "a volunteer worker out of your 49th and Wabash Campaign Headquarters."[25]

Other churches and religious groups were even much more explicit about their support for Washington. The minister of the Turner Memorial A.M.E.

Church on the city's South Side requested the appearance of Washington during a weekday evening. Giving Washington a choice of four dates, the Reverend Walter B. Johnson wrote, "We are very interested in seeing Congressman Washington elected Mayor of Chicago and are seeking to aid him in this endeavor." The minister anticipated "a gathering between 50–75 persons and would like him primarily speak to some of the issues that he seeks to tackle during his administration," adding, "Our prayers are with you as you seek to serve us."[26]

An ecumenical group with a spiritual focus, the Chicagoland Christian Women's Conference, invited Washington to "appear before and speak [to] approximately 1,400 Black Women at our Annual Retreat." As the letter stated, the group represented many different churches in the city, informing the candidate: "Our meeting is *not* political in nature, but rather spiritual, therefore if you plan to visit . . . we request you to limit your comments to 10–15 minutes duration." A similar spiritually focused group, the National Black Evangelical Association, an organization "committed to reaching the black community for Christ" and that is "committed to and disciplined by the Scripture," endorsed Washington in a statement that read, "We lament the apparent inconsistency of some other black Christians and churches who have detached themselves from their roots."[27]

After Washington's victory in the primary, support for the candidate through black church-based efforts became even more pronounced. The Park Manor Christian Church, a predominately black middle-class congregation, requested Washington to appear at a church-sponsored rally at the end of a Sunday service, "at which time we are asking members to make a financial contribution to help support the campaign."[28] Dr. Royce D. Cornelius also requested the appearance of Washington at a Sunday evening rally, where "the Pastor and members of Mount Pleasant Missionary Baptist Church are interested in our continued efforts to raise funds for you as a Mayoral candidate."[29] During Washington's run for mayor in 1983 church-based financial contributions to the candidate's campaign were common. These contributions ranged as little as $150 from Allen Temple C.M.E. Church to as large as $3,400 from South Park Baptist Church (see table 7.1 for other campaign contributions).

BLACK MINISTERS, THE SECOND DALEY REGIME, AND COOPTATION IN THE POST-WASHINGTON ERA

The death of Harold Washington in November 1987 splintered both secular and religious leadership in Chicago's black communities, returning Chicago politics back to its patronage-oriented tradition. Washington's election in 1983 and his reelection in 1987 had solidified the support of most religious

Table 7.1.   Contributions to Black Churches from the Richard M. Daley Campaign Committee, 1990–1993

Church	Donation	Year
St. Paul Church of God in Christ*	$5,500	1990
House of the Good Shepherd	$300	1990
Lighthouse Baptist Church*	$200	1990
First Church of Love and Faith*	$500	1990
	$550	1991
	$550	1992
Westside Center of Truth	$500	1991
New Friendship Baptist Church	$200	1991
Quinn Chapel A.M.E. Church*	$200	1993
African American Religious Connection	$400	1990
	$800	1991
	$3,000	1993
*Reverend Clay Evans Testimonial**	$500	1991

*Endorsed Daley in 1995
Source: Illinois Board of Elections.

and secular elites, who were pushed by grassroots activism to support Washington's administration. Patronage was no longer used to woo black ministers to support the regime. Indeed, the Washington administration fired ministers who had been on the city payroll during Byrne's administration.

However, offering symbolic and material incentives to activist black ministers has been revived under the new Daley regime. Because of the deep divisions over which black candidate would succeed Washington, Richard M. Daley was elected mayor over two black candidates in 1989. He has been reelected to office in each mayoral election since then, handily defeating black candidates in the Democratic primary and general elections. In the 1989 special election, Daley only netted 6 percent of the black vote in the April general election against independent candidate Timothy Evans, an alderman who many progressives thought was the appropriate choice to succeed Washington as mayor.

As a political entrepreneur who needed to make inroads into Chicago's black communities, Daley would use political patronage as a way to induce black clergy to support his candidacy and policy goals. Rudy Polk, who worked for Richard J. Daley during the 1960s and was the chief of staff for the former black congressman Gus Savage, was hired by the mayor to assist him with generating goodwill with Chicago blacks. Polk offered to help black ministers fund church-based social services, finance building initiatives, acquire vacant lots owned by the city, and lobby city and state agencies for various concerns. Reverend Joseph Wells, pastor of Mt. Pisgah Missionary Baptist Church, supported Jane Byrne in the 1983 mayoral election because she made a $5,000 contribution to an African Relief Fund: "This time I owed her because she cared enough to help those black babies in Africa."[30]

By 1989 Wells had switched his support to Richard M. Daley because he claimed being always "devoted to the Daleys." Richard J. Daley helped Mt. Pisgah pay off its $168,000 mortgage by renting the church for social service programs in the 1960s and 1970s. This time around Wells was seeking support for the church's $100,000-a-year food bank, which feeds residents in the Grand Boulevard neighborhood, one of Chicago's poorest neighborhoods. As Wells explains, "Rudy Polk can help the mayor if [Daley] empowers him to get funding for programs that help blacks. Right now I have to turn the city upside-down just to get a free case of pork and beans for my people."[31]

The actions of activist ministers such as Reverend Wells are not surprising. Wells comes from a tradition of activist clergy who have worked within the context of patronage-style politics, a strategy that he continues to employ even in the post-Washington era of Chicago politics. Again, clergy who employ this strategy exchange their support of vote-seeking elites for material and symbolic rewards for themselves and/or their congregations. Not only did Reverend Wells receive funding from the city for his social service programs, Daley also granted a symbolic gift to Wells by renaming a city street in the pastor's honor.

What is new about activist clergy under the new Daley regime is the convergence of old foes. Some ministers who were activists during the Chicago Freedom Movement and the Harold Washington campaigns have collaborated with patronage-oriented ministers who opposed or remained silent during the Freedom Movement and Washington's 1983 bid for mayor.

Contributions made from the Richard M. Daley Campaign Committee to black churches and ministers are revealing. Listed as "campaign expenses" in the Illinois Board of Elections campaign disclosure forms, nine black churches or ministerial groups received funding from the mayor's campaign coffers between 1990 and 1993 (see table 7.1). Of those nine, five endorsed Daley over two black candidates in 1995 (see table 7.2). The Reverend Clay Evans, who was punished by the machine for his participation in the Chicago Freedom Movement and whose church was an enthusiastic supporter of Washington in 1983 (see table 7.3), is also a beneficiary of the new Daley regime. The Daley campaign committee contributed $500 in 1991 to the "Reverend Clay Evans Testimonial" and $4,200 between 1990 and 1993 to the African American Religious Connection, an ecumenical group headed by Reverend Evans (See table 7.1).

The late Louis Ford, who was pastor of the St. Paul Church of God in Christ and who was the former presiding bishop of the Church of God in Christ, also appears to have been induced by patronage. Although Reverend Ford did not endorse Harold Washington, his church financially contributed to the candidate's campaign in 1983 (see table 7.3). In 1990 the Daley campaign committee contributed $5,500 to Bishop Ford's church. The bishop signed on with fifty black ministers who called themselves the

132   *Fredrick C. Harris*

Table 7.2. Black Ministers Who Endorsed Richard M. Daley in 1995

Minister	Church
Bishop Arthur Brazier	Apostolic Church of God
Reverend Wilber Daniels	Antioch Missionary Baptist Church
Reverend Clay Evans+	Fellowship Missionary Baptist Church
Reverend Leon Finney+	Christ Apostolic Church of God
Bishop Louis Ford+	St. Paul Church of God in Christ
Reverend George Henderson	Greater Garfield Missionary Baptist Church
Reverend Charles Murray+	New Galilee Missionary Baptist Church
Reverend Louis Rawls	Tabernacle Baptist Church
Reverend Addie Wyatt+	
Reverend Willie Upshire	Prince of Peace Baptist Church
Reverend Joseph Wells	Mt. Pisgah Missionary Baptist Church
Reverend Ben Butler	First Steadfast Baptist Church
Reverend George Butler	Haven Rest Baptist Church
Reverend Floyd Davis	Pilgram Baptist Church
Reverend Leonard Deville	Alpha Temple Missionary Baptist Church
Reverend Joseph E. Felker	Mt. Carmel Baptist Church
Reverend W. H. Foster	Pleasant Grove Baptist Church
Reverend J. Goodloe	Lighthouse Baptist Church
Reverend Lucius Hall	First Church of Love and Faith
Reverend Thomas Jackson	New Original Church of God in Christ
Reverend E. J. Jones	First Unity Baptist Church
Reverend Joseph Jones	Pleasant Grove Baptist Church
Bishop J. Hasko Mayo	4th Episcopal District of the African Methodist Episcopal Church
Dr. Johnny Miller	Mt. Vernon Baptist Church
Reverend O. C. Morgan	Evening Star Baptist Church
Dr. O. E. Piper	First Baptist Institutional Church of Lawndale
Reverend Willie Runnels	New Zion City Baptist Church
Reverend Phelmon Saunders	Quinn Chapel African Methodist Episcopal Church
Father Martini Shaw	St. Thomas Episcopal Church
Reverend Millard F. Southern	St. Paul African Methodist Episcopal Church
Dr. Amos Waller	Mercy Seat Baptist Church
Reverend Issac Whittmon	Greater Metropolitan Church of Christ
Reverend Charles B. Williams	Unity Fellowship Missionary Baptist Church
Reverend Marvell Williams	New Mt. Moriah Missionary Baptist Church

+Leading clergy who supported Washington in 1983 and 1987
Source: Endorsement Letter, Coalition of Concerned Clergy for Chicago, 1 January 1995.

Coalition of Concerned Clergy of Chicago. They endorsed Daley in 1995. Similarly, other ministers who received "contributions" from the Daley campaign also endorsed the mayor in 1995: Reverend J. Goodloe of the Lighthouse Baptist Church, Reverend Lucius Hall of the First Church of Love and Faith, and Reverend Phelmon Saunders of the Quinn Chapel A.M.E. Church. The endorsement of some activist ministers such as Reverend Wilber Daniels is not a surprise, given that minister's explicit endorsement of patronage pol-

Table 7.3.   Congregational and Ministerial Contributions to Harold Washington's 1983 Mayoral Campaign

Church/Minister	Donation
Fellowship Missionary Baptist Church	$300
First Baptist Church of Melrose	$1,000
First A.M.E. Church of Los Angeles	$350
Greater Mt. Eagle Baptist Church	$500
Greater Mt. Olive Missionary Baptist Church	$700
Life Center Church of Universal Awareness	$300
Mt. Calvary Baptist Church	$1,550
Mt. Pleasant Baptist Church	$300
Mt. Sinai Baptist Church	$250
New Gresham United Methodist Church	$200
Original Providence Baptist Church	$320
Park Manor Christian Church	$300
St. Mark United Methodist Church	$925
St. Paul C.M.E. Church	$512.83
St. Stephen A.M.E. Church	$325
The Calvary Baptist Church	$300
Trinity C.M.E. Church	$150
Union Baptist Church	$350
Union Hill Baptist Church	$213
United Methodist Women	$521.88
South Park Baptist Church	$3,400
St. James A.M.E. Church	$300
Bethlehem Healing Temple	$1,000
Bishop H. Hartford Brookins of the A.M.E. Church (Los Angeles)	$150
Baptist Ministers Conference of Chicago and Vicinity	$200
Berean Baptist Church	$365
St. Mark United Methodist	$405
St. Paul Church of God In Christ	$300
Oakdale Covenant Church	$200
Tabernacle Missionary Baptist Church	$800
First Baptist Church Relief Fund	$1,000
Second Baptist Church of Evanston	$513.80
Reverend Henry Hardy	$1,000
Dr. Arthur Brazier	$1,000
Reverend Eugene Gray	$1,000
Reverend Nathaniel Jarrett	$800

Source: Committee to Elect Harold Washington Mayor of the City of Chicago, 1983, State of Illinois Board of Elections.

itics and his silence during the Washington campaigns. On the other hand, the Daley support from traditionally reform-oriented clerical activists, such as Reverend Clay Evans, Reverend Addie Wyatt, Reverend William Upshire, Reverend Charles Murray, and Reverend George Henderson, suggests the development of a convergence between two traditional yet historically opposing groups of black activist clergy.

Despite these defections from the reform-oriented wing of black clergy, other reform-oriented clergy, as they had done during the 1983 mayoral election, protested against ministers' endorsement of Daley. A group called the Committee Against Plantation Politics attempted to alert church members of their minister's support of the Daley administration. Lay leaders received the following letter:

> As you know, your pastor is a member of the Coalition of Concerned Clergy for Chicago. Enclosed is proof that he is endorsing the candidacy and reelection of Richard M. Daley as Mayor of the City of Chicago. . . . It is our devout opinion that your pastor is a "Sell Out Preacher." As an African-American minister [your pastor] is taking advantage of his position as a trusted leader in the community and as head of your church he is falsely leading his flock.[32]

Two of the ministers who endorsed Daley had their church picketed by activists. With placards that read "Did God tell you to vote for Richie Daley?" activists marched in front of Bishop Arthur Brazier's Apostolic Church of God and Reverend Clay Evans's Fellowship Missionary Baptist Church.[33] Whether the defection of reform-oriented clergy signals a consolidation of two streams of the civic activism among black clergy remains to be seen. Of course, the alignment of reform-oriented black clergy with the Daley regime potentially indicates the growing black support of the Daley administration. Indeed, the Daley regime has many symbolic and material incentives to convert potential opposition to support, if it chooses to do so. Perhaps another insurgency for black empowerment in Chicago's black communities will realign the traditional strict boundaries between reform- and patronage-oriented clergy.

NOTES

1. Katherine Tate, *From Protest to Politics: The New Black Voters in American Elections* (Cambridge: Harvard University Press, 1993); Allison Calhoun-Brown, "African-American Churches and Political Mobilization: The Psychological Impact of Organizational Resources," *Journal of Politics* 58, no. 4 (1996): 935–53; Fredrick C. Harris, *Something Within: Religion in African-American Political Activism* (New York: Oxford University Press, 1999).

2. Harold Gosnell, *Negro Politicians: The Rise of Negro Politics in Chicago* (1935; repr., Chicago: University of Chicago Press, 1967), 95–96.

3. Quoted from Gosnell, *Negro Politicians*, 96–97n10. Originally published in *Whip* 3 (March 1928).

4. James Q. Wilson, *Negro Politics: The Search for Leadership* (New York: Free Press, 1960), 127.

5. Vernon Jarrett, "'Hired' Preachers Don't Always Win Votes," *Chicago Sun-Times*, 20 December 1988.

6. Grant Pick, "Daniel in the Loins' Den," *Chicago Reader*, 25 July 1980.

7. Pick, "Daniel in the Loins' Den."

8. Pick, "Daniel in the Loins' Den."

9. James R. Ralph Jr., *Northern Protest: Martin Luther King, Jr., Chicago, and the Civil Rights Movement* (Cambridge: Harvard University Press, 1993).

10. Ralph, *Northern Protest*, 204.

11. Dempsey J. Travis, *An Autobiography of Black Politics* (Chicago: Urban Research Press, 1987), 354.

12. Travis, *Autobiography of Black Politics*, 355.

13. Interview with A. Patterson Jackson, 14 November 1990.

14. Barnaby Dinges, "Mayor Daley Courting Black Ministers," *Chicago Reporter*, December 1989.

15. Dinges, "Mayor Daley Courting Black Ministers."

16. Claude Wyatt, "Formative Events in the Life of Harold Washington As Told by a Friend," in *The Black Church and the Harold Washington Story*, ed. Henry J. Young (Bristol, Indiana: Wyndham Hall Press, 1988).

17. Mitchell Locin and Jane Fritsch, "Black Clergy for Washington Hit Pro-Daley Colleagues," *Chicago Tribune*, 13 January 1983.

18. "The Black Church Supports Harold Washington for Mayor!!!," *Chicago Sun-Times*, 12 February 1983.

19. "Prophets For Profit," Dr. Jeremiah A. Wright Jr., Trinity United Church for Christ, 18 April 1982, cassette tape.

20. Reverend W. L. Upshire of the Prince of Peace M. B. Church to Harold Washington, 29 January 1983, Harold Washington Papers, box 35, Harold Washington Library, Chicago, Illinois.

21. "Mayor 'debate' scheduled for Bethel church," Newspaper clipping, box 35, n.d., Harold Washington Papers.

22. Evelyn N. Jefferson, President of Chicago Conference of the Laymen Organization for the African Methodist Episcopal Church, to Harold Washington, 22 December 1982 and 3 January 1983, box 35, Harold Washington Papers.

23. Dr. Donald Linder, chair, church and society of Southlawn United Methodist Church, 10 January 1983, box 35, Harold Washington Papers.

24. Reverend Paul Hall, Paul Hall Boys Club Community Services, to Harold Washington, c/o Ms. Velma Wilson, 19 January 1983, box 35, Harold Washington Papers.

25. Mrs. Laverne Bean, chairperson of the church and society committee of the Ingelside-Whitfield United Methodist Church, to Harold Washington, 6 January 1983, box 35, Harold Washington Papers.

26. Reverend Walter B. Johnson Jr., Turner Memorial African Methodist Episcopal Church, to Ms. Wilson, 20 January 1983, box 35, Harold Washington Papers.

27. Statement of Endorsement of the Candidacy of Harold Washington, National Black Evangelical Association—Chicago Chapter, box 36, Harold Washington Papers.

28. E. Toy Fletcher, Park Manor Christian Church, to Harold Washington, 28 February 28, 1983, box 36, Harold Washington Papers.

29. Dr. Royce D. Cornelius, pastor of the Mount Pleasant Missionary Baptist Church, to Harold Washington, 28 February 1983, box 37, Harold Washington Papers.

30. Travis, *Autobiography of Black Politics*, 581.

31. Dinges, "Mayor Daley Courting Black Ministers."

32. Citizens against the Coalition of Concerned Clergy of Chicago, 14 February 1995.

33. Chinta Strausberg, "Ministers Catch Heat for Backing Daley," *Chicago Defender*, 13 February 1995.

8

Black Clergy Electoral Involvement in Cleveland

Mittie Olion Chandler

There has been a seemingly immutable connection between the black community and black churches that has compelled ministers toward varying forms of political involvement. The present chapter outlines ways Cleveland's black clergy have impacted local electoral affairs, both as political brokers and as political candidates. By looking specifically at the involvement of black clergy in the political campaigns of Carl Stokes, Michael White, and Marvin McMickle, the chapter explores (1) the role of individual clergy in political pursuits; (2) the overlapping role of individual and collective political action through ministerial alliances; (3) the limitations of race-based endorsements when more than one black candidate is seeking an office; and (4) the unique issues that arise when an African American member of the clergy runs for office. The chapter argues that, while by no means universally involved in politics, Cleveland's black clergy have an especially strong legacy of political involvement that has been expressed through both individual and collective activism by these clergy.

BLACK CLERGY ACTIVISM IN CLEVELAND

A cadre of black clergy within Cleveland has been extensively involved in local political and social activism for decades. Ministers of Cleveland's Antioch Baptist Church were active in the NAACP and other organizations during the 1950s and 1960s. Reverend Horace Bailey Wade, minister of Antioch Baptist Church from 1903 to 1923, was a founder of the Cleveland NAACP.[1] Reverend Wade H. McKinney, Antioch's minister from 1928 to 1963, who was president of the Cleveland Baptist Association and the Cuyahoga Interdenominational

Ministerial Alliance, was the first black foreman of a Cuyahoga County grand jury, helped spearhead the Future Outlook League and the Cleveland Business League, and served on the Mayor's Committee under Mayor Frank Lausche.[2] Reverend Odie Millard Hoover, at the Olivet Institutional Baptist Church from 1952 to 1974, was on the board of the Southern Christian Leadership Conference.[3] He brought Reverend Dr. Martin Luther King and Reverend Jesse Jackson to the city during the turbulent sixties despite the fact that King and Jackson were generally not well-received by other local ministers. Reverend Marvin McMickle, who succeeded Reverend McKinney at Antioch, and Reverend Otis Moss, who succeeded Reverend Hoover at Olivet, maintained the activist tradition. Cleveland ministers have also sought or held political offices in Cleveland.

Cleveland's black clergy have also worked collectively through ministerial alliances, such as the Baptist Minister's Council and the Methodist Ministers Alliance, to produce the third strand of political participation. Black and white candidates have sought and continue to seek endorsements from the ministerial alliances extant in Cleveland at any given time. Some alliances have existed longer than others, but all hold or have held the promise of a voting bloc for endorsed candidates. Currently, Reverend McMickle heads United Pastors in Mission and Reverend Theophilus Caviness of Greater Abyssinia Baptist Church heads the Baptist Minister's Conference. Individual and collective political activism have combined in interesting ways in political campaigns over the last thirty-five years in Cleveland.

Carl Stokes and the Vital Electoral Role of Clergy

Black churches and their leaders, individually and collectively, surfaced as influential in electoral politics in the mid-1960s when Carl and Louis Stokes emerged as major political figures winning elections as mayor and congressman, respectively. Their campaigns and elections marked a new era for political participation within the black population—in both the secular and religious communities. With concerted voter registration and get-out-the-vote drives, the ability of the black community to influence the outcome of major elections was revealed. Black churches asserted themselves as vehicles for political action—reaching out to the community, serving as a gathering place for meetings and rallies, providing forums for candidates and their platforms, and compelling their members to participate politically and to vote. The two campaigns of Carl Stokes, particularly, provided a springboard for individual ministers and ministerial alliances to exercise political clout in subsequent decades.

The election of Carl Stokes marked a high point for black politics and the influence of the black church in politics in Cleveland. Clergy members were very involved in the voter mobilization that grounded Carl Stokes's 1967 campaign. Reverend John T. Weeden, head of the black Baptist Ministerial

Alliance (BMA), and Reverend Milan Brenkis, a white west side minister, led an interdenominational group of ministers who put together a voter registration drive in the black, Puerto Rican, and Appalachian communities. Historically, Puerto Rican and Appalachian households have resided primarily on the city's west side while blacks lived on the east side. By the time of the election, blacks were registered more solidly than whites.[4] What the Democratic Party failed to provide as a base for the Stokes campaign, the black church provided. Through the churches, Stokes was able to reach people on the black and white sides of town.

The unity and solidarity shown by the black clergy in Cleveland during the Stokes years are legend. However, even during those days when the black clergy seemed most galvanized and unified, there was dissension from within and without. When the church of Reverend O. M. Hoover, Olivet Institutional Baptist Church, provided Reverend Dr. Martin Luther King Jr. with his Cleveland base of operations, Dr. King's activism was apparently not well received throughout the black community. Stokes himself was worried about how overt support from Dr. King would affect the tenuous support from the white community. In *Promises of Power,* Stokes discussed the efforts of United Pastors, "a dozen ministers involved in an internal struggle with other ministers who were trying to establish their own community leadership," who invited Dr. King to Cleveland during the campaign. King limited his visits in response to Stokes's dilemma and curtailed his activities. Later, Stokes had to deal with a small group of black leaders from the Southern Christian Leadership Conference (SCLC) movement who were aware of his reservations about Dr. King's participation.[5]

After Stokes was elected, ministers were also important in his administration. He marshaled the political activism of black ministers, placed them in various capacities during his administration, sought counsel with them frequently, and treated them as adjunct to city hall.[6] Stokes appointed ministers to boards and commissions during his tenure in office (including the planning commission, building commission, and civil service commission). He appointed Reverend Arthur LeMon, from the Baptist Ministerial Alliance, as director of the Community Relations Board. Stokes recognized members of the Baptist Ministerial Alliance and other black and white religious organizations as the most important groups in his efforts to build white and black coalitions and politicize the poor in Cleveland.[7]

The engaged black churches and clergy remained politically viable after peaking in the 1960s and 1970s. The BMA, instrumental during the Stokes election, no longer exists, but other ministerial groups have been organized and are still active. Their effectiveness is due to a combination of individual and collective cachet that is difficult to separate. The cohesiveness of purpose among clergy and religious groups, however, did not persist through the 1980s and 1990s when the next African American mayor was elected.

Michael White and the Practical Politics of Clergy

Michael White served three four-year terms as mayor of Cleveland. His first election was the most difficult and he was not expected to win. He and George Forbes survived the primary field of five candidates made up of two blacks and three whites to run in the general election. Forbes had been a city council member for twenty-six years; seventeen of those years he was the city council president. White also served on the city council for seven years and in the Ohio Senate for five years. Forbes had been a mentor to White earlier in his career.

Observers expected that a black candidate and a white candidate would emerge from the mayoral primary based on past racial bloc voting and the population breakdown of almost equal numbers of black and white residents in the city at that time. When two black candidates moved on to the general election, White became the default candidate for many whites in the city. Over the years, a racially antagonistic relationship developed between Forbes and a large part of the white populace.

The usual black churches, ministers, and alliances were involved in the primary and general elections. Most of the politically active black clergy groups and ministers supported George Forbes as expected. Black churches had benefited from his actions as the powerful city council president. Some notable exceptions to those who backed Forbes included Reverend McMickle, who became a confidante to White during his first mayoral race, Reverend Sterling Glover, and Reverend Eugene Ward.

Michael White also struck a chord with some usually inactive churches. A group of about sixty primarily Protestant black ministers, led by Reverend Ward, a Baptist minister, supported Mike White from the fringes during the primary election. Afterward, Reverend Ward reached out to persons of other faiths, including Muslims, Jews, Catholics, and white clergy on both sides of town. Reverend Ward supported White as a spiritual undertaking because he believed that God's providence was over the election and portrayed the scenario as David versus Goliath.[8] In addition, candidate White frequented churches on Sundays, particularly those that had supported Forbes. With 30 percent of the black vote and 95 percent of the white vote, Michael White was elected mayor of Cleveland, and he became Cleveland's longest serving mayor for a total of twelve years.

White's electoral coalition did not withstand his years in office. He appointed Ward as a chaplain and special assistant where he remained until 1996, leaving the administration on sour terms. Ward became gradually disenchanted with White after he connected with mainline black clergy and groups that had initially supported his opponent. This sense of being cast aside discouraged some black clergy, making them cautious about participating in electoral politics.[9] In forming their governing coalitions, elected officials may not satisfy the expectations of their electoral coalitions.[10] Governing coalitions are formed for a different purpose—to expand the base for future elections—and may exclude some early supporters. The sense that he abandoned one group to appeal to another plagued White throughout his tenure in office.

When White ran the second time in 1993, he had no opposition and the support he received from the black clergy was perfunctory. The only candidate who opposed him was a novice described by the local media as a nonentity. White received 85 percent of the vote in the ten wards represented by black council members and 75 percent of the vote in the eleven wards represented by white council members. He was at the peak of his popularity going into the second term.

White's third campaign bore the effects of racial politics, which surfaced again when he faced Helen Smith, a white former city council member. His support had eroded among the grassroots clergy from the first campaign and he had the cursory backing of the clergy groups. The campaign strategy revealed by his campaign manager included several groups but not black churches. Instead, perhaps because they took the black vote for granted, voters casting absentee ballots (e.g., seniors residing in public housing) and west side voters were targeted. The strategy was a personal one—using phone calls and door-to-door contacts in low-income and blue-collar neighborhoods. Ultimately, the desired results were achieved as White won the general election with 60 percent of the vote. The significance of race was shown as Smith carried ten of the eleven wards represented by white council members. White lost the eleventh ward in the primary election, but picked it up in the general election. This downtown ward is where some of the city's young professionals that are more likely to rebuff racial appeals reside.

After winning the general election in 1989 with heavy support from whites, Michael White was labeled "White Mike" by detractors who believed that he catered to the white community. When White oversaw the successful negotiations to build sports facilities downtown, he was accused of neglecting the neighborhoods although his policies generated an unprecedented number of new housing starts. Particularly in his last term, Mayor White received much criticism about his management style and personality. Generally, though, he maintained a high level of popular appeal.

Toward the end of his tenure as mayor, White claimed to have appointed more ministers to boards and commissions that any of his predecessors. Among the most visible were Reverend Ward, who also chaired the Police Review Board, and Reverend Glover, who White appointed to the Cleveland Cuyahoga County Port Authority. White suggested the purpose of maintaining his relationship with the clergy when he said they are "the people in our neighborhood, with the most direct knowledge of residents and their problems."[11]

The *Cleveland Plain Dealer* disclosed that Mayor White maintained a list of 121 people who received faxes and news releases from the mayor when he wanted to get the word out. Using this list, it appears that White maintained his connections with the clergy, particularly the black clergy, for strategic purposes even if they were not among his key advisors. Twenty-seven clerics and religious activists were included: one was Republican, twenty-one were black, seventeen were Baptist, one was Jewish, two were westsiders (the area where most whites live in the city).[12] One could attach much or little significance to the list. Six of the African Americans who head politically active churches were also on the fax distribution list of Republican Governor Bob Taft. They obviously provide critical points of contact in the African American community but it is not clear that they were particularly close to Mayor White. White's actions and statements suggested that he was acutely aware of the role of ministers in the political success of all public officials—black and white.

The ecumenical group of clergy who supported Michael White's election was not maintained during his years as mayor. The backing of west side clergy may have been situational—when there was no viable west side/white candidate. Over the years, support for White became more nuanced. Some black clergy were clearly not supportive of the mayor's stances but appreciated the opportunity to communicate with him.

Marvin McMickle: Minister as Candidate

The 1994 campaign in which Reverend Marvin McMickle ran for the U.S. House of Representatives exposed crosscutting cleavages among the black religious community in Cleveland. Reverend McMickle's church is in the heart of inner-city Cleveland where the political interests of ministers, congregations, and individual church members intersect. Reverend Marvin McMickle was one of five candidates who sought the Democratic nomination in 1994 to replace Congressman Louis Stokes, who stepped down after thirty years of service. The winner of the Democratic primary was assured victory in the racially diverse, but solidly Democratic, district. Besides McMickle, there were two other strong candidates—Stephanie Tubbs Jones and Jeffrey Johnson. All three aspirants had prior political experience.

Stephanie Tubbs Jones was viewed as the heir apparent to the position. Congressman Stokes supported her in this and previous races. When she announced her plans to run for Congress, Jones was in her seventh year as Cuyahoga County prosecutor. After holding judgeships at the municipal and county levels for ten years, she had a broader base of support and wider name recognition than her opponents. Although not always victorious,

Jones's name had appeared six times on countywide ballots. She also ran unsuccessfully statewide for the Ohio Supreme Court. A popular and well-regarded public official, Jones received most of the major endorsements in the congressional primary, including that of the Cuyahoga County Democratic Party. Jones is a member of Bethany Baptist Church where the minister, the late Reverend Albert Rowan, consistently backed her political pursuits and had strong political contacts that included Reverend Caviness.

Jeffrey Johnson held public office for fourteen years before this campaign. He served on the Cleveland City Council for eight years and as an Ohio state senator for six years. Johnson's fortunes in the campaign were dashed by an indictment handed down just two weeks after announcing his candidacy that charged him with using his office to extort funds in violation of the federal Hobbs Act.[13] Throughout the campaign, he denied the charges and questioned the unfavorable timing of the allegations. Johnson was a lifetime member of Caviness's Greater Abyssinia Baptist Church. On the basis of that membership, Caviness claimed allegiance to Johnson during the campaign; however, the Baptist Minister's Conference (BMC) did not officially endorse a candidate. Some clergy members, including McMickle, showed moral support for Johnson after the indictment. The most outspoken, visible ministers in repudiating the charges were less well known and influential than the conventional leaders. Johnson was convicted after the election and incarcerated.

Reverend McMickle was the least experienced politician among the three top candidates. He was first elected to the Shaker Heights School Board in 1993 and later served as its president. He was also president of the Cleveland NAACP Chapter from 1989 to 1992. As a congressional candidate, McMickle developed a platform of the eight E's: employment, education, economic development, elderly, environment, equal opportunity, enforcement of the law, and enlargement. He secured the endorsement of the United Pastors in Mission (UPIM) although not all members lent their personal support. Some members of his church expressed misgivings about his candidacy.

The local media portrayed the contest as positive and cordial since there were no personal smears and character attacks. By some accounts, McMickle and Johnson appeared more knowledgeable about the issues than Jones at the outset, but Jones became more impressive as the campaign proceeded.[14] Jones won the primary handily with more than 51 percent of the votes cast and easily defeated the Republican and independent candidates in the general election. What the election revealed most was that the black religious community in Cleveland was not ready for a clergy member as politician.

Before running for office, Reverend McMickle and previous ministers of Antioch operated in the activist tradition without incident. As a candidate for elective office, however, McMickle faced the challenge of his limited involvement with Democratic Party machinery politics in the city and the county. When compared with the other candidates for the congressional seat who were not only involved with the party but the Black Elected Democrats of Cleveland, Ohio, his party affiliation was almost nonexistent. His two major competitors were considered among the most prominent black politicians in the county. Further, McMickle is not a Cleveland native, and, while active in the community, he does not command the sense of loyalty or allegiance that connected the Stokes brothers and others to the black electorate. Another obstacle to McMickle's successful candidacy was his opposition to the Million Man March. McMickle objected to the march's goals and to some of its organizers.[15] The result for McMickle was that his stance ostracized him from people in the Muslim community and the larger black community who viewed the march as a worthwhile gathering of mostly black men.

McMickle also encountered opposition to his candidacy among members of his congregation and among United Pastors in Mission. This opposition stemmed from questions about the appropriateness of ministers seeking political office. If the electorate were troubled by ministers running for office as a potential violation of church and state, the sentiment was riddled with contradictions. Black churches were so integral to the primary race that the *Plain Dealer* declared that the primary "was played out largely in black churches."[16]

McMickle asserts that the majority of black clergy were not supportive of his campaign in any substantive way, concluding that their reaction was due to an erroneous interpretation of the doctrine of church and state and to doubts about his ability to effectively serve as a member of Congress and as head of a large church simultaneously. He iterated, to no avail, the historic role of the black clergy in politics, recounted the fact that nine black clergy members have served in Congress in the past thirty years, and cited the experiences of black clergy who had ostensibly managed to maintain their ministerial responsibilities at the same time. Political clout in the black church is more diffuse now than thirty-five years ago. Comparing the involvement of the black church during the Carl Stokes era and the McMickle candidacy, clearly the black church played prominent but different roles in both. The black church was solidly behind Stokes and propelled him to victory. In the 1998 congressional campaign, competition for the predominantly black vote was played out largely in churches, but the collective clout of the ministers, however, was fragmented and moderated by the bigger political picture that included the ministerial alliances.

THE COLLECTIVE INFLUENCE OF MINISTERIAL ASSOCIATIONS

Despite the diversity and fragmentation among the black churches in Cleveland in the 1990s, black churches remained the most stable and independent organizations in the black community. As such, the black churches and black church leaders have been minimally effective in garnering respect among politicians and influencing public policy. Ministerial alliances have the potential to maximize the united political clout of the clergy. Among several groups in the city, two ministerial groups are most influential in endorsing political candidates and issues.

Baptist Minister's Conference: Strength in Leadership

Formed in 1910, the Baptist Minister's Conference (BMC) has three major functions. With fifty to sixty members, the BMC is the more traditional stalwart ministerial alliance. In addition to providing training for ministers who have not received formal education, BMC provides a platform for candidates running for public office to address several pastors at once and to seek their endorsement. Third, the organization considers public policy issues brought forward including those placed on the ballot. The BMC is the traditional black-only Baptist group primarily dominated by one person. Its power is found within the potential influence of its large membership. The BMC is readily identified with its leader, Reverend Emmett Theophilus Caviness, and its candidate screening function. A symbiotic relationship exists between Reverend Caviness and BMC—neither would be as secure without the other.

Reverend Caviness is one of the most political and outspoken ministers in Cleveland. His strength is grounded in longevity with the Greater Abyssinia Baptist Church where he has served as minister since 1961. In addition, he has experience in the secular political world beginning with an appointment to the Cleveland City Council in 1974—the first clergy member to serve. He has served on the Sewer District Board of Trustees and as executive assistant to Republican Mayor George Voinovich, acting as liaison to the Cleveland Public Schools, black ministers, and the city council. He helped Voinovich to increase his share of the black vote from 15 percent when he ran for mayor the first time to 85 percent the last time he ran for mayor. Reportedly, Voinovich received 40 percent of the black vote in his runs for statewide office as governor.[17] Until recently, Reverend Caviness chaired the Ohio Civil Rights Commission as an appointee of a Republican governor.

Reverend Caviness has the ability to build consensus and assuage contentious parties. He has forged links with members of the Democratic and Republican parties that have enabled him to secure employment for church members. He also employs his association with judges to intercede for youth faced with criminal prosecution. The church owns a $3 million senior citizens' complex located close to the church. The *Plain Dealer* reported that he supported each congressional candidate in the race to replace Louis Stokes. In reality, the ministerial group deferred to what other operatives (the unions, Congressman Stokes, Democratic Party) wanted—Stephanie Tubbs Jones. In this case, lack of overt action to the contrary was a show of approval for the preferred candidate.

United Pastors in Mission: In Pursuit of Diversity

The United Pastors in Mission (UPIM) is considered more progressive than the BMC although some clergy are members of both alliances. It was founded about fourteen years ago, drawing upon the vestiges of another 1960s-era ministerial group—United Pastors. Former participants in United Pastors are among the founding members of UPIM. Another predecessor organization, the Interdenominational Ministerial Alliance, apparently no longer exists. UPIM was primarily made up of black Baptist ministers initially but expanded to include an interdenominational and interracial membership. The membership remains about 80 percent African American, but it encompasses a wider segment of the community: suburban and urban, Protestant and Catholic (over a dozen denominations), and the east and west sides of the area. Eighty pastors are affiliated who represent more than fifty thousand congregants.

Ostensibly, the organization uses its broader base of support to pursue social justice issues. Racial reconciliation is an underlying theme for the membership. Black clergy with high public profiles within Cleveland are predominantly Baptist—with Marvin McMickle functioning as a primary spokesperson. Reverend McMickle is chairman and Reverend Larry Macon (minister of Mt. Zion Baptist Church in Oakwood) is president of UPIM. Conventional wisdom is that the Baptist members dominate the organization and its agenda.

The membership includes younger, more progressive ministers who some believe represent the changing of the guard. Compared with the BMC, the members are more educated with college degrees including doctorates.[18] An influential UPIM member, Reverend C. Jay Matthews, leads Mt. Sinai Baptist Church, which touts strong political underpinnings. John O. Holley, founder of the Future Outlook League (FOL) in the 1960s, was a Mt. Sinai member. The FOL successfully brought economic pressures to bear on Cleveland-area businesses to hire black employees.

UPIM members advance political stances collectively and individually. In 1996, UPIM supported Governor George Voinovich by taking a stance against two casino gambling proposals although they threw him a curve in opposing all forms of wagering including the state-sponsored lottery and expanded horse racing.[19] The ministers decided to oppose gambling after a meeting with the governor where they laid forth their issues, which included more black appointees to state boards and commissions, shoring up the state's affirmative action laws, and amending state proficiency testing policy to allow failing students to graduate with a full diploma. UPIM members constantly admonish blacks to vote—a move significantly short of the ubiquitous efforts of the 1960s when the churches organized van pools and transported voters to the polls.

With a large and multifaceted membership, UPIM decisions are not always unanimous. This was conspicuously clear when the campaigns by Reverend McMickle for Congress and Senate were not unanimously supported. In a similar vein, it is not always clear when members are speaking for themselves or for the organization. For example, when Reverend McMickle and Reverend Moss called upon Congress to abandon efforts to impeach President Clinton, UPIM was not mentioned, although the two pastors are clearly associated with the alliance.

UPIM supported state legislation that placed control of the Cleveland Public Schools in the hands of Mayor Michael White in 1997 for a trial period of four years. The ministers opined that the plan would restore accountability and local control to the district. Some segments of the community—including the local NAACP branch and the Cleveland Teachers' Union—vehemently opposed implementation of the plan without input from voters. When some state legislators spoke against the plan, suggesting that it gave the mayor too much power and took the democratic process away from the people, UPIM issued an ultimatum that lawmakers who did not meet with the group and/or support the plan might not be well received at the churches in the future. Two UPIM ministers served on the advisory board that developed the plan (Reverend Moss and Reverend Larry Harris). Reverend Larry Harris went on to serve on the eleven-person nominating committee that recommended applicants to the mayor for appointment to the school board.

REFLECTIONS ON CHURCH ACTIVISM, BOUNDARIES, AND TENSIONS

A number of contemporary black churches in Cleveland have legacies of political activism that build in important ways on long-standing traditions of congregational activism. Other ministers have carved individual niches for themselves in various political venues using their access to help establish the social standing of their churches while improving conditions in their communities. Ministerial alliances have also provided means for collective action among the clergy—although much of the political energy seems directed toward the individual goals of a minister or a congregation. Clergy activism in Cleveland has been highly visible and has produced both celebration and concerns.

Concerns have been related to the fact that public office holding and electioneering on the part of black clergy have sometimes resulted in conflicting interests and divided allegiances among clergy. Reverend Caviness, for example, worked for Republicans at the local and state level while the majority of black ministers and clergy are Democrats. In addition, as head of the Baptist Minister's Conference he was in an awkward position when a church member, a fellow clergyman, and a popular career politician sought BMC endorsement. Just as all black ministers were not supportive of civil rights activities at the national level,[20] black ministers in Cleveland have not been consistently mobilized around political goals or candidates. Black ministers have fallen on opposite sides of activities that constituted major milestones in the pursuit of equality. Black clergy opposed and supported efforts to boycott segregated streets in Southern states at the turn of the century. Some black ministers and ministerial groups opposed unionization efforts in the North, particularly in Chicago and Detroit.[21]

As the black electorate has more viable political options, the black clergy may be less unified in its support of particular candidates. Certainly, when more than one candidate is African American with clear commitment to the black community, some other basis of decision making must prevail. Reed suggests that the post–civil rights era is characterized by the emergence of competing criteria for the legitimization of claims to black leadership and the deepening socioeconomic stratification among African Americans.[22] The result of these divisive elements may be a candidate who has more difficulty mobilizing the community. Beyond racial identity, other criteria for selecting candidates may fragment black clergy support, such as allegiance to candidates, positions on issues, and membership in churches

Moreover, when African American clergy are candidates themselves, the likelihood for dissension and disunity increases. While clergy have enjoyed limited electoral success in Cleveland, it seems that the overall political culture is not receptive to the notion of ministers seeking political office. The politically active ministers have prior political connections and allegiances that come into play and complicate endorsement decisions. The same was apparently true among some of Reverend McMickle's church members who had prior political associations with other candidates.

While researchers have correctly challenged the notion that black churches are monolithic,[23] future research will need to determine whether these new levels of political division harm or benefit the black community in the long run.

NOTES

1. Antioch was founded in 1893.
2. The Future Outlook League worked to overcome employment discrimination. Lausche was Democratic mayor of Cleveland from 1941 to 1944 who went on to become the only five-term governor of Ohio.
3. Olivet Institutional Baptist Church was formed in 1931.

4. Carl B. Stokes, *Promises of Power: Then and Now* (Cleveland: Friends of Carl B. Stokes, 1989).

5. Stokes, *Promises of Power.*

6. Interview with Congressman Louis Stokes, Cleveland, 10 December 1998.

7. Stokes, *Promises of Power.*

8. Interview with Reverend Eugene Ward, Cleveland, 7 January 2004.

9. Interview with Ward.

10. Harold Washington faced this criticism when Latinos who had been part of his electoral coalition did not feel included in his administration. See John J. Betancur and Douglas C. Gills, "The African-American and Latino Coalition Experience in Chicago under Mayor Harold Washington," in *The Collaborative City,* ed. John J. Betancur and Douglas C. Gills (New York: Garland Publishing, 2000).

11. Karen L. Long, "The Platinum Clerics," *Plain Dealer,* 20 May 2000.

12. Long, "Platinum Clerics."

13. 18 U.S.C. § 1951.

14. Joe Hallett, "11th District Race Was Too Clean to See," *Plain Dealer,* 8 May 1998, 11B.

15. Marvin A. McMickle, *From Pulpit to Politics: Reflections on the Separation of Church and State* (Euclid, Ohio: Williams Custom Publishing, 1999).

16. Hallett, "11th District Race."

17. George Voinovich served as mayor of Cleveland from 1979 to 1989, governor of Ohio from 1991 to 1998, and has been U.S. senator since January 1999.

18. Thirteen area ministers contributed to a book of sermons distributed by the UPIM in 1999 entitled *Messages for Modern Times.*

19. The state legislature passed a bill to allow Ohio racetracks to simulcast horse races from tracks around the nation. The governor did not veto the bill but allowed it to become law without his signature.

20. William E. Nelson Jr., "The Role of the Black Church in Politics," prepared for the Committee on the Status of Black Americans of the National Research Council (unpublished paper on file with author).

21. Fredrick C. Harris, *Something Within: Religion in African-American Political Activism* (New York: Oxford University Press, 1999).

22. Adolph L. Reed Jr., *The Jesse Jackson Phenomenon: The Crisis of Purpose in Afro-American Politics* (New Haven: Yale University Press, 1986).

23. See C. Eric Lincoln and Lawrence Mamiya, *The Black Church in the African American Experience* (Durham: Duke University Press, 1990); Kenneth Wald, *Religion and Politics in the United States* (Washington, D.C.: Congressional Quarterly Press, 1997); and Nelson, "Role of the Black Church in Politics."

9

Black Churches and the Formation of Political Action Committees in Detroit

Ronald E. Brown and Carolyn Hartfield

This chapter discusses the historical evolution of church-based politics in the city of Detroit. It describes one outgrowth of this involvement, the creation of church-based political action committees that are active during electoral campaigns. Attention is focused on the Black Slate Committee and the Fannie Lou Hamer Political Action Committee during the 2000 national election. These grassroots/church-based political action organizations are registered with the Bureau of Elections in the Michigan Department of State. Both rely mainly on volunteer help during electoral campaigns. Theoretically, leaders from both faith-based organizations argue that they articulate the concern of the poor and the powerless, and they do so by maintaining a protest racial ideology—mainly that of black nationalism. The chapter concludes by focusing on challenges confronting church-based political action committees. Major problems confronting such grassroot organizations are finding volunteers, raising money in off election years, and avoiding being used by a more powerful ally, the Democratic Party.

While the major obligation, duty, and responsibility of clergy is to oversee and direct the spiritual life of his or her congregation, a number of pastors have been involved in the political life of the city. In 1925, the Reverend Robert Bradby, pastor of Second Baptist Church, ran unsuccessfully for a common council seat; the same would be true in 1947, for Reverend Charles Hill, of Hartford Memorial Baptist Church (city council).[1] However, Elvin L. Davenport, a black pastor with relatively quiet support from Baptist clergy, was elected in 1957 to Detroit Recorder's Court and served there until he retired in 1977.[2] By 1965, one pastor was on common council: Nicholas Hood II, the pastor of Plymouth United Church of Christ. He served on the council from 1965 to 1986. After retiring from the ministry and city council, his son,

Nicholas Hood III, succeeded him as church pastor and council member. Nicholas Hood III served on the council from 1986 to 2002. John Peoples, pastor of Calvary Baptist Church (now called Cosmopolitan Baptist Church), served one term on the council, from 1982 to 1986. This was also the case with Keith Butler, pastor of Word of Faith Christian Center, who served from 1990 to 1994. Essentially, at least one black clergy person has served on the city council from 1965 until 2002.

Mayor Coleman Young (the first African American mayor of the city, 1973–1993) and Mayor Dennis Archer (1993–2001) recognized the significance of clergy as political leaders. Young formally addressed the Council of Black Baptist Pastors, and, while upset about their unwillingness to support his casino projects (calling the group a "debating society"), Young nonetheless respected black pastors.[3] He credits church leaders for mobilizing volunteers who patrolled city blocks to ensure that arson fires were minimal on Devil's Night (the night before Halloween). Mayor Young appointed the president of the Council of Black Baptist Pastors, Reverend Charles Butler, to the police commission, and Archer followed suit by appointing Reverend Edgar Vann to the police commission. Finally, the political education of Mayor Kwame Kilpatrick (2002 to present) was nourished at the Shrine of the Black Madonna where his mother, U.S. House Representative Carolyn Cheeks Kilpatrick, and father, Bernard Kilpatrick, a former deputy Wayne County Commissioner, were members. Kwame Kilpatrick, much like Coleman Young, received the endorsement of the Council of Black Baptist Pastors in his 2001 electoral campaign. Kilpatrick also had the backing of prominent ministers, including Reverend Edgar Vann of Second Ebenezer Baptist Church, Reverend Wendell Anthony of Fellowship Baptist Church, and the former city council member, Reverend Keith Butler. Mayor Kilpatrick, following the tradition set by his predecessors, appointed Reverend Jim Holly to the police commission in 2004.

In addition to the activism of clergy, some church activists participate as campaign workers, others as poll watchers, and most vote in elections, and as stated, about one-third talk about politics at their place of worship. It is not at all surprising that religion and politics mix in the city of Detroit. Sidney Verba et al. find that African Americans are more likely than Latino Americans and Anglo-Americans to report a church setting as the place where political information is received.[4] That almost one-third of African American Detroit residents are exposed to church-based political communication is no small matter, given Robert Putnam's recent work showing a steady decline over the past three decades in religious as well as political activism.[5] An underlying theme in this chapter is that church-based political activism grew out of a historical struggle for racial justice that cast some clergy and their congregations in the middle of the fight. Moreover, today, about one third of the city residents are in churches where they expect to be engaged in some form of political discourse. Equally important, religious organizations pro-vide a place where people can volunteer time, energy, talent, and money to work on political matters.

THE ROLE OF THE BLACK CHURCH IN DETROIT[6]

Three interrelated reasons help explain why some black congregational leaders and members became involved in electoral politics. First, a ward-based election system decentralizes political power. This results in the mayor of the city not having the prestige, the organizational resources, or the loy-alty of followers to deter possible political rivals. Coleman Young felt that the nonpartisan ward system hurt the chances of any mayor to centralize power and rule effectively. He states in his autobiography:

> The revised city charter, while increasing the power of the mayor in some re-spects, disabled me in other ways. Detroit's non partisan system of electing councilmen-at-large designed in reaction to the Democratic machines that Richard Daley and other city bosses built around the ward systems by which municipal voting patterns can be localized and manipulated through the parti-san efforts of city employees has come to mean, in effect, that we have an extra nine would be . . . mayors sitting up there in the City-County Building.[7]

Thus unlike the powerful Cook County Democratic Party machinery that was so effectively used by Richard Daley (Chicago) at the height of his political career, Detroit has a more pluralist political culture which makes it difficult for the mayor of the city to use patronage and the prestige that comes with the office to determine how governmental resources are allocated. This al-lows politically astute pastors, such as Nicholas Hood II and Nicholas Hood III, to be among the many voices in the political process.

An important second determinant of church-based political activism is a political environment that includes large automotive companies, unions, and black militants. The large automotive companies—Ford, General Motors, and DaimlerChrysler—significantly affect the decision-making agenda of elected officials and citizens. Thomas Sugrue writes that corporate executives and managers who controlled the city's industry had a disproportionate influence on the city's development in the post–World War II era because of their eco-nomic power.[8] A single corporate decision could affect thousands of workers, and the introduction of new technologies and decisions about plant size, ex-pansion, and relocation affected the city's labor market and reshaped the economic geography of the Detroit region.[9] Yet, it was during the migration of African Americans from the rural South to the urban North, following the First World War, that one began to observe the role of black ministers as po-litical leaders interacting with political and economic power brokers. Robert

Bradby of Second Baptist Church, the most influential black pastor in the city during the 1920s, had many connections to powerful whites; one in particular was Henry Ford.[10] Bradby's importance to Henry Ford was based on his ability to recommend "very high type fellows"—those who were not black militants.[11] Ford also tapped St. Matthew's Father Everard Daniel and the Reverend William Peck of Bethel A.M.E. A recommendation from either Bradby or Daniel was considered tantamount to joining Ford's payroll, and historian David Levine speculates that many blacks joined Second Baptist or St. Matthew's "with an eye to secure a job at Ford."[12]

Thus, it is not surprising that in the early 1920s and 1930s, prominent church leaders, such as Robert Bradby, Everard Daniel, and William Peck, were against unions. Black pastors were not operating in a vacuum; the racism that existed within the plants in Detroit made their task easier.[13] Actually, black workers became more militant in the 1930s and 1940s. Blacks formed their own internal black groups to combat racism, voted against Ford's choice for mayor in 1931, and threatened to conduct wildcat strikes at the Dodge Chrysler plant in 1943.[14] In the end, the increasingly militant behavior of black autoworkers made it difficult for pastors like Bradby to keep a lid on black economic and political aspirations.

Blacks who were members of the United Auto Workers (UAW) and members of churches were instrumental in moving black church leaders to support unions.[15] The relationship that developed between black churches (those who have union members) and the UAW forged political activism among African Americans. Large black churches in Detroit, with greater resources, had become highly politicized during the 1930s mainly because more African Americans became members of the UAW. The relationship between clergy and Henry Ford therefore began to wane as the unions began to penetrate the black community. Nathaniel Leach remembered a split that developed within Second Baptist Church between Bradby (head pastor) and Reverend Charles Hill (associate pastor) over the church's role in unionization in the 1940s. Leach states, "Rev. Bradby was hired by Ford, and he could not afford to displease Ford. Therefore, he tried to be neutral. However, Hill courted the organization. But that became sort of a split because people sprang up all over the city [blacks became more supportive of unionization]. And this sort of left Bradby to slip down and cause him to lose power."[16] However, during the New Deal era, black clergy along with the union activists were beginning to become actively involved in recruiting blacks to register to vote and switch their partisan allegiance from the Republican to the Democratic Party. According to Wilbur Rich, black leadership switched its allegiance for several reasons including the Depression, Democratic Party support for unionization, and the party's rhetoric of equal treatment for workers.[17] Once church-based mobilization happened, political activism became the norm with respect to church life for many blacks, particularly those attending large churches where politics was discussed by both the pastor and members of the congregation.

The emergence of a black political consciousness during the civil rights and black power era is the third factor contributing to the political involvement of black clergy. In the 1960s, racial bullet voting was prevalent, and it became clear to black activists that white voters, despite the increase in the black population, would not support black political candidates for the common council.[18] The failure to elect a black to the 1965 city council primary election led to a proposal by the Interdenominational Ministers' Alliance (IMA), a group of black ministers, to boycott white candidates in the general election.[19] In addition to the IMA's proposal, Reverend Albert Cleage (known before his death as Jaramogi A. Agyeman) proposed a "Vote Black" campaign.[20] Even before the Vote Black Campaign, which produced the *Black Slate Digest*, a weekly newsletter, Reverend Cleage established a publication called *Illustrated News* in the late 1950s. The *Black Slate Digest* was an outgrowth of the *Illustrated News*. The goal of both publications was to educate black citizens about political matters. Additionally, the *Black Slate* (which is still in circulation) was designed so that citizens could make an informed choice at the polls. Citizens are given information about the policy positions of candidates and/or elected officials, exposed to editorials about pressing community matters, and provided a list of endorsed candidates. Black citizens are made aware of the Black Slate because the list is often published in the *Michigan Chronicle*, a newspaper with a wide black readership. It is also published in the *Michigan Citizen*, a grassroots newspaper, and it is placed in barbershops, beauty salons, and black churches that are supportive of the endorsed candidates.

The linkage between black racial consciousness and church-based activism is what helped Coleman Young win his initial mayoral race in 1976. Coleman Young cites Reverend Cleage as being one of the earliest supporters of his first mayoral campaign.[21] In addition to the Black Slate, the Council of Black Baptist Pastors, consisting of three hundred members that meet at least once a month, is a viable interest group in the city. As suggested earlier, Coleman Young saw the Council of Black Baptist Pastors as a formidable political organization. The 1989 mayoral election illustrates the centrality of church-based political support for any viable mayoral candidate. David Crumm, *Detroit Free Press* religious writer, reports that in 1989, prior to the Baptist church revival season, Young was trailing his opponent Tom Barrow in public opinion polls 47 percent to 37 percent. Once the revival season began, Young appeared in numerous packed churches, arm in arm with Aretha Franklin and the Reverend Jesse Jackson, quoting the Bible and singing "We Shall Overcome." After the revival season, Barrow fell at the polls, 56 percent to 44 percent, and subsequently lost the election.[22] The Council of Black Baptist Pastors does not always speak with one voice. In the early stages of the 1993 mayoral race, Charles Adams, pastor of Hartford Memorial Baptist Church, which has a large upper-middle-class African American membership, openly criticized the Archer candidacy. Adams viewed Archer in 1993 as a candidate beholden to the white power structure. In contrast, the Reverend Jim Holley, pastor of the Historic Little Rock Baptist Church and president of the Council of Black Pastors (1992–1995), openly supported Dennis Archer.[23]

Under Holley's leadership the council moved away from explicitly endorsing and slating political candidates. Holley met with the Internal Revenue Service (IRS) on several occasions and came away with an agreement in which the council would no longer get involved in "politics." Instead, there was discussion about establishing a separate organization to comply with IRS regulations.[24] The council rejected this plan because members felt that the overall purpose of the organization was fellowship as opposed to politics. Later, under the leadership of Reverend Edgar Vann Jr. (1995–1998), political awareness initiatives were launched to move black citizens from feelings "of being permanently disengaged from the system."[25] These initiatives included instruction at Vann's church in the use of computerized voting machines. In addition, at Reverend Holley's church, an employee at Little Rock Baptist Church registered citizens to vote until the state disallowed the practice.

Although the elections of Coleman Young, Dennis Archer, and Kwame Kilpatrick as mayors of Detroit have effectively integrated blacks into city government, some church-based organizations continue to have a protest ideology—believing that they must be the political voice of the black poor and powerless. Hence, for some activists, having a black administration does not necessarily denote articulation of the interests of the poor. As Wilbur Rich points out, "Whereas the clients of the labor unions and the black middle class were being elected and appointed to offices, the poor struggled with poverty and the police."[26]

After the riot in 1967, this tension was brought to the forefront. Members of the black working class and poor felt that the "established leadership had not adequately addressed the problems of downtrodden ghetto dwellers."[27] Black clergy were considered a part of that "established leadership." Sugrue maintains that the alienation of black poor within black civil rights groups began during the Second World War and continued into the Cold War era.[28] The Detroit NAACP is cited as an example. In the late 1940s it purged many of its more militant members, among them former Branch President Reverend Charles Hill, who left under a cloud of suspicion for his activism and his refusal to sever ties with communist-front civil rights organizations.[29] Sugrue also states that by the late 1950s and early 1960s groups like the Urban League and the NAACP in conjunction with powerful local black ministers worked to improve the status of skilled and white-collar workers. Hence, little effort was put into getting jobs for the unemployed and improving the working conditions for the unskilled.

SPEAKING ON BEHALF OF THE BLACK POOR

The Black Slate Political Action Committee (BS-PAC) and the Fannie Lou Hamer Political Action Committee (FLH-PAC) are two separate church-based political action committees seeking to mobilize and articulate the policy demands of the black poor during election campaigns. Both organizations attempt to provide poor people with access to communication networks, populist leaders, and political educational workshops that might increase their political knowledge and interest in becoming involved in grassroots political efforts. Essentially, by acting as linkage institutions that voice the demands and the needs of the black poor, these grassroots organizations attempt to increase the probability that elected officials will represent the interest of poor blacks in governmental corridors within Detroit, Lansing, and Washington, D.C. These PACs are affiliated with churches that strongly adhere to a black nationalistic theology. In addition, both PACs have leaders that believe that blacks should be skeptical of white political leadership, have knowledge and pride about their African past, and develop independent political organizations that articulate the interests of the poor. Both of these church-based organizations are registered with the Bureau of Elections within the Michigan Department of State as political action committees. Finally, each seeks to provide opportunities for those not normally involved in the political process to become activists. This is partially accomplished because the Michigan Department of State requires political committees to have at least twenty-five individual contributors. It is also accomplished because each PAC engages in endorsing political candidates, which requires the use of volunteers or paid individuals to get the word out to citizens about whom to support on election day.

BLACK SLATE, INC.

As stated, the Black Slate had its genesis in the 1960s. At the time, black power activists such as Malcolm X, H. Rap Brown, and Stokely Carmichael were arguing that too few black pastors were involved in the struggle for racial justice. Grace Boggs, a long-time resident and activist in the city of Detroit, states that at the start of the civil rights movement, black pastors and other black leaders were not ready for a black power movement that would challenge white supremacy.[30] By the mid-1960s, Albert Cleage, founder and pastor of the Central Congregational Christian Church (1953), began preaching a series of sermons centered on the idea that Jesus was a black revolutionary messiah whose primary objective was to construct a black nation. Cleage in 1966 changed the name of the church from Central Congregational Christian Church to the Shrine of the Black Madonna. Church leaders and members felt an obligation to "transform the spiritual emptiness, economic powerlessness and social disorganization which plagued the black community." The Black Slate is part of a number of efforts by the Shrine of the Black Madonna, including bookstores, community service centers, technological centers, a Beulah Land Farm Project, and educational centers. Essentially, this church seeks to create oppositional institutions that are independent of the white power structure.

Cleage (aka Jaramogi A. Agyeman) echoes this point in a written sermon entitled the "The Pentecost Experience," in which he states: "We are black. We are oppressed. . . . You do not realize that this world in which you live is organized. It is not run on automatic. We don't have anything to do with running it. . . . The system is an enemy system. . . . Our struggle for survival requires recognition of the fact that we are outside of the system and that we must build counter-institutions of our own."[31]

The Black Slate, Inc. became an official independent political action committee in the State of Michigan in 1977. As an independent political action committee, it raises and spends money on behalf of political issues and political candidates that are running for public office. It must also file campaign statements with the Bureau of Elections, showing receipts, contributions, expenditures, and a balance statement. Table 9.1 shows a summary of the activity of the committee between 1993 and 2000. The Black Slate PAC generates a slate of candidates endorsed within their committee meetings, as well as analysis of candidate positions and past voting records where applicable. Endorsed candidates pay a fee to have their name placed on the slate; fees range from $500 to $1,500, depending upon the office being sought. Between 1976 and 2000, the Black Slate endorsed Coleman Young, mayoral candidate Sharon McPhail, Congressman John Conyers, Senator Carl Levin,

Table 9.1.   Black Slate, Inc. Political Action Committee

	Total Receipts	Total Expenditures	Debts and Obligations	Ending Balance
1994	10,100.00	9,996.61	0.00	21,829.44
1995	0.00	0.00	0.00	17,927.67
1996	19,300.00	17,116.69	0.00	20,110.98
1997	0.00	1,531.09	0.00	10,886.69
1998	20,350	33,274.57	0.00	10,423.31
1999	15,772.00	15,336.52	0.00	941.52
2000	28,215.00	23,641.85	0.00	9,117.56

Source: Michigan Department of State, Elections Bureau, Tri-annual statements. All balances are from the October Tri-annual Campaign Statement.

Congresswoman Barbara Rose Collins, Congresswoman Carolyn Cheeks Kilpatrick, and the 1984 presidential candidacy of Reverend Jesse Jackson.

Disagreements on the part of the Black Slate Committee with Dennis Archer's administration led to a petition to recall Archer in 1998–1999. It failed largely because of improper ballot signatures. Nonetheless, the Black Slate Committee voiced its opposition in both the *Black Slate Digest* and the *Michigan Citizen*. In a special April 1999 edition of the *Black Slate Digest* it was asserted that Mayor Dennis Archer had refused to remove snow from neighborhoods, campaigned against black majority ownership of at least one casino, and had supported Republican Governor John Engler's efforts to take over Detroit public schools. In essence, he was a black mayor who was failing to represent the interest of the black community.

Campaign finance statements during the 2000 election cycle reveal that the Black Slate PAC rented space at the Shrine of the Black Madonna. Although the Black Slate embraces a black nationalist ideology, the ideology is pragmatic. The BS-PAC accepted $7,500 from the Democratic Party State Central Committee in October 2000. This money was to assist the political action committee in getting its message out to potential black voters. The Democratic Party may have given the Black Slate money because of its prior and present endorsement of progressive black and white Democrats. For example, at the state level during the 2000 elections, the Black Slate endorsed Judges E. Thomas Fitzgerald and Marietta Robinson for the Michigan Supreme Court—both are white Americans who received endorsements from the Michigan State Democratic Party. The Slate also endorsed Kwame Kilpatrick for the Michigan House of Representatives and his mother, Carolyn Cheeks Kilpatrick, for the U.S. House of Representatives. This is not surprising since both are members of the Shrine of the Black Madonna church. It is interesting to note, however, that being a church member does not qualify one for a free endorsement. In their respective campaigns in the year 2000, the Kilpatrick for United States Congress PAC paid $1,500 and the Committee to Elect Kwame Kilpatrick paid $600 to the Black Slate in endorsement fees.

The Black Slate Committee, which has a call-in talk radio show every Wednesday and Thursday evening, paid for political commercials throughout the electoral campaign. What is significant about radio ads and the talk show is that this political communication outlet provides opportunities for people to call in, listen, and/or talk to other listeners, friends, and family about issues being raised. A cursory analysis of the callers suggests a grassroots following who is supportive of grassroots black nationalist issues. Callers tend to be upset with the Archer administration's handling of city services and other issues and are generally distrustful of city, state, and federal government since all are controlled by the white power structure.

Nonetheless, the BS-PAC still supports the idea of civic involvement—or agitation. It has provided individuals with various opportunities for getting involved in the electoral cycle, including through participation in fundraisers and as paid poll workers on the day of the general election. It works its phone banks to encourage voters to turn out and vote for endorsed candidates. The Black Slate Committee spends most of its efforts providing political information to voters and attempting to get them to turn out on election day. In short, the Black Slate Committee spends most of its efforts providing political information to voters and encouraging voter turnout.

THE FANNIE LOU HAMER POLITICAL ACTION COMMITTEE

The Fannie Lou Hamer Political Action Committee (FLH-PAC) is an outgrowth of political activities at Fellowship Chapel, a ministry founded by Reverend James E. Wadsworth Jr. in 1981. Reverend Wadsworth was involved in the struggle for racial justice through his involvement in the NAACP and as chairperson of the 13th Congressional District democratic organization, and Fellowship Chapel's ministry reflects this racial justice emphasis. Each member that joined the church during Reverend Wadsworth's tenure attended a new members class every Sunday for several months, where they were exposed to the idea that it was their Christian duty to work for racial justice. Particular attention was devoted to the *Amistad* story, a story of fifty-three Mendi captives from Sierra Leone who rebelled on the slave ship *Amistad* in 1839. This was done to drive home the point that African Americans had to engage in political struggles as Africans to gain respect and recognition from white America.

Reverend Wadsworth established the Political Education Committee (PEC) at the church in the 1980s. The purpose of the PEC was to educate church members on the importance of political involvement and the impact on their lives. Reverend Wendell Anthony, the current pastor of the church, assumed the pastorate in December 1986, shortly after the death of Reverend Wadsworth. Reverend Anthony states that the concept of a church-based po-

Table 9.2. Fannie Lou Hamer Political Action Committee

	Total Receipts	Total Expenditures	Debts and Obligations	Ending Balance
1994	31,680.00	23,711.25	0.00	13,128.92
1995	3,942.32	4,136.23	0.00	5,972.85
1996	49,752.00	40,304.00	0.00	19,286.00
1997	34,403.00	39,311.78	5,000.00	5,200.22
1998	26,224.30	66,631.69	5,000.00	1,563.21
1999	421.98	1,210.14	5,000.00	576.45
2000	75,895.00	44,110.08	2,500.00	32,361.32

Source: Michigan Department of State, Elections Bureau, October Tri-annual statements.

litical action committee involved in all aspects of the electoral process began to take shape with him in 1989. Reverend Anthony often represented Reverend Wadsworth at political meetings, and it was through this involvement that Reverend Anthony began developing the idea of a formal political action committee. Reverend Anthony believes naming the PAC, which centers around black political consciousness, after Fannie Lou Hamer was appropriate because she gave everything for the cause of black Americans. He states:

> I have always been a student of Christian history and as a civil rights activist; I am one who is always looking for a way to bridge our history with our present. I look for those nuances in individuals, for example our men's choir is called the Paul Robeson Chorale, Paul Robeson was a strong solid civil rights social activist and that is what men want to be, as Fannie Lou Hamer was a woman as you know, who was very socially active who sacrificed her life for this cause, she was a Mississippi freedom fighter, working with the Mississippi Freedom Democratic Party, and going to the convention in '64 and not being given a seat and just making that statement, "I am sick and tired of being sick and tired."[32]

In 1993, the FLH-PAC filed a statement with the State of Michigan's Bureau of Election's Disclosure Division as a nonpartisan political organization. The stated purpose of the FLH-PAC is to endorse political candidates, to provide political information to prospective voters, and to encourage voter registration and turnout. It also provides opportunities for volunteers to work as poll workers, drive voters to the polls, work at the polls, and in some cases to participate as delegates at local, county, state, and national party conventions. The FLH-PAC has its own separate mailing address and treasurer who monitors contributions and expenditures by the PAC. The FLH-PAC is also registered as a federal PAC. The PAC accepts money from political candidates and from political organizations and other community-based organizations.

Table 9.2 shows a summary of the FLH-PAC's state activity from 1993 to 2000. In the 2000 campaign, the PAC spent a great deal of money on voter registration and voter education. For example in the 2000 election campaign, $2,000 was spent on radio advertising in an effort to increase voter turnout among young listeners. This effort was coordinated with the Detroit chapter of the NAACP. The slogan "Take Your Soles to the Polls" was played on various radio stations, written about in the *Detroit News* and *Free Press*, announced in area churches, and shown on billboards across the city. Mayor Dennis Archer, the Detroit City Council, and the Wayne County Commission endorsed this campaign, which started on Mothers' Day, May 14, 2000. More than two hundred churches in the Detroit metropolitan community conducted voter registration drives on Mothers' Day, including Fellowship Chapel, Pleasant Grove Baptist Church, and Sacred Heart Catholic Church.

The fact that leadership from the FLH-PAC (both state and federal) may have worked with the NAACP to increase voter interest is partially explained by the fact that the PAC is part of an organizational network, as illustrated in the appendix. Wendell Anthony is pastor of Fellowship Chapel, president of the NAACP, and founder of the PAC. In addition, the past executive director of the NAACP, John Johnson, directs the PAC and is a member of Fellowship Chapel. The PAC also benefits because several members of the executive committee of the PAC are themselves ministers, including Reverend Martin Bolton, Imam Abdullah El-Aim, Reverend Tony Curtis Henderson, and Reverend Robert Smith Jr.

In 2000, the Detroit NAACP Executive Board consisted of prominent political leaders such as U.S. Representative Carolyn Cheeks Kilpatrick, who was encouraged to run for Congress by Reverend Wendell Anthony in 1996. Both the NAACP and the FLH-PAC endorsed her candidacy and encouraged voters to support Kilpatrick, who ran against then-incumbent Barbara Rose Collins (endorsed at the time by the Black Slate). It should be noted that Collins like Kilpatrick is a member of the Shrine of the Black Madonna. The FLH-PAC endorsed and encouraged voters to support Kilpatrick again in the 2000 election cycle, which she won without much difficulty.

The FLH-PAC has been somewhat more successful than the Black Slate in getting contributions from PACs associated with interest groups that support mainly Democratic Party voter mobilization drives. For example, in the 2000 election campaign, the American Federation of State, County, Municipal Employees of the AFL/CIO national office contributed $5,000, and the Michigan Democratic Party contributed $7,500. Part of the success of the FLH-PAC is partially explained by the fact that its founder, Wendell Anthony, was a strong Clinton-Gore supporter. Records from the 1996 and 2000 campaign seasons from the Federal Election Commission reveal that either through Anthony's own contributions as a private citizen, as president of the NAACP, or founder of the FLH-PAC, the Clinton-Gore team received financial support and endorsements. Both Clinton and Gore made several stops to Detroit during the 1996 and 2000 presidential campaign seasons.

The PAC also spent money on fundraisers, the printing of slate cards, hiring poll workers, and renting buses so that people could be driven to the polls. In any event, the FLH-PAC, in conjunction with efforts by the NAACP and other political groups and elected officials, was able to increase voter turnout in the city from approximately 33 percent of registered voters in 1996 to 48 percent in 2000.

POLITICAL CRITICISM

Not everyone has been happy with the work of church-based political action committees. Bill Johnson, an African American editor at the *Detroit News*, wrote a critical essay on August 29, 1997, entitled, "Why Should Detroit Candidates Pay for PAC Endorsements?" In his essay, he named the FLH-PAC as an example of an organization that forces candidates to pay for endorsements that rarely result in the promised outcomes, for example, higher voter turnout. From Johnson's perspective, the FLH-PAC merely represents the interest of its founder, Reverend Wendell Anthony, and those that share an ideology of black nationalism.[33]

There are also criticisms from clergypersons, such as Reverend Jim Holley of the Historic Little Rock Baptist Church, who does not think that church-based political action committees lack integrity by charging candidates for endorsements. Holley states that whenever money is exchanged there is a problem. Nevertheless, Holley believes that pastors should be politically informed and that they should engage in political activities that will best serve the black community.[34] Reverend Hood III, pastor of Plymouth Congregational Church, also opposes the idea of church-based political action committees, believing that it is necessary to maintain the separation between church and state:

> The definition of political action committee as I understand it has to do with a forum where people contribute to it and agree to make decisions to support candidates. We do not have anything like that in this church. We are considered, probably, a very political church. But we do not have what I consider any formal or informal political action committees. I surmise that part of the reason why we don't have any formal or informal political action committees in the church is that the church has a history of elected officials and involvement—the last three consecutive pastors. Horace White, the pastor back in the '40s, actually served in the state legislature for a term and was also very involved in the initial organizing of the United Auto Workers. As I understand, there is a photograph in the Solidarity House of him . . . on the wall. Some of these guys . . . were beaten up for going out with some of the Ford workers who wanted to organize, along with Charles Hill from Hartford (Baptist Church). And then my father is my immediate predecessor—he served on the city council for twenty-eight years—and now I'm in my seventh year on city council. And so the church has a history of elected participation by its ministers, and because of that, to offset any negative criticism, within the church that the church is "too political," we are actually, I would say, less overtly politically than most churches in Detroit.[35]

DO THE BLACK SLATE AND THE FANNIE LOU HAMER PACS INCREASE VOLUNTEERISM AMONG THE POOR?

Given the criticisms of church-based political action committees and the caution echoed by Reverend Hood III, one must ask whether such organizations actually achieve stated objectives such as increasing political engagement. The Black Slate Committee and the Fannie Lou Hamer Political

Action Committee attempt to build church-based political communities that possess high degrees of social trust, group identity, pride, and commitment to political advocacy and that convert this into concrete forms of political volunteerism within the black community. While we lack data to support our claim, we posit that both PACs are probably most successful at increasing political interest among black nationalist–oriented political activists, which are activists who already have heightened group consciousness. Yet, pragmatism guides the behavior of both groups. As stated, both PACs have received money from the state central committee of the Democratic Party. In addition, in 1997 Reverend Anthony reversed his previous opposition to Mayor Dennis Archer and announced that the FLH-PAC was supportive of his administrative efforts to improve the plight of the poor in the city. Finally, Al Gore, a centrist Democrat and 2000 Democratic presidential nominee, benefited from the volunteers who worked for the FLH-PAC or the NAACP to get out the vote in the 2000 presidential campaign.

The political actions of these two church-based political action committees may not be in vain. U.S. Representative Carolyn Cheeks Kilpatrick has sought to represent the poor in the halls of Congress. In the 105th Congress, she sponsored and cosponsored legislation to improve the economic and social conditions of blacks residing in central cities and other urban communities. Representative Kilpatrick was also the primary sponsor of legislation that provided opportunities for low- to moderate-income people to own homes. This legislation was critical for the 15th Congressional District since only 40 percent of the residents in the district are homeowners and over 35 percent of the families in the district are classified as living in poverty.

CHALLENGES CONFRONTING THE BLACK SLATE AND FLH-PAC

A major challenge confronting church-based PACs is their reliance on a small volunteer staff in an era when people are less likely to engage in volunteer work. The fact that some of the leaders may be called to be active simultaneously in church and political work could prove taxing. Both PACs may wish to engage in fundraising activities in nonelection years to raise money to hire full-time staff persons whose primary responsibilities would be to raise money, keep a close watch on changes in reporting procedures by the state and federal election commissions, and write position papers on policy issues. Such papers could be the basis of questions asked during the political forums that have been used in the past to scrutinize candidates seeking endorsements from the PACs. Having a permanent staff would institutionalize the PACS and potentially shield them from criticism that these organizations have no true vision outside that of their own desire to exercise leadership. Moreover, a permanent organization that also operates during nonelection years could engage in political education activities to increase interest in politics among the uninformed and the poor. Certainly, media ads are a start, but the sponsoring of recreational sporting events, dance parties, poetry slams, gospel choir events, and other black social events is a way to raise the consciousness of people whom the PACs seek to influence. A call-in radio talk show, such as the one facilitated by the Black Slate, is also an effective means to reach people, as is the *Black Slate Digest* publication. However, reliance on radio or television to reach black voters presents increasing challenges. For example, in April 2004, WCHB, a locally owned radio station known for airing talk shows of interest to African Americans, became part of California-based Salem Communications, a conglomerate that owns ninety-two radio stations.[36] Many of the stations owned by this company tend to broadcast conservative Christian programs centering on sermons and Bible studies.[37] An important consideration is the degree to which the new owners share the same political and social concerns of Detroiters.[38] If, in fact, there is little affinity between the concerns of Salem Communications and black Detroiters, then it may be more difficult for stations such as WCBH to have programs that speak to the issues and needs of blacks in the city.

Capitalizing on its early history of endorsing women candidates—Sharon McPhail for mayor (1992) and city council (2003), Joann Watson for city council (2003), and Kilpatrick for Congress (1998, 2000, 2002, 2004)—the FLH-PAC hopes this commitment to leadership by women will help it generate a volunteer pool of women. These women volunteers could provide the PAC with people who would be in contact with individuals who are in both formal and informal support networks at the grassroots level. Another challenge is increasing the involvement of the poor in the electoral process. Doing so will be a difficult challenge because it will require a greater deployment of personnel representing the PACs to organize among the poor, and increasing personnel will require convincing many more black pastors and citizens about the connection between personal faith and political activism. This point is critical because while the NAACP 2000 presidential voter registration drive was relatively successful, the Black Slate Committee was not formally involved in the process, nor were other church-based activists such as Reverend Jim Holley or Reverend Nicholas Hood III. Given the low organizational involvement of the black poor and high amount of organizational resources needed to mobilize this segment of the population, having the assistance of other civic leaders is necessary to produce a more effective voter mobilization effort.

The final challenge confronting both PACs is avoiding being perceived as clients of the centrist wing of the Democratic Party. Although the Democratic Party is strongly supported by black voters (over 95 percent of Detroit voters cast ballots for Democrats in the 2000 election), the party works hard to distance itself from radical blacks, largely so that potential white voters do not leave the party or split their tickets. National Democratic Party leaders, such as former President Bill Clinton, openly criticized Louis Farrakhan, the organizer of the Million Man March in 1995—attended by people such as former Mayor Dennis Archer. In addition, when Reverend Wendell Anthony went to Florida and Washington following the 2000 national election returns to protest unfair treatment of black voters, Al Gore was not supportive of such protest efforts.

In the end, grassroots PACs with a black nationalist ideology have to find a balance between an electoral realism (where winning elections is the emphasis) and a commitment to voicing the concerns of the poor and powerless. Doing this will likely require taking money from the Democratic Party, but in a way that does not repeat the kind of control Henry Ford exercised over black pastors in the 1920s and 1930s. Currently, the FLH-PAC and the Black Slate Committee must guard against being captured by a more powerful ally—the Democratic Party. This may be accomplished through closer collaborations between the two PACs during election campaigns and even during nonelection seasons. The sharing of information, ideas, and volunteers could help these groups, as well as the NAACP and the Council of Black Baptist Pastors, to facilitate an informal network that provides a basis for mobilizing the poor. In addition, these organizations may wish to work more closely with union organizations who might also give them access to resources that could be used in their struggle to represent the poor.

As the cases here make clear, black church-based PACs provide a number of benefits, ranging from the social capital (as opposed to monetary capital) they extend to candidates, to the community service they provide by evaluating candidates' commitment to the black poor and to black concerns in general. In order to more effectively carry out these tasks, as well as the important work they do in recruiting potential officeholders and offering training in running successful campaigns, greater collaboration between these PACs is essential. Moreover, these PACs could pursue more creative community education strategies, such as the development of newsletters to assist voters in determining how to evaluate political candidates. Unless church-based PACs make some of these adjustments, they will continue to have an uphill battle maintaining their political independence and being an effective voice for the powerless.

NOTES

1. Cara L. Shelly, "Bradby's Baptists: Second Baptist Church of Detroit, 1919–1946," *Michigan Historical Review* 17, no. 1 (Spring 1991): 19; Coleman Young and Lonnie Wheeler, *Hard Stuff: The Autobiography of Coleman Young* (New York: Viking, 1994), 94.

2. Interview with prominent Detroit clergy by the late Henry Pratt, 5 December 1996.

3. Interview with Coleman Young by Sabrina Williams and Ronald E. Brown, 17 June 1998.

4. Sidney Verba, Key Lehman Schlozamn, Henry Brady, and Norman Nie, "Race, Ethnicity and Political Resources: Participation in the United States," *British Journal of Political Science* 23 (1993): 453–97.

5. Robert D. Putnam, *Bowling Alone: The Collapse and Revival of American Community* (New York: Simon & Schuster, 2000), 45, 70–71.

6. This section of the chapter is significantly influenced by Ronald E. Brown and Sabrina Williams, "African-American Church-Based Political Discourse and Political Mobilization," paper delivered at the 1997 Annual Meeting of the American Political Science Association Meeting, Sheraton Washington Hotel, 28–31 August 1997, and chapter 2 of Sabrina Williams's dissertation, "Church-Based Civic Awareness and Political Participation in the City of Detroit," Wayne State University, 1999.

7. Young and Wheeler, *Hard Stuff,* 316.

8. Thomas J. Sugrue, *The Origins of the Urban Crisis: Race and Inequality in Postwar Detroit* (Princeton, N.J.: Princeton University Press, 1996), 11.

9. Sugrue, *Origins of the Urban Crisis*, 11.

10. Shelly, "Bradby's Baptists," 17.

11. Shelly, "Bradby's Baptists," 17.

12. Shelly, "Bradby's Baptists," 17.

13. August Meier and Elliot Rudwick, *Black Detroit and the Rise of the UAW* (New York: Oxford University Press, 1979).

14. Charles Denby, *Indignant Heart: A Black Worker's Journal* (Detroit: Wayne State University Press, 1978), 100–1; and Shelly, "Bradby's Baptists," 18.

15. Elaine L. Moon, *Untold Tales, Unsung Heroes: An Oral History of Detroit's African American Community, 1918–1968* (Detroit: Detroit Urban League and Wayne State University Press, 1994).

16. Moon, *Untold Tales, Unsung Heroes*, 97.

17. Wilbur Rich, *Coleman Young and Detroit Politics: From Social Activist to Power Broker* (Detroit: Wayne State University Press, 1989).

18. Sabrina Williams, "Church-Based Civic Awareness and Political Participation," chapter 2.

19. Rich, *Coleman Young,* 78.

20. Rich, *Coleman Young,* 79; and Grace L. Boggs, *Living for Change: An Autobiography* (Minneapolis: University of Minnesota Press, 1998), 118–24.

21. Young and Wheeler, *Hard Stuff,* 199.

22. See Ronald Brown, "The Black Church in a Post-Church Federation Era," in *Churches and Urban Government in Detroit and New York 1895–1994*, ed. Henry Pratt (Detroit: Wayne State University Press, 2004); and David Crumm, "Secret Sermon Helped End Ford Site Battle," *Detroit Free Press,* 17 October 1991, 12A.

23. See Brown, "Post-Church Federation."

24. Brown, "Post-Church Federation."

25. Kevin Fobbs, "Community Concerns: Getting out the Vote Still Ranks High in Community Awareness," *Detroit News*, 29 July 1998, detnews.com/1998/9807.

26. Rich, *Coleman Young,* 81.

27. Rich, *Coleman Young*, 81.

28. Sugrue, *Origins of the Urban Crisis*, 171.

29. Sugrue, *Origins of the Urban Crisis*, 175.

30. Boggs, *Living for Change*, 117.

31. Jaramogi Abebe Agyeman, "The Pentecost Experience (Part III): The Struggle for Enlightenment the Healing Ministry of the Church," in *Review, Tribute and Conclave 95 Edition* 5, no. 1 (August/September 1995): 42.

32. Author interview with Reverend Wendell Anthony, 14 August 2000.

33. Bill Johnson, Editor Notebook, and "Why Should Detroit Candidates Pay For PAC Endorsements?" *Detroit News*, 29 August 1997.

34. Author interview with Reverend Jim Holley, 11 August 2000.

35. Author interview with Reverend Nicholas Hood III, 20 August 2000.

36. Susan Whithall, "WQBH-AM Fans Dismayed to Learn of Sale of Station," *Detroit News*, 1 April 2004, www.detnews.com.

37. Whithall, "WQBG-AM Fans Dismayed."

38. Whithall, "WQBG-AM Fans Dismayed."

APPENDIX: 2000 SOCIAL RELATIONSHIPS

NAACP	*FLH-PAC*	*Fellowship Chapel*
Rev. Wendell Anthony	Rev. Wendell Anthony	Rev. Wendell Anthony
Ernest Lofton, 1st VP, Ex. Bd.	Ernest Lofton, Ex. Bd.	Ernest Lofton
Geneva Williams, 2nd VP, Ex. Bd.		Geneva Williams
Bernice Sheilds, 3rd VP, Ex. Bd.		
Ellen Griffin, Treasurer, Ex. Bd.		Ellen Griffin
Evelyn Hankins, Secretary, Ex. Bd.		Evelyn Hankins
Shekitra Frazier, Asst. Secretary, Ex. Bd.		
Karen Allen, Ex. Bd.		
Gerald Bantum, Ex. Bd.		
Marvin Beatty*, Ex. Bd.	Marvin Beatty, Ex. Bd.	Marvin Beatty
Emma Bell, Ex. Bd.		
Sharon Bernard, Ex. Bd.		
Dr. Robert O. Bland, Ex. Bd.		
Rev. Martin Bolton, Ex. Bd.		
Hon. Margie Braxton, Ex. Bd.		
Mark Carter, Ex. Bd.		
Marvel Cheeks, Ex. Bd.	Marvel Cheeks, Ex. Bd.	Marvel Cheeks
Hon. Sheila Cockrel, Ex. Bd.	Sheila Cockrel	
Imam Abdullah El-Amin		
John Elliott		
Rosa Floyd		
Joyce Hayes-Giles		
Nathan Gooden		

NAACP	FLH-PAC	Fellowship Chapel
Henry Griffin**		Henry Griffin
Rev. Tony Curtis Henderson		
Denise Ilitch		
Hiram Jackson		
Frankie James	Frankie James, Ex. Bd.	Frankie James
Atty. John E. Johnson	John E. Johnson, Ex. Bd.	John E. Johnson
Hon. Carolyn Cheeks-Kilpatrick		
Hon. Bernard Parker		
Bertha Poe		
Katie Riley	Katie Riley, Ex. Bd.	Katie Riley
Roger Robinson		
Nate Shapiro		
Beverly Smith		
Rev. Robert Smith Jr.		
Hon. Ricardo Solomon		
Jerry Sullivan		
Patricia Williams-Taitt		
Khary Turner, Ex. Bd.		Khary Turner
Jeff Washington, Ex. Bd.		
Yvonne White, Ex. Bd.	Yvonne White, Mem.	Yvonne White
Rochelle Wicks, Ex. Bd.		
Beulah W. Works, Ex. Bd.		
Beverly Chatman, Member	Beverly Chatman, Ex. Bd.	Beverly Chatman
Clifton Williams, Member.	Clifton Williams, Ex. Bd.	Clifton Williams
Frank Woods, Member	Frank Woods, Ex. Bd.	Frank Woods
Helen Bell, Member	Helen Bell, Ex. Bd.	Helen Bell
Darnelle Dickerson, Member	Darnelle Dickerson, Ex. Bd.	Darnelle Dickerson
Heaster Wheeler, Ex. Dir.	Heaster Wheeler, Mem	

Religious Connections		
Rev. Martin Bolton	People's Community Church	8601 Woodward, Detroit
Imam Abdullah El-Amin	Muslim Center	1605 W. Davison, Detroit
Rev. Tony Curtis Henderson	St. John C.M.E.	8715 Woodward, Detroit
Rev. Robert Smith Jr.	New Bethel Baptist Church	8430 C. L. Franklin, Detroit

*Marvin Beatty can no longer be connected with the FLH-PAC due to his involvement with the Greektown Casino.
** Henry Griffin is the husband of Ellen Griffin who is the treasurer of the Detroit Branch NAACP; both are active members of Fellowship Chapel.
Most members of Fellowship Chapel support the activities of the FLH-PAC.

10

Party Politics and Black Church Political Organization in Queens, New York

Michael Leo Owens

Appearing alongside the dominant political parties in the electoral process are alternative political organizations seeking to influence partisan politics and to pressure government. These alternative political organizations may assume the form of either parties or interest groups. As increasingly influential alternative organizations, they span the spectrum of class, religion, ethnicity, issue, and race. For blacks the impetus for the formation of alternative organizations, particularly church-based political organizations, appears to be the same as for other groups—unresponsive political parties. Similar to their precursors in the post-Emancipation period, today's black churches provide organizational, financial, and spiritual resources for collective political mobilization. According to social scientists Charles Green and Basil Wilson, rising church-based political activism within black communities, along with the contemporary black church's "demonstrated . . . willingness to experiment with new approaches to organization . . . could fundamentally alter the relationship of the black community to established power structures [e.g., the Democratic Party]."[1]

While attention has been focused on blacks' participation in the formation of third parties,[2] scant attention has been focused on black alternative *nonparty* organizations, especially organization linked to activist black churches. This neglect in the scholarship in political parties and urban politics is remarkable when one considers the extent to which black churches and their clerics will, and do, engage in nonparty political activity. Yet, as Alan J. Ware has observed: "While white liberal Democrats in the 1980s were becoming worried about the intertwining of politics and religion by right-wing fundamentalists, most forgot or ignored the fact that, for their black allies also, the separation of religion and politics had rarely been sustained."[3]

Church-based, black nonparty organizations are visible in the partisan politics of urban areas. As a consequence, the dominant political parties, as well as minor political parties and "others seeking to influence the black community assume the black church and its ministers to be the means to do so. In the absence of other viable institutions, the black church has been assumed to be the principle focal point for political activity, both electoral and otherwise."[4] But how influential can church-based, black nonparty organizations be in the electoral process? Can they successfully challenge political parties? Specifically, can church-based, black nonparty organizations provide a means for black empowerment, especially with regard to candidate selection and local party nominations? This chapter provides some answers to these questions by analyzing the circumstances that led to the creation of one church-based, black nonparty organization in New York City—the Southeast Queens Clergy for Community Empowerment (SQCCE). Detailing the organization's involvement in the electoral system, particularly its competitive relationship with the Democratic Party in Queens and its support of the election of former Congressman (Reverend) Floyd Flake, this chapter concludes that, in the case of local electoral politics, church-based, black nonparty organizations can influence the electoral process, successfully challenge dominant political parties, and increase the sense of empowerment and political efficacy in black communities.

THE DEVELOPMENT OF A CHURCH-BASED, BLACK NONPARTY ORGANIZATION

Increasingly, alternative political organizations are joining the dominant political parties in the electoral arena, sometimes contesting them for predominance.[5] Three theories of party failure can be identified that offer varying insights into the establishment of alternative political organizations. The first of these is the theory of linkage failure. This theory, advanced by Kay Lawson, postulates that the rise in alternative political organizations is the result of the failure of contemporary dominant political parties to form and maintain "adequate linkages between the state and its citizens."[6] Because political parties are unable to unite the demands of citizens with the policy outcomes of their governments, citizens have looked to institutions other than political parties for pursuing their political objectives. Consequently, alternative political organizations have appeared to reconnect citizens to the state, and *vice versa*.

The second theory posits that party failure is a consequence of weak political competition, whereby there is a disjunction between parties and particular groups that comprise a portion of their membership.[7] History shows that in the presence of weak political competition among parties, one political party will eventually dominate. This domination leads to the development of a one-party system in which the options and alternatives available to voters are limited. It is the lack of competition and the prevention of citizens from fully participating in the electoral process which is said to give rise to alternative political organizations that eventually challenge the dominant political party and open the process to once-neglected interests.

The third theory holds that party failure results from a lack of understanding on the part of the party leadership concerning the trade-offs inherent in party politics.[8] Specifically, this theory states that alternative political organizations appear because party leaders, in attempting to respond to pressures external and internal to their parties, incorrectly choose to deal with one type of pressure over another. For example, when party leaders side with the particular interests within their party instead of pursuing a more general or societal interest, party failure may result because voters no longer identify the party as interest optimizers.

As parties have failed to clear the theoreticians' and citizens' bars, new entities have been organized to take their place, or at least share their space, within the electoral system. Each of the three theories of party failure that have been highlighted is useful in the discourse on the emergence of black alternative political organizations, both in the form of parties and nonparties. In particular, these theories offer sound explanations for the appearance of church-based, black nonparty organizations. If party failure occurs, it is most obvious at the local level. As the following case study illustrates, the formation of church-based, independent political organizations occurs in response to the black electorate feeling that the local Democratic Party is failing to link its concerns to government action. Furthermore, the emergence of church-based, black nonparty organizations can be attributed to an increasingly negative black perception of local Democratic parties as inhibitors of participation. Moreover, when the leadership of local Democratic parties respond to internal party pressures instead of external party pressures, like endorsing and nominating party regulars with ties to the leadership over party insurgents supported by an important constituency that has broad-based appeal, one is likely to see alternative black nonparty organizations appear.

Historically, black Americans have found it difficult to extricate themselves from their contemporary political position in the United States. In particular, when it has come to bargaining with the Democratic Party over political concessions, such as endorsements, appointments, and funds, black "leaders" have found themselves faced with the reality that bolting to the Republicans is not a plausible alternative. Nevertheless, black Americans have discovered options for exercising their political influence as an interest group in the electoral system. As Hardy T. Frye noted in his research on black political participation in the Southern region of the United States during the late 1970s and early 1980s, in those places where "the Democratic party remains the dominant political organization, blacks are trying new strategies both within and *outside* the party to increase their political strength."[9] These internal and external activities also occur in parts of the North, where blacks are relying on innovative methods and new types of organizations for achieving empowerment within the Democratic Party. Much of the attention on these options, however, has been on alternative party organizations in the form of independent black political parties.

Throughout their history in America, blacks have been involved, directly and indirectly, in third-party politics, often joining other racial and ethnic groups in forming third parties.[10] Yet they also have founded all-black political parties, primarily in deep Southern states like Mississippi and Alabama during the era of racial segregation.[11] These independent black political parties have been formed for two reasons. One, black participation has been denied within one or the other major party. Two, blacks decided that aspects of their political and socioeconomic concerns could not, or would not, be met by the established majority parties. However, the formation of alternative political organizations in the form of black third parties has proven difficult to start and sustain over time.

There is, however, another option that blacks have chosen besides direct participation in the activities of the established majority or the formation of minor parties. Specifically, some blacks have elected to form alternative *nonparty* political organizations. The subsequent sections of this chapter discuss church-based, nonparty organizations, which constitute a particular type of alternative nonparty organization that has been used by blacks seeking to exercise their political influence in pursuit of empowerment in Queens. As the chapter documents, the formation of, and participation in, an alternative organization by the black clergy in the 6th Congressional District, which was financially and organizationally supported by their congregants, developed in response to the local Democratic Party's unresponsiveness to black concerns, which is considered by some party theorists to be a strong form of party failure.

THE 6TH CONGRESSIONAL DISTRICT
AND ACTIVIST BLACK CLERGY

In *The Struggle for Black Empowerment in New York City*, Green and Wilson contend that the "rising of political activism of the black church have increased the political power of the church in the black community."[12] Emanating from places like Manhattan's Abyssinian Baptist Church, Brooklyn's St. Paul's Community Church, and the Bronx's Walker-Memorial, black church-based politics has been ascending in New York City. In the borough of Queens political activity on the part of black churches has been just as strong. Since the middle part of the 1980s, a network of black clergy has exercised political influence in Southeast Queens, particularly within the 6th Congressional District. This black church-based political activism has brought new actors into the political process. It has also led to the creation and endurance of an alternative political organization that has continually prodded the local Democratic Party to remain responsive to the needs, grievances, and desires of a considerable segment of its membership.

The 6th district is located in the southeastern section of Queens County. Like the county in which it is contained, the district is mostly middle class, but it is also predominantly black. In large measure, the residents of the district live in cross-class communities in which the black middle class and its institutions, particularly black churches, serve the district through organizational development, political leadership, and entrepreneurship. Up through the middle 1980s, when blacks comprised a minority of the district's constituents, the involvement of the black clergy in the electoral politics of the district was confined to a supporting role in mobilizing voters for the Democratic Party. Midway through the 1980s, when blacks came to numerical predominance in the district, the black clergy became politically radicalized. This resulted in the transference of a considerable amount of black political participation to extraparty political activity.

THE SOUTHEAST QUEENS CLERGY
FOR COMMUNITY EMPOWERMENT

In 1984, a cadre of black clergy joined together to assist Jesse Jackson's effort to win the New York Democratic presidential primary election. While Jackson did not win the primary, this collection of black clergy, acting through their churches and their congregants, mobilized a considerable number of black voters and, most importantly, delegates for the Jackson campaign. The results of the election show that Jackson received more than forty thousand votes in Queen's 6th Congressional District, outpacing Walter Mondale's and Gary Hart's primary vote totals. Indeed, Jackson's vote totals in the district were twice the number of the combined votes of Mondale and Hart. This successful mobilization of the black communities found among the precincts of Southeast Queens impressed upon the informal group of black clergy that (1) they could be influential in local Democratic party politics and (2) they needed to organize themselves as an institution.[13] The result of their institutionalization was the formation of the Southeast Queens Clergy for Community Empowerment (SQCCE).

Cognizant that a single church could not affect the overall conditions of blacks and that political parties tend to be responsive to those interests that are organized, the pastors of the largest black churches in Southeast Queens joined together to create an organization that would pursue black political empowerment through party and extraparty channels. Comprised of pastors from approximately seventy churches, the SQCCE was founded in 1984 with the specific aim of enhancing the participation and influence of blacks within the Queens Democratic Party organization. The SQCCE, however, has not operated as a mass organization. Membership in the organization has been limited to the black clergy, with each member-pastor required to contribute monthly to the organization. Additionally, member churches have been annually assessed a fee for supporting SQCCE's political mobilization and community development activities. The executive committee of the SQCCE is democratically elected, with provisions for term limits among the leadership positions of the organization. Moreover, the SQCCE tends toward professional rather than protest politics. Whereas other black church-based nonparty organizations may engage in confrontational acts along the lines of the Saul Alinsky school of community politics, the SQCCE, with its middle-class organizational base, prefers to engage in the politics of bargaining, compromise, and reconciliation. However, it has maintained an oppositional stance toward the local Democratic Party.

CHURCH-BASED, BLACK POLITICAL ACTIVISM IN LOCAL ELECTORAL POLITICS

The summer of 1984 witnessed the SQCCE insinuating itself in the local electoral politics of Southeast Queens. In the months leading up to the Democratic primary for the 6th Congressional District, the SQCCE became a pivotal actor in the election's outcome. Having served the district for twenty-four years, Joseph Addabbo, the white incumbent congressman, sought reelection to a thirteenth term. However, Addabbo, despite his tenure in the district and seniority in Congress, was not guaranteed victory in the autumn primary. Unlike prior elections, the district had become majority black. The new district was the product of redistricting following the 1980 Census.[14] As the *New York Times* proclaimed at the time, the new 6th district provided "certainty among people in New York politics that . . . a black politician [soon would] represent the district in Congress."[15] In the 1982 Democratic primary election, a black candidate did challenge Addabbo. Simeon Golar, a former New York City housing commissioner during the Lindsay administration and a prosperous real-estate developer, ran strong against Addabbo in the primary, capturing 43 percent of the votes cast. Two years later, Golar again challenged Addabbo for his congressional seat.

Noting the relationship between politicians and the black clergy, Fredrick Harris observes that "although some commentators criticize the appropriateness of black clerics as representatives of black interests in the American polity, political entrepreneurs certainly woo the activist clergy within black communities as a means to legitimize and garner support for their political goals."[16] As the black population of Southeast Queens multiplied during the 1970s, Addabbo formed ties with activist black clergy. Acknowledging the significant role black churches have often played in partisan politics in New York City, Addabbo rightly believed that an endorsement from SQCCE would be critical to his reelection bid in the newly formed majority-minority district. Therefore, he actively sought the backing of the SQCCE in order to legitimize his candidacy and energize black support for his reelection bid. Golar, on the other hand, neglected to pursue the support of the black clergy, or a grassroots campaign, in the district. Instead, he focused on developing technical resources for his campaign by using phone banks, polling, fundraising, and speaking engagements before local business interests.

In the end, the SQCCE gave Addabbo their support. The group's rationale was straightforward. Golar was, figuratively and literally, an outsider to the district and Addabbo was a close ally of the clergy and their churches. As one member of the SQCCE stated: "This is not a black issue; we're going by performance and Mr. Addabbo has been very representative of the community. . . . It would serve no purpose to have Congressman Addabbo replaced by a freshman representative."[17] With the endorsement of the SQCCE, Addabbo won the election by more than seventeen thousand votes.[18] Of the nearly fifty thousand ballots cast in behalf of the two candidates, Golar received only a third of the votes. But into the second year of his term in Congress, Addabbo died and a special election was called for the summer of 1986.

The research of Thomas Kazee and Mary Thornberry on congressional candidate recruitment informs us that in many congressional districts local political parties play both direct and indirect roles in determining who the candidates will be in congressional elections.[19] In the special election to replace Addabbo, four candidates actively sought the nomination of the Democratic Party. In Southeast Queens, as is the case in other Democratic strongholds throughout New York City, the endorsement of the Democratic Party is tantamount to victory in almost any election, especially a congressional election. Among the candidates seeking the party's formal support were State Assemblyman Alton Waldon, State Senator Andrew Jenkins, and Assistant New York City Health Commissioner Kevin McCabe. Another candidate vying for the office was the Reverend Floyd Flake. Flake, pastor of the Allen A.M.E. Church, where two-thirds of its four thousand members were registered Democrats, was active in the black clerical community and had lived in the district since 1976.

Though a novice to electoral politics, the SQCCE chose Flake as its candidate of choice to complete Addabbo's term in office. It recruited him, financed and staffed his campaign, and lobbied the Queens Democratic Party leadership to consider him for the nomination. The SQCCE predicted, along with other political actors in the district, that Flake would receive the party's endorsement. This expectation was driven by three specific factors. First, Addabbo maintained an attentive relationship with the membership of the SQCCE, especially Flake. For example, while in Congress, Addabbo provided Flake with funds that underwrote many of the Allen A.M.E. Church's community and economic development activities. In particular, Addabbo secured federal funding for the church's development of an $11 million senior citizens complex and the construction of its private elementary school. Second, the SQCCE had proven itself a serious political actor in the 1984 Democratic presidential primary. In general, the SQCCE was credited with ensuring Jackson's victory in the 6th district. Specifically, the SQCCE was acknowledged as the primary reason Jackson carried the district by 63 percent of the vote.[20] Furthermore, up to this point, the SQCCE's influence in local Democratic politics was, like the Jackson campaign and the Democratic National Committee, dependent on the fear that if the leaders of the Queens Democratic Party did not negotiate, black voters would lose faith with the party and resort to extraparty activities. And third, the SQCCE banked on the legacy of the black church and its connection with black voters and their subsequent support for candidates endorsed by the black clergy. Despite the strong relationship between Addabbo and the SQCCE, the leadership of the Queens Democratic Party endorsed State Assemblyman Waldon over Flake.

Ware, in his research on the demise of the Democratic Party organization, observed that one of the successes of black churches over time has been their ability to be "a major power base *independent* of the parties in many cities."[21] The Queens Democratic Party, however, overlooked this observation, probably because of the truism of nomination politics: unless they have enough members to control a majority party, "an interest group seeking to determine the outcome of a nomination must either run its own candidate as an independent, as a candidate among a host of others in a primary battle, or seek to establish a party in its own name,"[22] all of which are difficult tasks to achieve. Yet the SQCCE opted for the first alternative. In turn, Flake, backed by a successful petition campaign conducted by the SQCCE, acquired enough signatures from the district to secure a place on the ballot as an independent candidate under the "Unity Party" banner. And in the initial counting of the special election ballots, Flake was declared the winner. But a recount, which included absentee ballots that were not previously counted, resulted in the election of the Democratic Party nominee by less than three hundred votes.[23]

Waldon's victory in the special election ultimately proved illusory. For instead of uniting behind him and the Democratic Party, the SQCCE filed a new set of petitions for Flake to run in the primary for a full term. In the fall primary election, Waldon, who was supported by then Governor Mario Cuomo and a host of other party regulars, again faced Flake, who by the time of the election was endorsed by the *New York Times* and then Mayor Edward I. Koch. In the weeks leading up to this contest, the SQCCE mobilized the congregations of their member churches, which provided resources to Flake that rivaled or surpassed the resources available to Waldon from the Queens Democratic Party. In particular, Flake's church-based candidacy allowed for him to directly tap into the most visible and influential institutions in the 6th Congressional District—the black churches. The resources the SQCCE and its member churches provided to Flake were those that politically active black churches have often provided to political candidates: group endorsements by ministers and religious groups, clerical appeals, church-sponsored political forums and rallies, candidate contacts at religious services, and fundraising for political candidates.

Responding to the leadership of their churches, the individual congregations of the SQCCE turned out in large numbers to volunteer for Flake's campaign. Similar to Harold Washington's mayoral campaign in Chicago (see chapter 7), the people who joined Flake's campaign, both registered and unregistered voters, "performed all of the conventional activities: distributing literature, putting up posters, and knocking on doors to target voters for election day."[24] Church congregants also raised campaign funds, carried his petitions, and extended invitations to Flake to appear before them during their Sunday services. In the end, like Washington's "church connection," Flake's affiliation with SQCCE was "instrumental in transforming the political campaign into a civil rights movement, a politico-religious crusade."[25] The result of this crusade in the district was a three-thousand-vote margin of victory for Flake and the SQCCE over Waldon and the Queens Democratic Party in the fall primary election. Soon after, Flake and the SQCCE went on to win the general election. This victory was achieved under the banner of the Democratic Party.

INSIGHTS INTO ALTERNATIVE BLACK POLITICAL ORGANIZATIONS AND ACTIVISM

Since Reconstruction, blacks have been active participants in the political process. The most noted illustration of this participation has been their involvement with the major political parties as voters, activists, and candidates. The enduring involvement of blacks within both the Republican and Democratic parties has been fostered by civic duty and political and economic expediency. Blacks have been drawn to partisan politics mostly out of a belief that partisan politics would allow them to achieve what other racial and ethnic groups are believed to already possess—empowerment. Consequently, blacks have used partisan politics to pursue two complementary objectives. The first goal of black partisan participation has been to insinuate themselves fully into the processes of public decision making. The second aim of black involvement with the dominant political parties has been to share political power with other groups. In short, black politics, as Mary D. Coleman has observed, constitutes nothing short of "a systematic struggle to acquire equal formal and informal access to, and effective control of, the available political, economic, and institutional resources of this country."[26]

Most students of black empowerment and black partisan politics tend to focus their attention at the national level. But some of the most important struggles for black political advancement have or are occurring at the municipal level of politics. While not as strong as they used to be, local parties are still influential in structuring the politics of cities, especially in those places where political machines endure. In many instances, these local parties have served as agents for black advancement. That is to say, they have been open to black participation at all levels and they have been responsive to black concerns, especially with regard to descriptive representation among the personnel of parties and municipal government. Nevertheless, there have been those instances where local parties have imposed barriers to the full political incorporation and advancement of blacks. In these situations, local parties have been successful at limiting the participation of blacks in party decision making; they have overlooked the desires of black constituents with regard to policy outcomes; and they have generally taken the black vote for granted. All of these actions have been made possible by the fact that one-party systems dominate most election districts,[27] if not all majority-black election districts.

Yet history provides examples where, faced with barriers to participation and influence over, for example, the selection of candidates for local office, blacks have formed alternative organizations and challenged the hegemony of dominant local parties. In these instances, it has often been black churches that have afforded blacks critical organizational resources for the mobilization of protest "through clerical leadership and through formal and informal networks of communication."[28] Consequently, throughout the history of blacks in America, churches have been recognized as the traditional bases of political power within black communities. Most scholars and commentators on the black political experience agree that the church has served as the foundation for political mobilization and participation among black Americans.[29] Some, however, have viewed the institution of the black church as negligible, even oppositional to the mobilization and participation of blacks in the political system.[30] Nonetheless, many black churches in the contemporary period, as the survey research of Fredrick Harris attests, "have a strong commitment to political activism, and black church goers generally approve of that commitment."[31]

To date, the most visible demonstrations of church-based, black political organization and activism were the involvement of black clerics and their congregations in the 1984 and 1988 presidential campaigns of Jesse Jackson and the 1983 Chicago mayoral campaign of the late Harold Washington. In these instances, politically active black clergy and their institutions basically functioned as nonparty bosses and ward organizations, who skillfully conducted voter registration drives, canvassed registered voters, organized get-out-the-vote events, raised campaign funds, and transported voters to the polls. In the case of Queens County and the SQCCE, the primary objective behind the creation of an alternative black political organization, which manifested itself in the form of church-based, black political activism, was to enhance the influence of blacks within the local Democratic Party.

As a consequence of its activism over the last twelve years, the SQCCE has become a significant force in the local politics of Southeast Queens. Its visibility and acceptance as an elemental unit in the politics of the 6th Congressional District is largely the result of one of its members—Floyd Flake, pastor of the Allen A.M.E. Church. Taken together, as Green and Wilson note, "the election of the Reverend Floyd Flake to Congress and the emergence of the [SQCCE] have created new opportunities for blacks to exercise power in the borough of Queens."[32] By successfully operating beyond the confines of party organizations, the SQCCE has not only furthered the reputation of politically active black churches as important conduits for black political participation, but it has provided black voters in the district with a instrument for responding to various levels of failure on the part of the Queens County Democratic Party. This is not to say that blacks in Southeast Queens have disaligned from the Democratic Party and realigned with the SQCCE. On the contrary, blacks in the district solidly remain Democratic. It is to admit, however, that blacks in Southeast Queens have identified a supplemental means of participating in the electoral process, one that holds out the possibility for the achievement of greater influence over the outcomes of local electoral politics.

Recognizing that at the level of the states and counties, local parties truly are "the weakest link in the party organizational chain" due to their limited influence and scant resources,[33] it seems plausible that blacks seeking to be more influential in the local politics of other majority-black and urban places will, in the face of party failure, form alternative nonparty organizations. If so, local Democratic parties, which are often *the* political institutions dominating the electoral systems of majority-black districts, may face increasing challenges from alternative black political organizations seeking to provide black voters and nonvoters alike with opportunities for participation, input, and empowerment, especially with regard to candidate selection and party nominations. Due to their ability to provide critical organizational resources for protest mobilization and political organizing in urban black communities, it seems highly likely that future pursuits of black empowerment with regard to local Democratic parties, and urban politics in general, will be led by church-based, black nonparty organizations along the lines of the Southeast Queens Clergy for Community Empowerment.

The appearance—or disappearance—of alternative black political organizations is tied to the opportunity structures local political parties provide for black participation and political advancement. If the dominant political parties are open to black participation and receptive to calls for black empowerment, blacks will channel all of their political activity through them. In the absence of openness and responsiveness, blacks can be expected to channel much, but not all, of their political activity into alternative political organizations formed by blacks. However, due to the constraints that alternative party organizations can expect to face, along with the fact that black clerics are increasingly involving themselves and their churches in urban electoral politics today, the type of alternative black political organization that will tend to predominate will be the church-based, black nonparty organization. For in the face of local party failure, black churches, with their "communication networks, their capacity to stimulate social interaction, provide material resources, and give individuals the opportunity to learn organizing skills, and, perhaps most importantly, their sustainability over time and physical space,"[34] offer the best hope for blacks to correct local Democratic Party failure when it occurs.

NOTES

1. Charles Green and Basil Wilson, *The Struggle for Black Empowerment in New York City: Beyond the Politics of Pigmentation* (New York: McGraw-Hill, 1992), 59.

2. For examples, see Hardy T. Frye, *Black Parties and Political Power: A Case Study* (Boston: G. K. Hall and Co., 1980) and Hanes Walton Jr., *Black Political Parties: An Historical and Political Analysis* (1972; repr., New York: Free Press, 1975).

3. Alan Ware, *The Breakdown of Democratic Party Organization, 1940–1980* (Oxford: Clarendon Press, 1985), 212.

4. Allison Calhoun-Brown, "African American Churches and Political Mobilization: The Psychological Impact of Organizational Resources," *Journal of Politics* 58, no. 4 (November 1996): 936.

5. See Kay Lawson and Peter H. Merkl, eds., *When Parties Fail: Emerging Alternative Organizations* (Princeton: Princeton University Press, 1988), particularly chs. 7, 11, and 14.

6. See Kay Lawson, "When Linkage Fails," in *When Parties Fail*, 13–38.

7. See Peter H. Merkl, "Challengers and Party Systems," in *When Parties Fail*, 574–78.

8. See Richard Rose and Thomas T. Mackie, "Do Parties Persist or Fail? The Big Trade-off Facing Organizations," in *When Parties Fail*, 533–58.

9. Frye, *Black Parties and Political Power*, xv (emphasis added).

10. See the following by Hanes Walton Jr.: "Blacks and the 1968 Third Parties," *Negro Educational Review*, January 1970, 19–23; *The Negro in Third Party Politics*

(Philadelphia: Dorrance and Co., 1969); and "The Negro in Early Third Party Movements," *Negro Educational Review*, April–July 1968, 73–82.

11. Hanes Walton Jr., *Black Political Parties: An Historical and Political Analysis*; "The National Democratic Party of Alabama and Party Failure in America"; *Black Republicans: The Politics of the Black and Tans* (Metuchen, N.J.: Scarecrow Press, 1975); and Frye, *Black Parties and Political Power*.

12. Green and Wilson, *Struggle for Black Empowerment*, 59.

13. Green and Wilson, *Struggle for Black Empowerment*, 59.

14. Addabbo was offered an opportunity to run in a majority-white district. The party leadership afforded Addabbo the option of running for the congressional seat vacated by Geraldine Ferraro. Had he accepted, the Queens Democratic party could have nominated a black candidate for the sixth congressional district. Addabbo, however, declined the offer. See "Addabbo Staying Put," *New York Times*, 28 July 1984, B3.

15. "Addabbo's Seat Focus of New Black Hopes," *New York Times*, 2 May 1984, B1.

16. Harris, "Religious Institutions and African American Political Mobilization," 295.

17. "Group of Black Clergymen Backs the Re-election of Rep. Addabbo," *New York Times*, 4 July 1984, B2.

18. Queens County Board of Elections, *Statement and Return of Primary and General Elections* (Queens, N.Y.: Queens County Board of Elections, 1984).

19. Thomas A. Kazee and Mary C. Thornberry, "Where's the Party? Congressional Candidate Recruitment and American Party Organizations," *Western Political Quarterly*, March 1990, 77.

20. Adolph L. Reed Jr., *The Jesse Jackson Phenomenon: The Crisis of Purpose in Afro-American Politics* (New Haven: Yale University Press, 1986), 23.

21. Ware, *Breakdown of Democratic Party Organization*, 210 (emphasis added).

22. Xandra Kayden and Eddie Mahe Jr., *The Party Goes On: The Persistence of the Two-Party System in the United States* (New York: Basic Books, 1985), 145.

23. Flake's name was omitted from the ballot by the board of elections due to a technicality in his petition filings. His name was reinstated by the State Supreme Court after the mail ballots had been sent out.

24. William J. Grimshaw, "Unraveling the Enigma: Mayor Harold Washington and the Black Political Tradition," *Urban Affairs Quarterly* 23, no. 2 (1987): 203.

25. Grimshaw, "Unraveling the Enigma," 203.

26. Mary D. Coleman, "The Black Elected Elites in Mississippi: The Post-Civil Rights Apportionment Era," in *Black Politics and Political Behavior: A Linkage Analysis,* ed. Hanes Walton Jr. (Westport, Conn.: Praeger, 1994), 69.

27. According to Theodore J. Lowi, "two-party systems have prevailed in only a minority of all electoral districts in the United States since 1896. Most of the districts, from those that elect members of state legislatures up to the state as a whole in presidential elections, have in fact been dominated by one-party systems." See Theodore J. Lowi, "Toward a Responsible Three-Party System," in *The State of the Parties*, ed. John C. Green and Daniel M. Shea (Lanham, Md.: Rowman & Littlefield, 1999), 46.

28. Harris, "Religious Institutions and African American Political Mobilization," 278.

29. For examples, see C. Eric Lincoln and Lawrence Mamiya, *The Black Church in the African American Experience* (Durham: Duke University Press, 1990); Gayraud Wilmore, *Black Religion and Black Radicalism* (Maryknoll, N.Y.: Orbis, 1985); Benjamin E. Mays and James Nicholson, *The Negro's Church* (New York: Institute of Social and Religious Research, 1933); and W. E. B. DuBois, *The Souls of Black Folk* (Greenwich, Conn.: Fawcett Publications, 1968).

30. For examples, see Reed, *Jesse Jackson Phenomenon*, particularly ch. 4, and E. Franklin Frazier, *The Negro Church in America* (New York: Schoken, 1964).

31. Harris, "Religious Institutions and African American Political Mobilization," 307.

32. Green and Wilson, *Struggle for Black Empowerment*, 75.

33. Kayden and Mahe, *Party Goes On*, 105.

34. Harris, "Religious Institutions and African American Political Mobilization," 279.

III

EPILOGUE

11

Black Clergy and the Governmental Sector during George W. Bush's Presidency

R. Drew Smith

Black clergy relations with the governmental sector during George W. Bush's presidency have centered around two strategic instincts that appear fundamentally in tension—a tension that President Bush and national, state, and local Republican officials have hoped to turn to their political advantage. On the one hand, there is the civil rights tradition with its emphasis on holding government accountable for promoting and protecting social fairness and justice. Black churches became most strongly associated with this tradition through their high-profile civil rights activism during the mid-twentieth century, although black church demands for black rights began at least with nineteenth-century black church involvement in abolitionism and carried forward through active alliances with the NAACP and other civic groups during the first half of the twentieth century. On the other hand, there is the community development tradition, which focuses less on structural reform than on unleashing the institutional and human capacities resident within the black community and within the broader society that contribute to black social progress and improvement. This tradition dates back at least to eighteenth-century efforts to form independent black institutions—with black churches serving as a prototype of sorts of this institutional independence and as an incubator for the formation of independent black educational, fraternal, civic, social service, and business institutions.

Potential divergences in the way these two traditions respond to government were spotlighted when President Bush traveled to Atlanta and New Orleans for Martin Luther King Day observances in January 2004. In New Orleans, President Bush visited an inner-city African Methodist Episcopal church where he promoted government funding of faith-based social services in a speech before the congregation and at a roundtable for select

187

clergy and community leaders. Bush's remarks outlined a central role for the faith community in responding to social needs, stating: "Problems that face our society are oftentimes problems that . . . require something greater than just a government program or a government counselor to solve." Bush viewed faith as an answer to intractable social problems because, said Bush, "faith is a power greater than all others."[1] The president's remarks reportedly played well among the numerous black clergy and congregants in attendance. The church where Bush spoke and the New Orleans setting were both strategic because the congregation reportedly engages in "the kind of social ministries the Bush administration believes work effectively, and ought to be fed with more federal dollars" and Louisiana is a state that "steers more than $430,000 a year in federal block-grant money to faith-based groups."[2]

The second leg of Bush's Southern swing was to Atlanta (and to the heart of the Auburn Avenue district discussed by Alton Pollard in chapter 1 of this volume), where his decision to lay a wreath at Dr. King's grave generated a firestorm of criticism from black Atlantans. They were upset about the disruptive effect of the president's visit upon their own King Day activities but, even more so, about what they perceived as the disingenuousness of a Bush visit to King's grave when the policies of his administration run counter to so much of what King stood for. Bush's arrival at King's gravesite was greeted by hundreds of protesters who booed him, chanted slogans such as "Bush go home," and carried signs with messages such as "Money for jobs and housing, not war." A press release issued by organizers of the protests, including the Georgia Peace and Justice Coalition headed by civil rights veteran Joseph Lowery and the Concerned Black Clergy, referred to Bush's visit as "transparent opportunism" and stated that "President Bush's domestic and foreign policies contradict every value for which Dr. King lived and died." Reverend Timothy McDonald, who heads Concerned Black Clergy, led a prayer vigil and held a press conference at the site where he referred to Bush's visit as "the epitome of insult." Another representative of Concerned Black Clergy, Reverend Raphael Allen, accused the Bush administration of "never supporting anything to help the poor, education, or children." At the King Day service held at Ebenezer Baptist Church a few days after Bush's visit, Atlanta Mayor Shirley Franklin reiterated the disconnect between Bush's policies and his symbolic tribute to King: "Perhaps some prefer to honor the dreamer while ignoring or fighting the dream. For those of us who hold elective office, the public policy we advocate and adopt—from foreign affairs to domestic budgeting— tells the real story of our celebration of Dr. King's legacy."[3] Clearly, then, if President Bush's visit to the King site was intended to score points with black voters, it missed the mark—especially, it would seem, among black Atlantans.

In certain respects, the contrasting black church responses to Bush's Atlanta and New Orleans visits point to real divergences between civil rights and community development traditions, but they also feed a dichotomization between these two traditions that may be more apparent than real. That is to say that while Bush's experience may suggest at first glance that these two traditions are mutually exclusive, a greater overlap and convergence may actually exist between the two traditions than is sometimes assumed. The present discussion (1) examines points of political divergence and convergence between these two traditions as embraced by black clergy and (2) details Republican Party efforts during George W. Bush's presidency to magnify and exploit perceived or actual political divergences between various black clergy. Data are also analyzed from a 1999–2000 survey of 1,956 African American churches that point to elements of black religious affinity with aspects of the current Republican political agenda, especially the faith-based agenda and vouchers. Nevertheless, the conclusion is that none of this suggests a lessening of black commitments to civil rights or to political leaders and institutions that embody those civil rights commitments.

TIP OF THE ICEBERG? TENSIONS AMONG ACTIVIST BLACK CLERGY

There is a certain level of tension between black civil rights advocates and community development advocates that seems verifiable, longstanding, and rooted in part in disagreements over the most effective political strategies for achieving two things: optimizing structural opportunities for black progress and opposing structural constraints. That is to say, given the strategic disadvantages resulting from their minority numerical status and distorted developmental process within the United States, how do African Americans pursue a practical balance between confronting oppressive aspects of America's social systems and cooperating with beneficial aspects of its social systems? The concern in both instances is with advancing the interests of black people, but the challenge has been determining which strategy is likely to yield the greater advantage in a given instance.

This debate among African Americans over optimizing opportunities versus opposing constraints dates back at least to the late nineteenth century and early twentieth century. The two positions were embodied in a very public way by Tuskegee Institute founder Booker T. Washington and by NAACP cofounder and Harvard trained sociologist W. E. B. Du Bois. Washington's assessment was that black progress, particularly within the racially hostile context of the post-Reconstruction South, was best achieved by leveraging resources for black self-improvement and social capacity building from within the black community and from sympathetic whites in charge of public and private resources rather than by agitating for political rights. Washington stated: "I believe it is the duty of the Negro . . . to deport himself modestly in regard to political claims, depending upon the slow but sure influences that proceed from the possession of property, intelligence, and high character for the full recognition of his political rights."[4] Washington's position gained broad support within the Southern white community and among a large number of blacks as well. His position was strongly criticized, however, by Du Bois and others who felt that it played directly into the hands of those determined to withhold political rights from blacks. Du Bois put the matter this way: "But so far as Mr. Washington apologizes for injustice, North or South, does not rightly value the privilege and duty of voting, belittles the emasculating effects of caste distinctions, and opposes the higher training and ambition of our brighter minds . . . we must unceasingly and firmly oppose [him]. By every civilized and peaceful method we must strive for the rights which the world accords to men."[5] The social circumstances and political context for this debate have shifted over the last century, but in many ways the tension between optimizing opportunities and opposing constraints has remained a point of separation between a black *conservative* and *liberal* politics—with *conservative* suggesting operating within the status quo and *liberal* suggesting working to reform the social context so as to provide maximum benefits to a maximum number of people.[6]

Strategic tensions between contemporary clergy activists over whether to focus on opportunities or on constraints are captured within a number of chapters in the present volume. For example, Sherri Wallace argues in chapter 3 that black clergy in Buffalo tended to be more receptive to community economic development than they were to civil rights activism, both during and after the civil rights movement. Wallace details how Reverend Bennett W. Smith, cognizant of this dynamic, facilitated community development partnerships among Buffalo-area clergy as a means of generating trust, social engagement, and institutional networking among clergy that could lead to greater clergy willingness and capacity to engage in civil rights activism. Also, Yvette Alex-Assensoh's chapter points out that clergy in Columbus recognized the need for an activism strategy that focuses simultaneously on economic and civic empowerment, with the economic empowerment initiatives emphasizing church partnerships with the governmental and private sector. Fredrick Harris's chapter on Chicago, however, makes clear that community development commitments by clergy can sometimes privilege cooperation with government in ways that undermine or preclude the ability, and even the will, of churches to pursue urgently needed criticism and reform of social and political systems.

Certainly there are political tensions between black civil rights traditions and community development traditions, but are these two positions as divergent or mutually exclusive as they appear and as some pundits and political strategists suggest? Trends and patterns revealed through examination of the 1999–2000 BCAP survey bear in important ways on the extent of strategic division between black clergy and the likelihood that Republicans might effectively exploit these divisions in order to increase black voter support.

FROM IDEOLOGICAL TENSIONS TO POLITICAL BEHAVIOR

How does the ideological positioning of black clergy translate into public policy support? Important details about black clergy public policy positioning are captured in the 1999–2000 Black Churches and Politics Survey (BCAP), including black clergy support of civil rights and government funding of church-related social services.[7]

One of the questions clergy were asked was whether their congregation had been involved in civil rights policies as part of their congregational mission during the previous ten years. Thirty-one percent of the 1,956 respondents answered yes to the question. Respondents were also asked three separate questions that bear on their support for government funding of church-based social services. First, they were asked whether their congregation had programs for which it receives government funding. Twenty-four percent said yes. Second, they were asked whether they agreed or disagreed with the government encouraging churches to apply for and use government funds to provide social services. Forty-six percent of the respondents expressed agreement with the policy.[8] Third, they were asked whether they agreed or disagreed with tax dollars for public education being made available to parents in the form of vouchers that can be applied toward private education for their children. (Studies have shown that in many cases these vouchers have been applied toward church-related schools.)[9] Forty-three percent of the BCAP survey respondents expressed agreement with the policy (see table 11.1).[10]

Although almost one-half of the respondents expressed agreement with government funding of church-related social services and with voucher programs, only about one-quarter of the congregations represented by the respondents actually had programs that received government funding. There are several potential reasons for this gap between opinion and behavior, not least of which are insufficient information and expertise by churches relative to government funding procedures. It could also be that while certain black clergy agree in theory with the idea of government funding of church-related social services, implementing this idea is not a priority. For example, churches may view the time and energy required to build new partnerships with institutions outside their normal sphere of operation as outweighing any potential advantages of such partnerships—especially if churches have more immediate sources of institutional support upon which they can rely.

Table 11.1.   Geographic Distinctions among Black Churches on Civil Rights and Government Funding

		Political Actions			Political Attitudes	
		CivilRts[a]	GovFundProg[b]		GovtFund[c]	Vouch[d]
	N	% Yes	% Yes	N	% Agree	%Agree
General	1,956	31	24	324	46	43
Chicago	160	41	20	31	74	48
Philadelphia	116	26	25	25	68	68
Detroit	150	29	24	24	66	70
Atlanta	159	23	16	49	30	24
Washington	92	28	43	53	39	39

Source: 1999–2000 BCAP Survey.
[a] During the past ten years, has your congregation been directly involved in [civil rights policies] as part of their congregational mission?
[b] Does your congregation have any programs for which it receives government funding?
[c] It is helpful that the government is now encouraging churches to apply for and use government funds to provide social services.
[d] Tax dollars for public education can be put to better use in the form of vouchers that parents can apply toward private school fees for their children.

It is instructive to note that 31 percent stated congregational involvement with civil rights advocacy as opposed to 24 percent whose congregation received government funding—which, while not a significant difference in the proportions of these two types of clergy involvement, is consistent with general findings about African American political priorities. African Americans, and churchgoing African Americans as a subgroup, have identified civil rights as their top political priority with great regularity, as in the case of a Gallup survey conducted in the late 1980s. The Gallup survey (which was a general population survey) showed that 84 percent of black Protestant respondents strongly identified with civil rights, which was roughly 25 percentage points higher than the next two highest categories on the list (peace and anticommunism) and at least double the percentage of any of the other eight categories.[11] Among BCAP survey respondents, the next highest categories of political involvement after civil rights were public welfare, affirmative action, and criminal justice—each arguably a civil rights–related policy itself, and each indicated by approximately 25 percent of the BCAP respondents. Nineteen percent indicated involvement with government economic development policies.[12] Interestingly, polling data from the Pew Forum and the Pew Research Center show essentially the same amount of black Protestant support for government funding of church-based social services (83 percent) as Gallup polling data show for black Protestant support for civil rights issues.[13] Implications of this parallel issue support will be discussed below.

These national-level data on black church political priorities provide insights into how various issues rank in importance among black churchgoers.

Also revealing are variations in black church issue priorities from city to city (see table 11.1). Among the few select cities analyzed in the table, BCAP respondents from Chicago and Detroit had the highest rate of civil rights involvement (41 and 29 percent respectively) followed closely by Washington, D.C. (28 percent). The rate of civil rights involvement in Philadelphia and Atlanta was slightly lower. While there were not significant differences between these cities in rates of civil rights involvement (except for Chicago's somewhat higher rate), there were real differences in rates of support for government funding of church-based social services. Seventy-four percent of Chicago respondents and 66 percent of Detroit respondents supported government funding of church-related social services, while 70 percent of Detroit respondents and 48 percent of Chicago respondents supported vouchers. These Chicago and Detroit results would seem to reinforce the entrepreneurial characterizations of black clergy in these two cities as conveyed in chapter 7 by Harris and in chapter 9 by Brown and Hartfield. By contrast, BCAP respondents in the southeastern cities of Washington, D.C., and Atlanta—a region often characterized as possessing higher rates of black religiosity than other regions of the United States[14]—expressed little support for involvement by government in the provision of their social and educational services. Support for government-funded social services and for vouchers was 39 percent for both categories among Washington, D.C., respondents, and 30 percent for social services and 24 percent for vouchers among Atlanta respondents. This suggests, among other things, that high levels of religiosity do not necessarily translate into support for government funding of church-based programs—as demonstrated by opposition to Bush's faith-based initiative by white Evangelicals.

THE FEDERAL GOVERNMENT AND ELECTORAL RECRUITMENT AMONG BLACK CHURCHES

The chapters in this volume have situated black church activism within the local political trajectories and contexts of various cities. But it is important in assessing tactical and strategic tensions among activist black churches to reflect briefly on possible implications of those political tensions within the current national political context. Since George W. Bush took office in 2001, Bush and other Republican Party leaders have engaged in a fairly concerted campaign to exploit weak and divided party loyalties within the black electorate. Special attention has been given in this effort to churchgoing blacks—no doubt because of the preponderance of churchgoing blacks and because of calculations about stronger conservative tendencies and affinities among black churchgoers. Black churchgoers have in fact displayed strong anti–gay rights tendencies, as in early 2004 when three black clergy associations in the

Boston area and a group of black Baptist ministers in Chicago issued public statements condemning same-sex marriage.[15] (As Jennings shows in chapter 5 and Harris in chapter 7, there are other elements of the political position-ing of black clergy in these two cities that appear more status quo than re-formist in nature—mainly, the unusually close collaboration between black clergy and police in Boston and the strong patronage relationships between black clergy and government officials in Chicago.) Republican assessments about a general moral conservatism on the part of black churchgoers and clergy, and about the potential receptivity of black churchgoers and clergy to governmental funding of faith-based social service programs, has led Re-publican strategists to believe that a strategic targeting of black churchgoers and clergy could result in perhaps a doubling of their current voter share within the African American community.

A few weeks after the November 2000 elections, President-elect Bush convened a meeting in Austin with approximately thirty hand-picked reli-gious leaders, many of whom were black, to signal the importance his ad-ministration would place on partnering with the faith community on social services and other matters. The African American clergy invited to the meet-ing were in many cases clergy known to emphasize community develop-ment involvements more than political rights involvements and who tended to operate independently of the historically black ecclesiastical structures that many would regard as the black religious mainstream and as the back-bone of black church-based civic activism. The list of black clergy invitees included, for example, a number of black Pentecostal and charismatic clergy such as Bishop Charles Blake of the Church of God in Christ, Bishop Carlton Pearson of Higher Dimensions Church, and Reverend Eugene Rivers, cofounder of the Ten Point Coalition, whose crime reduction em-phasis is discussed in the Jennings chapter. Also in attendance were former Democratic Congressman Floyd Flake, who is an African Methodist Episco-pal Church pastor and was a prospect at the time for a possible Bush cabi-net appointment (and who is discussed more fully in chapter 10 by Owens); Reverend Kirbyjon Caldwell, a United Methodist pastor and strong Bush supporter who gave the invocation prayer at Bush's inauguration; and Rev-erend Herbert Lusk, a Baptist pastor and another close ally of Bush and his faith-based initiative proposal. Noticeably absent from the meeting were principal denominational leaders from the historically black Baptist and Methodist denominations and conventions (which account for roughly two-thirds of African American Christians)[16] and activist clergy such as Jesse Jackson or Al Sharpton.

The Congress of National Black Churches (CNBC), an ecumenical group that has facilitated community development and policy advocacy initiatives on behalf of the historically black Baptists, Methodists, and the Church of God in Christ, complained about being excluded from the meeting (despite the fact that a number of persons affiliated with its organization or its member denominations were in attendance at the meeting with Bush). CNBC co-founder Bishop John Hurst Adams wrote a letter to the *Washington Post* that stated: "to have a 'national' meeting and not to include [leadership from the historically black denominations] is an affront to the black church, its leadership, and all African Americans."[17] The sentiments of CNBC leadership were consistent with those of a number of prominent black clergy around the country who, in the words of Reverend Amos Brown of Third Street Baptist Church in San Francisco, viewed Bush's meeting as "another one of those old schemes of divide and conquer."[18]

No doubt in response to these criticisms, Bush convened a March 2001 meeting at the White House with religious leaders that included fifteen leaders from historically black denominations, including William Shaw, president of the National Baptist Convention, USA Inc.; Cecil Bishop, senior bishop of the African Methodist Episcopal Zion Church; and Gilbert Patterson, presiding bishop of the Church of God in Christ. Many of these black church leaders, however, were disappointed with the meeting's lack of substance and were angry about being misled into participating in what was little more than a public relations ploy by Bush and the meeting's organizers.[19] The White House and Republican allies in the U.S. Congress have also sponsored a series of subsequent meetings to promote Bush's faith-based initiative that have targeted black religious leaders. In April 2001, Congressman J. C. Watts (R-OK), Senator Rick Santorum (R-PA), and Bishop Harold Ray (a Bush ally and Miami-based pastor who heads an ecclesiastical network called the National Center for Faith Based Initiative) convened a meeting in Washington to build support for Bush's faith-based policies. Approximately four hundred black ministers were invited and, as was the case in the Austin meeting, few denominational leaders from the historically black denominations were on the invitation list. During 2002, the White House took steps to broaden its support base among black religious leaders for the faith-based initiative by sponsoring a series of seminars around the country aimed at informing clergy about the mechanics of the faith-based initiative. These events attracted hundreds of mainly black clergy, although there were religious leaders in attendance from various faiths, races, and political persuasions.[20]

The Bush administration and key Republicans in the U.S Congress argue that this systematic outreach to black churches simply acknowledges the strategic role black churches play in reaching the urban poor. And, as J. C. Watts comments, Republicans want to show black leaders that they are "just as interested as Democrats in helping lift people out of poverty."[21]

Black clergy, on their part, have had varying interpretations of the cost and benefits of embracing these Republican overtures. As mentioned above, there are those who have viewed it as a divide-and-conquer strategy by Republicans, and they would certainly find support for this interpretation in remarks made by Reverend Eugene Rivers, who was an early supporter of Bush's faith-based initiative and attended Bush's Austin meeting in 2000 and White House meeting in March 2001. Rivers stated shortly after attending the Austin meeting that black clergy advocates of the faith-based initiative were trying to distance themselves from "a declining civil rights industry." Bishop Charles Blake, who also attended the Austin meeting and was an early supporter of Bush's faith-based initiative, qualified Rivers's remarks by suggesting that black clergy advocates of Bush's initiative "have not taken any kind of adversarial approach toward any of our liberal friends."[22]

A black denominational leader strongly connected to the civil rights tradition, Reverend C. Mackey Daniels, who succeeded Bennett W. Smith (discussed by Wallace in chapter 3) as president of the Progressive National Baptist Convention, issued a press release in early 2001 condemning Bush's faith-based initiative and targeting of black churches as "an effort to muffle the prophetic voice of the African American church." Daniels also suggested that support of Bush's initiative was equivalent to accepting "thirty pieces of silver." About the same time, Jesse Jackson advanced the following assessment during a sermon delivered to a large black congregation in Maryland: "I am for faith based programs . . . but I fear federally funded, faith-based initiatives. Don't let them get into your books, because they are wolves in sheep's clothing. Money is seductive; the church needs money, but it needs independence even more."[23]

Then there are black clergy who do not have a strong opinion either way but are willing to give the initiative a hearing. Reverend Lewis Flowers who heads Chicago's Westside Ministers Coalition articulated the matter this way: "For those who've got millions of dollars in funding from other sources, it's OK to say, 'Don't take the money.' When we're scuffling to pay phone bills, we ought to be able to accept funds to keep programs in the community."[24]

As numerous chapters in this volume point out, civil rights commitments do not prevent black clergy from supporting church-state social service partnerships, nor does support for church-state partnerships prevent black clergy from supporting civil rights activism. If that is the case, then what might the implications of that be for black church voting behavior and for the Republican Party black church strategy? Despite moral conservative tendencies on the part of black churchgoers, such tendencies do not appear to have contributed to any greater support for the Republican Party among black churchgoers than among blacks in general. Public opinion data from the late 1980s show black Protestant support of the Republican Party at about 9 percent.[25] Moreover, election data from the 2000 elections show that only 4 percent of black Protestants who voted in the election supported Bush.[26] Republicans may detect hopeful trends, however, in recent polling data that show an increase in blacks identifying as Republicans. According to the polling data, 4 percent of blacks identified as Republicans in 2000 while 10 percent did in 2002.[27] Moreover, polling figures from the Joint Center for Political and Economic Studies show that blacks who identified with the Republican Party increased from 9 percent in their 2000 survey to 18 percent in their October 2004 survey.[28] Nevertheless, 2004 election-day exit polls showed that President Bush's support from African American voters was only about a percentage point or two better than the roughly 9 percent he received in the 2000 election.[29] Bush fared better in some states than he did in others, however—for example, in Ohio, where approximately 16 percent of black voters indicated that they voted for Bush and in Florida where Bush received 13 percent of the black vote.[30]

Given continuously strong indicators of African American commitments to social justice and civil rights, and given the systematic but largely unsuccessful Republican strategy during Bush's first term to win over black voters, the expectation would be that black voting and political alignments will remain relatively unchanged during Bush's second term. Black churches may express some level of support for church-state social service partnerships, but accepting government monies for social services will not necessarily erode black church commitments to black political rights or black church support of political leaders and institutions that embody commitments to black political rights. There is a pragmatism that has guided African American politics, captured in the motto of the Congressional Black Caucus, and perhaps usefully applied to black churches: "[we] have no permanent friends, no permanent enemies . . . just permanent interests."

NOTES

1. "Bush Honors King, Draws Protest," Fox News, 16 January 2004; Bruce Nolan, "Historic N. O. Church Provides Presidential Pulpit," *Times-Picayune*, 16 January 2004.

2. Nolan, "Historic N. O. Church Provides Presidential Pulpit."

3. "Nation Marks Martin Luther King Day," Associated Press, 19 January 2004; Jeffrey Gettleman and Ariel Hart, *New York Times*, 15 January 2004; Randal Mikkelsen, "Bush Booed at Martin Luther King Gravesite," Reuters, 16 January 2004.

4. Booker T. Washington, *Up from Slavery* (1903), in *Three Negro Classics* (New York: Avon Books, 1965), 156.

5. W. E. B. Du Bois, *The Souls of Black Folks*, in *Three Negro Classics* (New York: Avon Books, 1965), 252.

6. This definition of liberalism draws on William Gerber, *American Liberalism: Laudable Ends, Controversial Means* (Lanham, Md.: University Press of America, 1987), 111.

7. The Black Churches and Politics Survey was conducted by the Public Influences of African-American Churches Project at Morehouse College. The survey was administered to a representative cross-section of predominantly black churches, drawn

from nineteen cities, twenty-six predominantly black rural counties, and two predominantly black suburbs.

8. There are significant differences between black clergy and laity attitudes about this policy. A general population of black Protestants (N=131) who were part of a larger public opinion survey (N=2002) conducted by the Pew Forum on Religion and Public Life and the Pew Research Center for the People and the Press showed that 83 percent of black Protestant respondents favored churches applying for government funding. See *American Views on Religion, Politics, and Public Policy*, April 2002, 44.

9. Scott Stephens points out that 99 percent of Cleveland's 4,202 voucher students attend a religious school. See "Study: Most Voucher Schools Religious," *Cleveland Plain Dealer*, 24 January 2002.

10. There are also differences between black clergy and the black general public in levels of support for vouchers. According to a national public opinion survey conducted by Gallup, 59 percent of black respondents expressed support for vouchers. See Peter Schrag, "The Voucher Seduction," *American Prospect* 11, no. 1 (23 November 1999).

11. George Gallup Jr. and Jim Castelli, *The People's Religion: American Faith in the '90's* (New York: MacMillan, 1989), 215. On the prominence of civil rights among blacks in general, see Dona Hamilton and Charles Hamilton, *Political Science Quarterly* 107, no. 3 (Fall 1992): 435–52.

12. R. Drew Smith, ed., *New Day Begun: African American Churches and Civic Culture in Post-Civil Rights America* (Durham: Duke University Press 2003), 302–3.

13. Pew Forum on Religion and Public Life and the Pew Research Center for the People and the Press, *American Views on Religion, Politics and Public Policy*, April 2002, 44.

14. Roger Stump points out that church attendance is much higher among blacks in the South, and their attendance less dependent on the strength of their religious commitment than in the "more secular North," where attendance is smaller and usually "limited to individuals possessing high levels of religiosity." See, "Regional Contrasts within Black Protestantism: A Research Note," *Social Forces* 66, no. 1 (September 1987): 145. Christopher Ellison and Darren Sherkat make similar observations, noting that approximately 70 percent of blacks in the urban South attend church at least a few times per month while only about 55 percent of blacks outside the South attend church a few times or more per month. They also stress the fact that churches are much more central to black social life in the South than they are outside the South where there is a wider "availability of alternative lifestyles and secular opportunities for status and resources." See, "The 'Semi-involuntary Institution' Revisited: Regional Variations in Church Participation Among Black Americans," *Social Forces* 73, no. 4 (June 1995): 1423 and 1415.

15. See Michael Paulson, "Black Clergy Rejection Stirs Gay Marriage Backers," *Boston Globe*, 10 February 2004; and Lynette Clemetson, "Both Sides Court Black Churches in the Debate Over Gay Marriage," *New York Times*, 1 March 2004.

16. C. Eric Lincoln and Lawrence Mamiya, *The Black Church in the African American Experience* (Durham: Duke University Press, 1990), 407.

17. Quoted in Joshua Green, "Bad Faith," *American Prospect*, 30 July 2001.

18. "Black Clergy Wary of W.'s Overture," CBS News, 20 December 2000.

19. See, for example, Green, "Bad Faith."

20. Thomas Edsall and Alan Cooperman, "GOP Using Faith Initiative to Woo Voters," *New York Times*, 15 September 2002, A5.

21. Rebecca Carr, "GOP Looks for Black Faith-Based Allies," *Atlanta Journal Constitution*, 25 April 2001, A7.

22. John Leland, "Some Black Pastors See New Aid Under Bush," *New York Times*, 2 February 2001.

23. Hamil Harris, "Bush Proposal is Worrisome, Jackson Says," *Washington Post*, 5 February 2001, B3.

24. Julia Liblich, "At Black Churches, Bush Plan is Welcome," *Chicago Tribune*, 6 April 2001.

25. Gallup and Castelli, *People's Religion*, 222.

26. University of Akron Survey Research Center, "The Third National Survey of Religion and Politics," 2000.

27. David Bositis, *2002 National Opinion Poll* (Washington, D.C.: Joint Center for Political and Economic Studies, 2002), 16.

28. However, preelection polling from other sources showed little or no gain in support for George Bush within the black community. See Jim Dwyer and Jodi Wilgoern, "Gore and Kerry Unite in Search for Black Votes," *New York Times*, 25 October 2004.

29. David Broder and Richard Morin, "Four Years Later, Voters More Deeply Split," *Washington Post*, 3 November 2004, 1.

30. Melissa Harris and Victor Manuel Ramos, "Strong Minority Turnout Affects Voting Dynamics," *Orlando Sentinel*, 4 November 2004.

Index

About the Editors and Contributors

R. Drew Smith is scholar-in-residence and director of Religion and Public Life Projects at the Leadership Center at Morehouse College.

Fredrick C. Harris is associate professor of political science and director of the Center for the Study of African American Politics at the University of Rochester.

Yvette Alex-Assensoh is associate professor of political science at Indiana University.

Ronald E. Brown is associate professor of political science at Wayne State University.

Mittie Olion Chandler is associate professor of urban affairs at Cleveland State University.

Carolyn Hartfield is a doctoral candidate in the Political Science Department at Wayne State University.

James Jennings is associate professor of political science at Tufts University.

Michael Leo Owens is assistant professor of political science at Emory University.

Alton B. Pollard III is associate professor of Christian ethics and director of Black Church Studies at Candler School of Theology at Emory University.

Clarence Taylor is professor of history at Baruch College and the City University of New York Graduate Center.

Tamelyn Tucker-Worgs is assistant professor of political science at Hood College.

Sherri Leronda Wallace is assistant professor of political science at the University of Louisville.

Ronald Walters is distinguished scholar and director of the African American Leadership Institute at the James McGregor Burns Academy of Leadership at the University of Maryland.